U.S.A. FIFTIES

Volume 4

Lebanon — Pauling, Linus

GROLIER

an imprint of

SCHOLASTIC

www.scholastic.com/librarypublishing

First published 2005 by Grolier,
an imprint of Scholastic Library Publishing,
Old Sherman Turnpike,
Danbury, Connecticut 06816

Set ISBN 0-7172-6082-8
Volume ISBN 0-7172-6086-0

Library of Congress Cataloging-in-Publication Data
USA 1950s.
         p. cm.
     Includes indexes.
     Contents: v. 1. Abstract Expressionism–China—v. 2. Chosin
Reservoir–Foreign policy—v. 3. Formosa/Taiwan–Law and order—v. 4.
Lebanon–Pauling, Linus—v. 5. Phillips, Sam–South America—v. 6.
Southeast Asia–Zhou Enlai.
     ISBN 0-7172-6082-8 (set : alk. paper)—ISBN 0-7172-6083-6 (v. 1 :
alk. paper)—ISBN 0-7172-6084-4 (v. 2 : alk. paper)—ISBN 0-7172-
6085-2 (v. 3 : alk. paper)—ISBN 0-7172-6086-0 (v. 4 : alk. paper)—
ISBN 0-7172-6087-9 (v. 5 : alk. paper)—ISBN 0-7172-6088-7 (v. 6 :
alk. paper)
     1. United States—Civilization—1945—Encyclopedias, Juvenile. 2.
Nineteen fifties—Encyclopedias, Juvenile. I. Grolier (Firm)

     E169.12.U78 2005
     973.921—dc22   2004061903

For information address the publisher:
Grolier, Scholastic Library Publishing,
Old Sherman Turnpike,
Danbury, Connecticut 06816

Printed and bound in Singapore

For The Brown Reference Group plc
Project Editor: Claire Chandler
Deputy Editor: Chris King
Editors: Felicity Crowe, Jonathan Dore,
                               Jane Edmonds, Mark Fletcher,
                               Lee Stacy, David Tombesi-Walton,
                               Sylvia Tombesi-Walton, Elizabeth Wyse
Designers: Ron Callow, Q2A
Picture Researchers: Becky Cox, Laila Torsun
Cartography: Darren Awuah, Mark Walker
Index: Kay Ollerenshaw
Production Director: Alastair Gourlay
Senior Managing Editor: Tim Cooke
Editorial Director: Lindsey Lowe
Consultants: Professor Mina Carson, Oregon State
                               University; Professor Richard C. Crepeau,
                               University of Central Florida; Professor
                               Sharon Ullman, Bryn Mawr College

ABOUT THIS SET

This book is part of a six-volume reference set that explores all aspects of life in the United States in the 1950s. The set covers not only the major political events of the decade but also developments in the arts, sciences, and popular culture.

Politically the 1950s were dominated by the Cold War, the hostile relationship that developed after World War II between the United States and the Soviet Union and their respective allies. At the beginning of the decade the United States' commitment to fighting communism drew it into the Korean War, a conflict that lasted from 1950 to 1953 and cost thousands of American lives. Anticommunist suspicion at home, meanwhile, was stoked by the investigations of Senator Joseph McCarthy and the House Un-American Activities Committee.

The rivalry between the superpowers also manifested itself in efforts to develop ever more devastating nuclear weapons. By 1953 both the Americans and the Soviets had tested hydrogen bombs. Four years later the Soviet Union became the first country to send an artificial satellite into orbit, marking the beginning of the space race that would continue throughout the 1960s.

The 1950s were a decade of great cultural change. Popular music was transformed with the birth of rock 'n' roll, musical theater flourished on Broadway, and there was continued experimentation in the world of jazz. Television came to dominate all other media and had a huge influence on the daily life of the average American family.

Growing prosperity after the deprivations of the Great Depression and the war meant that families had more money to spend on consumer goods and more time to spend on leisure activities. By the end of the decade most families owned a car, and many white Americans had moved to the suburbs. The good times were not shared by all, however. Black Americans faced discrimination in many areas of public life, and racial segregation was still a reality in the southern states. During the decade key Supreme Court decisions regarding desegregation paved the way for further successes for the growing civil rights movement in the 1960s.

This set contains more than 270 illustrated articles, arranged alphabetically for ease of reference. Many contain boxes that provide more detailed examination of key topics. Each entry contains cross-references to related articles, while every volume features a comprehensive set index, together with a timeline, a reading list, and useful websites for further research.

CONTENTS

LEBANON

The 1950s were a time of volatility and change in Lebanon. Religious tensions were running high, and there were calls for an end to corruption within the government. A Muslim uprising led to the U.S. Marines being called in to help restore peace to the country.

In 1944 Lebanon achieved full independence after having been under French administration since 1920. Under Lebanon's first elected president, Bishara al-Khuri (1890–1964), the country took its first fragile steps into self-government. French troops withdrew in 1946, and Lebanon became a member of the United Nations (UN) and the Arab League.

Following an initial six-year term in office, Khuri was reelected in 1949. Yet despite a reasonably stable government, Lebanese society was unsettled. As it entered the 1950s, Lebanon was divided between religious communities. Historically its population comprised largely Maronite Christians and Druze, a sect who follow a monotheistic religion that shares elements of doctrine with Christianity, Islam, and other religions. The French, however, had enlarged the borders of Lebanon to include numerous Muslim communities. A possibly more significant division in Lebanon was between those who favored unification with other Arab states (known as pan-Arabists) and those who preferred independence. Lebanese politics were also riddled with sectarianism, with influential families all vying for power and influence.

A new regime

By the early 1950s discontent with Khuri's management of the economy and some of his autocratic policies led to widespread opposition to his rule. One of the most influential groups that opposed Khuri was the Social National Front (SNF), led by a group of high-profile politicians and businessmen, including Kamal Jumblatt, Camille Chamoun, and Emile Bustani. With considerable popular backing the SNF called for an end to governmental corruption and sectarianism.

Matters came to a head in 1952. Following a rally attended by 50,000 people, the SNF leaders called on Khuri to resign. He refused, so in September

The uprising of the Muslim community in 1958 led to President Chamoun's request for help from the United States. Peace was restored, but Chamoun's presidency was all but over.

SNF supporters launched a general strike and effectively brought the country to a halt. Khuri appealed to the military to break the strike, but no help was forthcoming. Finally, on September 18 Khuri resigned, and Camille Chamoun (1900–1987) took his place.

Within less than a year members of the new government were fighting among themselves. Jumblatt felt that Chamoun had backed away from his original revolutionary policies. Muslim leaders complained that Christians dominated both government and the civil service, and they called for a national census to prove that Muslims were in the majority in Lebanon and should therefore have greater rights. Christian leaders refused, saying that Christians provided 80 percent of Lebanon's taxes and consequently had a right to occupy the highest positions.

Tensions in Lebanon came to a head, however, over the issue of pan-Arabism. In 1956 Britain and France took military action against Egypt in an attempt to secure their use of the Suez Canal. Their action was condemned and halted by UN intervention, and Egyptian President Gamal Abdel Nasser (1918–1970) became an Arab hero, especially among Lebanese Muslims. Chamoun, however, refused to break off diplomatic relations with Britain and France. In 1958 Nasser united Egypt with Syria to create the United Arab Republic (UAR). Many Muslim leaders in Lebanon also felt that their country should unite with the UAR, but Chamoun refused to consider such a move. His position was even more unpopular because, in 1957, he had modified the Lebanese constitution to extend his term as president.

Muslim rebellion

During 1958 Lebanese Muslims became more vocal, and riots and demonstrations spread throughout the country. The interest of the United States was awakened, partly because of its objective to protect its sources of oil in the region. In 1957 President Dwight D. Eisenhower (1953–1961) had offered armed forces to help any country "against overt armed aggression

from any nation controlled by international communism." In July 1958 the Iraqi royal family was murdered by Muslim revolutionaries, and Chamoun feared that Lebanon's Muslims would be inspired to act against him. He appealed for U.S. troops to restore calm, claiming that communist forces in Syria were assisting the Lebanese rebels. The United States deployed a large force of U.S. Marines onto the streets of Beirut, the capital, to act as peacekeepers. The Eisenhower Doctrine was used to justify the action, although Lebanon faced no armed aggression. A measure of peace returned to Lebanon.

After U.S.-led negotiations Chamoun agreed to resign. He was succeeded by General Fuad Chehab (1902–1973), commander of the army and a moderate who had not allied himself with any

Camille Chamoun was president of Lebanon for six years. However, his pro-Western policies were not popular with the country's Muslim leaders, and Muslim groups rebelled against his government.

faction and was acceptable to Muslims, Christians, and Druze alike. He brought in measures to include members of all factions in the government. He strengthened infrastructure, improving roads, water and electricity supply, and medical care. He also requested that U.S. forces withdraw, which they did in October 1958. The following decade was one of relative calm in Lebanon.

See Also:

Eisenhower Doctrine • Foreign Policy • Middle East • Suez Crisis

LEGION OF DECENCY

The Legion of Decency was a Roman Catholic organization originally founded in the 1930s to counter the perceived immorality of the movies. Although the film industry was increasingly effectively regulated by the 1950s, the legion still occasionally played a significant role.

The Legion of Decency was created in 1934 by a group of Catholic bishops who were concerned about the possible negative moral effects of film. The legion issued its own ratings on movies and black-listed or boycotted offensive films. Under pressure, partly from the legion itself, the trade organization the Motion Picture Producers and Distributors of America (MPPDA) established the Production Code Administration (PCA) as a formal means to maintain standards. All movies released or distributed by members of the MPPDA had to have a PCA seal of approval. The legion, meanwhile, continued to issue its own film ratings. Its decisions, although they had no formal status, influenced the moviegoing decisions of millions of Catholics.

Pope Pius XII, in white, meets with Catholic film commissioners from around the world in May 1953. In 1957 Pius called for a more positive attitude toward the movies.

The courts and the church

During the 1950s Hollywood shared the general trend toward more relaxed moral attitudes. The influence of the communist witch hunts led by Senator Joseph McCarthy, meanwhile, meant that the industry was increasingly policed on political rather than moral grounds. The legion continued to object to movies of which it disapproved, however.

The most celebrated case came in 1950, when *The Miracle*, by Italian director Roberto Rossellini, reached America. In the movie a drunken peasant girl is seduced by a vagrant she imagines is Saint Joseph; the "miracle" of the film's title is her resulting pregnancy. The Legion of Decency denounced the movie as "a sacrilegious and blasphemous mockery of Christian religious truth." Under pressure from the legion and the Catholic Church the New York State Board of Regents withdrew the license to distribute the movie. When the distributor, Joseph

Burstyn, went to the New York Court of Appeals to overturn the decision, he lost. He then appealed to the U.S. Supreme Court, which in May 1952 handed down its landmark decision *Burstyn v. Wilson*. The court ruled that movies were a form of free speech and were therefore protected under the First Amendment to the Constitution.

Following the "Miracle decision," more filmmakers began to challenge the PCA. In 1953 director Otto Preminger released the sex comedy *The Moon Is Blue* without a PCA code and to condemnation by the legion. The film received three Oscar nominations. The legion also criticized Elia Kazan's 1956 movie of the Tennessee Williams screenplay *Baby Doll* and a billboard in New York City's Times Square showing the movie's star, Carroll Baker, curled up on a cot sucking her thumb.

The success of such movies helped weaken the importance of the PCA and the legion. Meanwhile, inconsistency between the two bodies further undermined their message. When the PCA condemned the 1955 movie *The Man with the Golden Arm*, starring Frank Sinatra as a heroin addict, the legion did not. In 1957 Pope Pius XII signaled a relaxation in the church's attitude when he issued an encyclical (a formal papal letter) calling for a more positive attitude toward film, emphasizing its potential for good rather than evil.

The Legion of Decency continued to comment on film throughout the 1960s. By the time it ceased to issue ratings in 1971, it had previewed and classified more than 16,000 movies.

See Also:

Movie Industry • Oscars • Religion

LEISURE INDUSTRY

Increasing incomes and shorter working hours during the 1950s gave many Americans more leisure hours than ever before and a wide range of ways to fill them. Favorite activities varied from watching television or entertaining friends at home to exploring the United States by car.

Compared with previous decades, in the 1950s America was a nation at leisure. *Business Week* magazine commented, "Never have so many people had so much time on their hands—with pay—as today in the United States." Since the end of World War II (1939–1945) working conditions had undergone a revolution. The average work week had fallen to 40 hours, including lunch and coffee breaks. Three-weeks' paid vacation and two-day weekends were standard, and early retirement on a company pension was increasingly normal.

As the amount of free time expanded, leisure became big business. Growing postwar prosperity meant that a large number of Americans found themselves with both the time and the money to enjoy the many new recreations that became popular during the decade. Businesses sprang up to cater to leisure requirements. After the austerity of the Great Depression and the war years white middle-class Americans relished the new opportunities. In 1954 *Fortune* magazine calculated that the leisure industry was worth $30 billion a year. That figure represented a 50 percent increase on the $20 billion that Americans spent each year on clothing and housing.

Not everyone benefited. Around half of African Americans, for example, who comprised some 11 percent of the population, lived below the poverty line. Travel, moviegoing, and other activities remained beyond their budget.

At home and on the road

Two of the most popular pastimes summed up the broad range of ways in which Americans enjoyed their leisure: recreational travel on the one hand and staying home on the other. At home people watched television or took up popular hobbies, such as painting-by-numbers, reading, photography, cooking, barbecuing in the backyard, listening to music, and do-it-yourself, or DIY. At the heart of such activities was the concept of family life. In 1954 *McCall's* magazine coined the notion of "togetherness," by which it intended to suggest the idea of families doing things together. Home-based hobbies were also essentially suburban, appealing to people with their own homes and backyards. As the population of the suburbs grew—of the 13 million new

Shoppers enjoy the Southdale Regional Shopping Center, the first fully enclosed mall, which opened in Minnesota in 1956. The mall soon became an important leisure destination.

suburban family the greatest symbol of freedom was the automobile. Auto manufacturers responded to the growing market between 1949 and 1950 by dramatically changing the shape and style of their vehicles. Cars became bigger, more powerful, and more fun to drive than earlier models. In 1950 twice as many people owned cars as they had in 1935. By 1954 some 47 million cars were registered in the United States, and by the end of the decade four-fifths of all American families owned a car.

Cars were not just an important means of transport. For men in particular they became a leisure industry in themselves. Cars were status symbols that made a statement about professional success. Keeping them clean, tinkering with their mechanics and generally maintaining them, and repainting or otherwise customizing them was a time-consuming activity for both men and teenagers, who were eager to get their own car as soon as

homes built between 1948 and 1958, 85 percent were in the suburbs—more families moved from downtown areas to new homes, around which their leisure activities often revolved.

While the suburban boom of the fifties brought increased comfort for many Americans, the conformity of suburban life also bred a desire to escape from daily routine. For the

KEMMONS WILSON'S HOLIDAY INN

A successful homebuilder from Memphis, Tennessee, transformed the hotel industry in the 1950s. When Kemmons Wilson (1913–2003) took his wife and five children for a vacation to Washington, D.C., in the summer of 1951, they needed somewhere to stay en route. Motels, roadside hotels that provided rooms with plenty of carparking out front, were a new concept, and no industry standard existed. The quality of motels varied dramatically, but what most irritated Wilson was that each child was charged as an extra, usually $2 each.

By the end of the vacation Wilson had resolved to address the problem. Having measured different motel rooms on the way home, he decided that the optimum size for a room was 12 feet by 30 feet (3.7m x 9m) plus a bathroom. Wilson had a draftsman called Eddie Bluestein sketch out a simple design for a motel. When Bluestein produced his sketches, he had written "Holiday Inn" on top of the drawing, inspired by the 1942 movie starring

Bing Crosby and Fred Astaire that he was watching as he sketched. Wilson decided to keep the name.

Location was key to the project's success. For the first Holiday Inn Wilson found a site on the highway between Memphis and Nashville. He costed the motel at $325,000, which he borrowed, but brought the project in at $280,000, allowing him to use what was left over for his next motel. The first Holiday Inn, with 120 rooms, was built in 90 days and opened for business in August 1952. It had a restaurant, gift shop, swimming pool, and free air-conditioning and television in the rooms. It charged $6 each night, and children stayed for free.

Within two years Wilson had built three more motels. He decided to franchise the popular chain, allowing it to spread faster as the new interstate highways were built. By 1959 there were 100 Holiday Inns across the country. They set a benchmark for good, affordable family accommodation that was soon copied by Wilson's rivals.

Students at the Brooklyn School of Automotive Trades prepare a car for a paint job in this image from 1956. The driving boom brought increased demand for trained mechanics.

they could drive legally at age 16. By 1958 nearly six million teenagers held driving licenses. The teenage obsession with cars was epitomized in the 1955 movie *Rebel without a Cause*, in which James Dean played a youth who becomes involved in racing cars toward a cliff in games of "chicken."

Recreation and consumer boom

The auto industry led a more general consumer boom, which itself fueled much of the 1950s leisure boom. Families were buying on credit—Diners Club had introduced the first universal charge card in 1950—and buying not because they needed things but because they wanted them. Car manufacturer General Motors responded with a series of ads promoting the idea of the "two car family." Families, the ads suggested, would be able to spend more time together if mom and dad each had a car to get their chores done simultaneously, freeing up more leisure time.

As consumer attitudes changed, many families came to expect to change their cars every couple of years; manufacturers, eager to stimulate interest, continually updated their models. Fins on the back of autos grew larger and larger as the decade went on, reaching their most outrageous on the Cadillac, designed by Harley Earl. By the late 1950s the average car carried over 44 pounds (20kg) of chrome trimming. Auto colors grew more outlandish, and convertibles became highly popular. So powerful was the car as a symbol of freedom that many Americans rejected such safety features as seatbelts, which they believed compromised that freedom. Partly as a result, more Americans died in auto wrecks in the 1950s than in the whole of World War II.

Driving destinations

Families with cars needed somewhere to go. A process was already underway of relocating shopping and other activities from downtown areas to sites that required consumers to drive there. Increasingly, recreational shopping became a new pastime as families traveled substantial distances to shop. The opening of the first fully enclosed suburban shopping mall in 1956 in Southdale, near Minneapolis, signaled the transformation of how people shopped. Earlier shopping malls had been attached to other buildings, such as the indoor shopping arcade attached to the lobby of the Fontainebleau Hotel, which opened in Miami Beach, Florida, in 1953. Now consumers were able to drive to the mall, leave their cars in the ample carpark, and then, safely ignoring the weather outside, shop in the mall's many stores and eat in its food facilities.

Driving became an integral part of vacations as well as shopping. For much of the decade, however, vacation driving in some places or at peak times meant being stuck in traffic jams on roads that were largely inadequate for the new volume of cars. The Federal-Aid Highway Act of 1944 had called for a national system of interstate highways, but by the start of the 1950s few roads had been built. It was not until the Federal-Aid Highway Act of 1956 that road building began in earnest. The project, the largest public works program then undertaken, aimed to link 90 percent of all cities with a population of over 50,000. The new road system shortened journey times and made places more accessible. With gas costing less than 25 cents a gallon, families traveled an average of 1,108 miles (1,780 km) on their vacations.

By the end of March 1953 the travel industry was worth between $7.5 and $8 billion a year. Depending on its income, the average family took two trips of 10 days each year; most of the trips were made by car—in 1953, 85.5 percent of all trips. More people on the

formal activity generally saved for business or special occasions. The coming of informal, low-priced restaurants for the whole family transformed America's dining habits. None typified the change more than the decision of the first McDonald's restaurant to cater specifically to the family market.

In 1948 the McDonald brothers, Richard and Maurice, relaunched their popular drive-in in San Bernardino, California, as a cheaper restaurant aimed at young families. To cut costs, they automated the making of hamburgers, their most popular menu item, concentrating on speed and volume of production. They cut their prices and did away with crockery and cutlery, replacing them with paper and plastic.

The response from working families was remarkable. By 1950 they and their children were the restaurant's key customers. The restaurant was a huge hit, with long lines every lunchtime. It appealed to families because the food was cheap—hamburgers retailed at 15 cents, with a cheese slice for 4 cents more; shakes were 20 cents and coffee a nickel—and there was no tipping. Families came, ordered their meals, ate them in their cars, and left.

The McDonald brothers had no ambitions to develop their business as a chain. However, when Ray Kroc, an ambitious salesman, bought into the McDonald franchise in 1954, he set about making it nationwide. By 1959 there were 145 McDonald's restaurants and by 1960, 228.

A similar expansion benefited the older Dairy Queen chain, which grew from 1,156 franchises in 1950 to more than 3,000 by 1959. Both McDonald's and Dairy Queen offered a predictable

roads meant that more facilities were required to service their needs. A whole industry sprang up along the highways and the two-lane roads that still dominated the country. Families spent the night in motels, which also provided parking. One of America's largest hotel chains, Holiday Inn, had its origins in founder Kemmons Wilson's irritation with the unfriendly child policies of motels (*see box on p. 8*). Gas stations and restaurants also appeared to meet travelers' needs.

Eating out

Family restaurants became a popular destination in themselves during the fifties. In the past eating out had been a

LAS VEGAS

The 1950s were a period of dramatic growth in the Nevada desert city of Las Vegas. Following the outlawing of gambling and prostitution in Los Angeles in 1938, Las Vegas became the new center for both in the Southwest, drawing huge investment from organized crime. The opening of the El Rancho Vegas in 1941 launched a spate of resort hotel building that lasted throughout the decade.

The resort hotels were destinations in themselves. Air-conditioned rooms were a big draw, as were the hotels' swimming pools, shops, restaurants, travel agencies, horse-riding facilities, and on-site gambling and entertainment. By the start of the 1950s Las Vegas was being heavily marketed on its reputation for being "naughty but nice."

As the decade went on, bigger and more extravagant hotels were built. When the Desert Inn opened in April 1950, it had Nevada's largest casino, at 2,400 square feet (223 sq. m). But it was the Sands hotel, which opened in December 1952, that put Las Vegas on the map. The city's most popular hotel of the decade, the Sands provided legendary entertainment. Frank Sinatra performed there throughout the 1950s, as did the other members of the so-called Rat Pack: Dean Martin, Sammy Davis, Jr., Peter Lawford, and Joey Bishop. Movie stars stayed at the hotel, including Lauren Bacall and Doris Day. The hotel's main showroom, the Copa, featured the Copa dancing girls, the classiest, best-looking dancers in Las Vegas.

As Las Vegas gained popularity as a vacation destination, more hotels sprang up. A craze for unusual-shaped hotels started in 1954 with the Showboat, whose design was based on an 1840s Mississippi paddle wheeler. With the increasing number of hotel rooms Las Vegas's Chamber of Commerce began to promote the town as a convention center. A specially built convention center opened in 1959.

The Las Vegas Club, seen here in around 1950, was one of the town's earliest institutions. Its promotional literature boasted that it had the largest parking lots in Nevada—a must for attracting the tourists who drove to the desert resort from Southern California and elsewhere in the Southwest.

eating experience that Americans found appealing. When families were on the road, they knew they could rely on a McDonald's or Dairy Queen for exactly the meal they were expecting. Reliable restaurants and motels were a key part of making the vacation a success.

Disneyland

Family road trips had a range of traditional destinations, such as the nation's great cities or national parks.

The decade also brought wholly new types of destination, including the first theme park and the leisure city of Las Vegas (*see p. 11*).

Walt Disney (1901–1966) opened his first resort park, which he called a family entertainment complex, in Anaheim, California, in 1955. Overcoming initial teething problems, Disneyland soon became a hit. It had attracted 10 million visitors by New Year's Eve 1957, 40 percent of whom

had driven by car from outside California. The idea for the park came from the drives Disney took with his daughters to play areas that were generally of a poor standard. He envisioned a park that would help families make the most of their time together. Disneyland's Main Street remained essentially a shopping mall, but it was a mall hidden behind the storefronts of a make-believe U.S. main street in 1900. For entertainment the park provided a variety of rides through themed areas such as Tomorrowland, Disney's vision of what the future might hold.

To get to Disneyland, families drove their cars there, parked, and then transferred to Disney's transport to take rides around the park. People loved it. Disney was giving them a sanitized version of America, peopled with the characters families had grown up with. Disneyland became a destination in itself, like Las Vegas. Hotels were built to accommodate all the tourists who wanted to visit.

Other popular tourist destinations had been around for millennia. The road network opened up even sites that had been largely remote and inaccessible, such as the Grand Canyon in Arizona or Yosemite in California. Such sites, like national parks across the country, became more visited. The idea of escaping from the suburbs and returning to nature was a popular one. Families drove to the parks, camped, and cooked out of doors. The fact that they were surrounded by thousands of other families doing the same thing did not detract from the sense of freedom their trip engendered. Double the number of people were visiting national parks each year by the end of the 1950s than at the start of the decade.

When Hawaii—a popular but expensive tourist destination since the end of World War II—achieved statehood in 1959, the minds of many citizens of the continental United States turned to all things tropical. At home

This poster for United States Lines appeared in 1955. Sea travel remained popular but was increasingly challenged by air travel: The first nonstop transatlantic flights began in 1958.

A family relaxes outside its trailer in Grand Canyon National Park. Trailers, introduced in the 1920s, allowed Americans to get right to the heart of the great outdoors.

and away from the office men wore brightly colored Hawaiian leisure shirts, and palm trees became a popular decorative motif. Honeymooning in Hawaii became fashionable for the well-off.

Air travel

At the start of the 1950s leisure air travel was still in its infancy. However, with many Air Force pilots home from war and looking for work, it was not long until commercial airlines employed them to fly their growing fleets. Since people had more money to spend, the idea of flying to a vacation destination became increasingly attractive. Carriers such as Pan Am and Trans World Airlines started to fly leisure passengers on domestic and international routes. In 1956 American vacationers spent $1.75 billion abroad, an increase of 12.5 percent on 1955 and a greater sum than all of the

country's coffee and petroleum imports. Of the 1,239,000 Americans who went overseas in 1956, half traveled to either Central America, Mexico, or the West Indies, and 42 percent visited Europe. Newspapers responded to the growth in foreign travel by including a travel section in the weekend editions, featuring articles on favored destinations. In the summer of 1958 American students traveled to the Soviet Union for the first time on an exchange program organized by the Council for Student Travel.

Home pursuits

It seemed as though the whole country was on the move. In fact, most families also spent increasing amounts of time in their living and family rooms, where television, and to a lesser degree recorded music, dominated leisure hours. The high-fidelity record player, or hi-fi, was an important element of leisure time. The 12-inch, 33⅓-rpm (revolutions per minute) long-playing (LP) vinyl phonograph record had been introduced in 1948 and offered a vast improvement in quality over the old

78-rpm records. People started to buy LPs to listen to at home. Stereophonic sound was introduced in the 1950s, and manufacturers adapted hi-fi systems to play stereo sound. Popular with teenagers were the cheaper 7-inch, 45-rpm records, even though they only held two songs. Teenagers often had small portable record players in their bedrooms, where they could listen to their own choice of music rather than their parents'.

Television developed from a fledgling industry at the start of the 1950s into a sophisticated money-making business by the end of the decade. By then programs were being specifically scheduled for children and housewives, as well as for general family entertainment. Television ownership grew from four million sets in 1950 to 45 million in 1957; during the same period the total ownership in Europe and the Soviet Union was some 11,725 sets.

An integral feature of television shows was advertising or sponsorship, which were key factors in both paying for the shows and promoting consumerism. There was widespread evidence

TV DINNERS

One of the lasting effects of the 1950s was the establishment of convenience food as an important part of the U.S. diet. Created to allow the housewife to save time but still feel good about the food she served, ready meals were also evidence of the popularity of the television, in front of which they were designed to be eaten. Market leader Swanson packaged its dinners in cartons designed to resemble television sets.

The emphasis was on making food look appetizing—it was often brightly colored using dyes—and easy to serve. The first Swanson TV dinner appeared in 1954 and was served in an aluminum tray. It featured turkey, which was then regarded as a luxury eaten mainly at Thanksgiving. The turkey, sweet potatoes, and vegetables were kept separate from each other, and the potatoes and vegetables both had their own separate bit of butter. The success of the first meal soon led to other dishes being introduced.

TV dinners cost substantially more than equivalent meals prepared from scratch. However, market research suggested that Americans were prepared to pay as much as 45 percent more for the convenience of having their meal already prepared and their time saved.

This 1955 photograph shows an empty molded aluminum tray that kept the three different parts of the meal separate and the same tray filled with a chicken dinner.

of the commercial power of television: Children wanted the latest Davy Crockett outfits, particularly coonskin hats, after seeing the popular Disney TV show; Barbie, launched in 1959, took off after being advertised on television. The first toy ever advertised on television, Mr. Potato Head, is still available today.

Advertising both responded to and shaped demand. Women wanted to be like women on television—good home-keepers, wives, and mothers. Television shows such as *The Adventures of Ozzie and Harriet* promoted an ideal of sub-urban life. For women, however, there was an inherent contradiction. Although many women worked, they were still supposed to find time to do all their chores during the day so that the family's leisure time together could be maximized.

Food manufacturers eagerly seized on the average housewife's shortage of time. A whole range of time-saving cooking products appeared. Rather than bake a cake from scratch, housewives turned to labor-saving packages that just required the addition of water or eggs. Such conveniences made it possible for them to play their role as provider and creator of a welcoming home in the shortest possible time. The next logical step in time-saving meal preparation was complete dinners. A new concept, the TV dinner, became a fashionable product from the middle of the decade (*see box*).

The movies

The rise of television had a dramatic effect on the movie industry. Audiences declined sharply. At the start of the

decade audience numbers had already dropped to 36 million from a high of 82 million in 1946. Movie making was still a huge business throughout the 1950s, however. Epics and musicals, two genres that did not work well on the television screen, boomed. Popular movie musicals included *Singin' in the Rain* (1952) and *Guys and Dolls* (1955). Movies also continued to be influential. Marlon Brando (1924– 2004) became a new idol with the release of the movie version of Tennessee Williams's play *A Streetcar Named Desire* in 1951. James Dean (1931–1955) captured the growing disenchantment of some teenagers with suburban life in *Rebel without a Cause* (1955).

One area in which movie audiences continued to grow was the drive-in. Drive-in theaters allowed audiences in their cars to watch the latest movies projected onto a large screen. Extremely popular with teenagers, partly because of the opportunity they offered for private dating, drive-ins soon appeared all over the country.

Reading and magazines

Another predicted casualty of the rise of television was reading. In fact, however, reading had never been so popular. Many people read before bed after the television stopped transmission. In 1957, 13,142 new titles were published, the highest number since 1900. Popular genres included westerns, detective fiction—particularly the Mickey Spillane novels, which sold three million paperback copies—war novels in the aftermath of World War II, and science fiction. Women read romance novels. One of the most popular and controversial books of the decade was *Peyton Place* (published in 1956). The novel, written by Grace Metalious (1924–1964), was a titillating mixture of sex and scandal that sold 60,000 copies within 10 days of its release. Other popular titles were self-help manuals from which people sought advice about everything from living longer to dealing with arthritis. The sales of paperback books grew from 231 million copies sold in 1951 to 260 million in 1953. Among the sales were a remarkable million copies of *The Illiad* and *The Odyssey*, epics by the ancient Greek poet Homer.

Magazines also enjoyed a boom period. Women read *Ladies' Home Journal, McCall's, Good Housekeeping,* and *Redbook* not only to keep up with the latest fashions but also to read articles about how to perform their role as a housewife. Recipes and handy household hints were plentiful. Romance magazines, such as *True Confessions* and *Modern Romance,* were popular among young working women. Children loved comic books such as *Little Lulu* and *Spooky;* at

the peak of comic book popularity in 1954 there were more than 650 titles with a combined circulation of 100 million each month. Families subscribed to magazines such as *Reader's Digest* and *Life* that told them what was going on in the world. Business magazines reflected the country's growing prosperity with articles about new wealth. Men's magazines encouraged the idea of virility and masculinity, and true adventure pulp magazines were also popular. Teenage girls read *Seventeen* magazine, which became a bestseller by advising girls on how to appeal to boys. Movie magazines were hugely popular, while a magazine created specifically to list the growing number of television programs, *TV Guide,* was launched nationally in 1953.

Hobbies and activities

Partly perhaps as a way to break out of suburban conformity, people pursued many activities that involved some degree of creativity. For example, as cameras improved and became more affordable, amateur photography boomed. Capturing the family on vacation, at home in the backyard, or on important occasions became an essential part of a family record.

Model making and crafts whose popularity had peaked during the Great Depression of the 1930s became popular pastimes once again, including wood carving, train building, and making model aircraft. Such hobbies were essentially lone activities, although they were perhaps shared between a father and son or a "couple of buddies." They provided a counter to the need to be sociable at work and with neighbors. "Basement tinkerings" were in many ways a means for men to rediscover their childhood and a past that was almost always idealized. They also, however, answered people's need to be creative, a need that was best illustrated by the boom in painting-by-numbers that swept the nation during the decade (*see box on p. 16*).

Other activities that were creative but also practical included the DIY boom. By the end of the 1950s the powertool and DIY accessories industry was worth $12 billion. Do-it-yourself was popular for a number of reasons. First, it allowed people to save money. First-time homeowners often bought their tract home with an unfinished basement and attic to get a cheaper price and then finished them themselves. Second, great emphasis was placed on the father and head of the

Teenagers listen to new releases in a record store in 1959. Allowances and weekend or vacation jobs made teenagers an economically important group of consumers.

family being able to do all the practical household jobs. Apart from earning the family income, father was expected to mend and build things around the house and to be able to barbecue. Sales of power tools boomed, but often owning them appealed more than actually using them. In 1954 some 11 million tools were stored away in basement workshops and seldom, if ever, used.

Art boomed through the decade, and not simply in the form of painting-by-numbers. Many people also turned to painting as a creative outlet. Some two million Americans claimed to paint regularly, and the amateur art supplies market was worth $30 million annually. Visits to art galleries rose, fueled by the emergence of exciting new art movements, such as the abstract expressionism of artists like Jackson Pollock and Mark Rothko.

The most popular artist of the 1950s, however, was a grandmother who had never taken an art class in her life and who took up painting at the age of 78. Anna Mary Robertson Moses, known as Grandma Moses (1860–1961), whose images summed up a naive, nostalgic view of American life, became a role model for every kind of hobbyist. The painter's fans included President Dwight D. Eisenhower. When she was interviewed by Ed Murrow in 1955, it provided an opportunity for those people who had color TV sets to see her work at its best.

Creative activities took over from more traditional hobbies such as collecting stamps, coins, dolls, and autographs, which had been popular at the start of the decade. Companies and the government encouraged Americans to participate in creative pastimes. Boeing was just one company to sponsor employee hobby shows. Its 1952 exhibition drew 27,652 visitors and displayed work in 13 different competitive categories, varying from tablecloths crocheted on the bus on the way to work to elaborate model trains. Eisenhower's secretary of Health, Education, and Welfare, herself named Oveta Culp Hobby, declared that hobbies were an essential part of the nation's sense of wellbeing.

The social suburbs

In addition to time spent on creative pastimes the average suburban family had a busy social calendar. Socializing with neighbors was a significant part of leisure time. The most relaxed form of mixing was to have friends over to watch television or enjoy a barbecue in the backyard. The barbecue was the domain of the father, who cooked the meat for the meal. The relaxed barbecue was a mainstay of 1950s suburban life. The more formal equivalent was the cocktail party (*see box opposite*).

Another popular suburban activity was the bridge party. Card games had always been popular, but in the 1950s bridge had a particular appeal that lay not only in the game itself but also in its ability to bring people together to socialize without the need to make much conversation. By 1955, 57 percent of adults were playing regularly. Meanwhile, in a reflection of the extremes of the Cold War, in 1954 the Soviet Union denounced card playing—along with drinking and smoking—as being against the state.

Attending classical music concerts or even playing in an amateur orchestra was also popular. In 1900 the United States had 10 symphony orchestras; by 1958 there were more than 1,000. In the previous year the American public had spent $500 million on concert tickets, $80 million on classical records, $160 million on hi-fi equipment, and $40 million on sheet music. The piano remained the most popular musical instrument to learn at home.

PAINTING-BY-NUMBERS

Among the most popular crazes of the 1950s was painting-by-numbers, in which consumers bought a kit containing a picture divided into numbered areas and paints that corresponded to those numbers. The precise origins of the idea remain disputed. Children's numbered painting had already been around for some time, but the refinement of supplying the exact paints with the picture was new, as was the idea of aiming the kits at adults.

By Christmas 1953 a painting-by-numbers kit was on almost everyone's Christmas list. Retailing for as little as $1.79, the kits gave everyone the opportunity to create their own masterpiece regardless of their talent or lack of it. The craze swept the country. President Dwight D. Eisenhower gave sets to his staff for Christmas presents. The much-admired British Prime Minister Winston Churchill was an eager painter-by-numbers, as well as an accomplished artist in his own right. Television's most popular family, the Nelsons, promoted their own kits and painted-by-numbers on their show.

The kits were particularly popular with women and often featured such subjects as kittens and landscapes. The most popular single painting was an $11.50 kit of *The Last Supper* by Leonardo Da Vinci, which was highly complex and time-consuming.

Despite the popularity and financial success of painting-by-numbers—yearly sales in 1954 reached $200 million—the kits were not universally popular. Artists, in particular, hated the idea that painting could be reduced to a mindless activity. Other critics saw the kits as a metaphor for the emphasis placed throughout the decade on social conformity: The kits had to be filled in exactly as instructed, with no individual input or creativity.

A SUBURBAN COCKTAIL PARTY

Cocktail parties were an integral part of suburban life in the 1950s. They helped counter the isolation felt by many people and offered a chance for them to get to know their neighbors. The parties followed a set pattern. Formal invitations were sent out and replied to. People dressed up for the occasion, with women wearing their latest cocktail dress and high heels, while men wore suits.

Refreshments comprised cocktails in special cocktail glasses and snacks. Liquor, such as whisky, gin, and vodka, was placed on side tables in decorative decanters. Most people smoked, and one of the hostess's jobs was to make sure that enough cigarettes and ashtrays were put out. It was the man's job to mix and serve cocktails, while his wife concentrated on serving coffee and the food. Wine was not served; it was expensive and not readily available at that time.

One consequence of the popularity of cocktail parties was a boom in sales of associated goods. Gin production tripled from 6 million gallons (23 million liters) in 1950 to 19 million gallons (72 million liters) in 1960. Vodka consumption was negligible in the United States before 1950 but had reached 9 million gallons (34 million liters) by 1960. The sales of aspirin—a popular choice of hangover cure—increased by one-third during the decade.

This 1956 cocktail party, hosted by millionaire Robert P. McCulloch, was echoed throughout America by similar, albeit less ostentatious, gatherings, where people chatted or played bridge.

Teenagers, meanwhile, had little to do with their parents' social life. They went to dances and listened to rock 'n' roll. Along with their interest in new music came a newfound rebellion against their parents' lifestyle. Drive-in movies and hot-rodding—customizing cars and racing them at high speeds— were popular pastimes for young men, while girls became increasingly interested in their appearance and went shopping for clothes and makeup. In 1956, 35 percent of boys and 22 percent of girls aged between 13 and 18 had permanent part-time jobs. During the summer vacation the figure rose much higher. Working gave teenagers annual spending money of $9 billion, making the teen leisure market a highly significant economic sector.

By the late 1950s beach culture inspired by the California lifestyle had become important for teenagers. Surfing and sunbathing were fashionable, particularly once portable radios appeared on the market that could be taken to the beach.

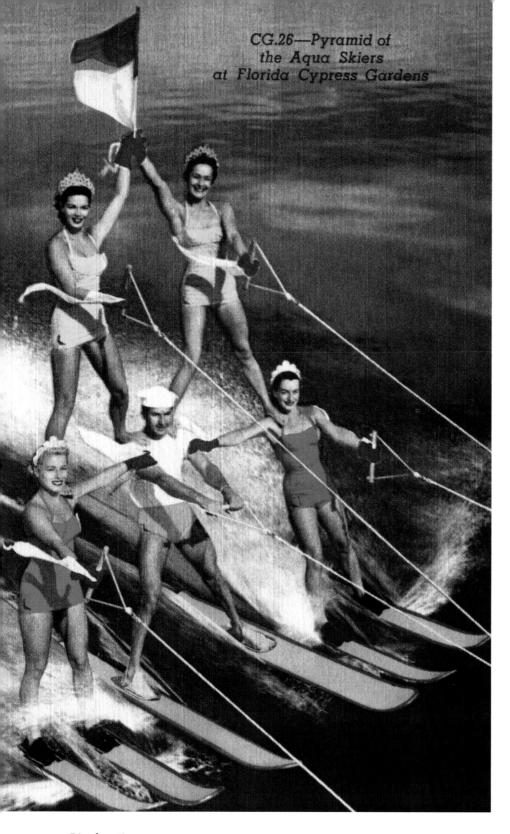

CG.26—*Pyramid of the Aqua Skiers at Florida Cypress Gardens*

The Aqua Skiers perform at Cypress Gardens in Florida in 1954. The state had extensive facilities for water sports, with 30,000 lakes and 1,440 miles (2,230km) of coastline.

related sports enjoyed huge popularity. The number of boaters increased from 20 to 30 million during the decade. They spent $240 million on boats and boating accessories; meanwhile, anglers spent $150 million on their sport.

Before the war activities such as tennis and golf had been considered the preserve of the rich. With the building of public golf courses and tennis courts more people started to play. They were also sociable activities to be enjoyed with friends and neighbors on the weekends. Perhaps the most sociable of all sports was bowling. A weekend visit to the local bowling alley was as much about catching up with friends as it was about bowling.

Children played sports, too. Particularly in the suburbs, moms ferried their kids to Little League games, and playing in the backyard with the neighbors' kids passed many hours. Hula Hoops also became a massive craze, reaching a peak of popularity in 1958.

For many Americans the 1950s were indeed an era of leisure. Increased income, shorter working hours, and greater mechanization in the kitchen allowed families in the newly built suburbs to enjoy more activities than ever before. Technological advances in broadcasting widened the choice of things to do. Critics, however, protested the pressure to be active: Doing nothing did not seem to be an option.

See Also:

Air Travel • Automobile Culture • Barbie Doll • Book Publishing • Cartoons and Animation • Children's Books • Classical Music • Disney, Walt • Fashion and Dress • Games and Pastimes • Highway Network • Magazines • Movie Industry • Popular Music • Radio • Recording Industry • Retail Industry • Rock 'n' Roll • Sports • Sports and TV • Suburbs • Teenage Culture • Television • Visual Arts

Playing the game

Participatory sport also became popular in the 1950s. During the Great Depression of the 1930s, when people had little money to spend, they had yearned to play tennis or golf, swim, skate, or enjoy other sports that cost more than they could dream of. In the more prosperous 1950s sports became a major leisure activity. While audiences declined for some spectator sports, notably baseball, people wanted to be out doing some activity, particularly after working in an office all week.

With the construction of many more reservoirs to meet the extra demand for water created by the growing population, boating and water-

LITERATURE

At odds with the optimistic mood of postwar America, fiction writers of the 1950s confronted unsettling themes such as war, crime, and sexuality. Their disquiet crystallized around the figure of the misunderstood and nonconformist "outsider."

By the 1950s American literature enjoyed an international reputation, largely owing to the achievements of the prewar writers Ernest Hemingway (1899–1961), William Faulkner (1897–1962), and John Steinbeck (1902–1968), all of whom became Nobel laureates in this period. Experimental, socially conscious, and often politically radical, the writers of the 1930s had offered a distinctly American version of modernism, the early 20th-century movement that had sought to break with traditional forms and ways of writing.

The "age of anxiety"

The older generation of great American writers exerted a powerful influence on their postwar successors, who were ambitious to match their achievements and to create a fictional masterpiece that in some way encapsulated American life and experience: the so-called "Great American Novel." However, between prewar and postwar generations there was a deep division caused by the trauma of World War II (1939–1945)—in which many 1950s writers took part as combatants—and

John Steinbeck was one of the great prewar writers; his 1930s novels included Of *Mice and Men* and *The Grapes of Wrath*. In 1952 he published *East of Eden*, a family saga.

WINNERS OF THE NATIONAL BOOK AWARD FOR FICTION

1950 Nelson Algren, *The Man with the Golden Arm*
1951 William Faulkner, *The Collected Stories*
1952 James Jones, *From Here to Eternity*
1953 Ralph Ellison, *Invisible Man*
1954 Saul Bellow, *The Adventures of Augie March*

1955 William Faulkner, *A Fable*
1956 John O'Hara, *Ten North Frederick*
1957 Wright Morris, *The Field of Vision*
1958 John Cheever, *The Wapshot Chronicle*
1959 Bernard Malamud, *The Magic Barrel*

THE OUTSIDER

The theme of the disturbed, troubled, and persecuted "outsider" or "misfit" was to recur in the works of many 1950s writers. It was a theme that can be traced back at least as far as Mark Twain's *The Adventures of Huckleberry Finn* (1884), whose hero's innocence and natural rebelliousness highlight the hypocrisy of the adult world. In the postwar period, however, the theme took on a new urgency.

During the 1950s many commentators were already criticizing the period's stifling culture of conformism and materialism. Sociological studies such as William Whyte's *The Organization Man* (1956) and C. Wright Mills's *White Collar* (1951) decried the rise of a corporate, suburban man who relinquished his individuality in order to gain materialistic success and societal status. The flipside of this critique was an interest in those who failed to conform or "achieve," whether because of their race, ethnicity, sexuality, age, or class, or simply owing to their vulnerability or idealism.

Alienation, it seemed, was the American condition. Owing to society's racism, African Americans continued to be largely excluded from participating in the "American Dream," while members of immigrant cultures were suspended in a kind of limbo between the culture of their forefathers and the American culture they had yet to join. Alienation of another kind was felt by many former servicemen who found it difficult to settle down to civilian life after their wartime experiences, while a developing youth culture led to a further estrangement between adults and teenagers.

Holden Caulfield, the central character of J.D. Salinger's 1951 cult novel *The Catcher in the Rye*, feels alienated from what he sees as the corrupt adult world.

The theme of the outsider was given a philosophical focus by the intellectual movement that was known as existentialism, which exerted a powerful influence on American literature in this period. Existentialism's leaders, the French writers Jean-Paul Sartre (1905–1980) and Albert Camus (1913–1960), argued that alienation was not only an attribute of the poor or of minorities but part of the human condition itself. Camus's novel *L'Etranger* ("The Outsider"; 1942) offered an archetypal figure of the misfit in its portrait of a murderer who refuses to submit to society's expectations even when he is threatened with the death penalty.

In American fiction the classic 1950s statement of the outsider theme was J.D. Salinger's *The Catcher in the Rye* (1951), in which the adolescent Holden Caulfield instinctively rebels against the adult world. The outsider was prevalent too in black writing: in Ralph Ellison's *Invisible Man* (1952), whose nameless narrator ends up alone in a Harlem cellar, and in Richard Wright's *The Outsider* (1953), often billed as the first American existentialist novel. Alienation also marks the war novel, in which soldiers are at odds with their regimented life, and also the crime "pulp" paperback, in which both murderer and detective share a common urban angst.

Toward the end of the decade the Beats—Jack Kerouac and Allen Ginsberg, among others—made the outsider not an object of sympathy but a modern hero, whose rebellion against society's conventions promised to rejuvenate the jaded American spirit.

the overwhelming horrors of the Holocaust and the bombing of Hiroshima and Nagasaki in Japan.

Writers shaped in the prewar era were fundamentally optimistic—both about human nature and the American way of life—and often used their work to fight against injustice and in order to win social change. Postwar writers, by contrast, found themselves faced with what the English-born poet W.H. Auden in 1947 described as "the age of anxiety." The events of the war had left many disillusioned about human nature and haunted by the specter of nuclear annihilation, especially as the Cold War gathered pace. Many were troubled too by the self-righteousness

of America in its position as a world superpower and the complacency of a public that seemed to have so whole-heartedly embraced the twin spirits of consumerism and conformism.

It was a cultural pessimism that led many writers to ponder what kinds of novels, poems, or plays they ought to be writing. They wondered if it was any longer possible to write meaningfully about individual lives in the face of the crushing economic, military, and historic forces that seemed to play havoc with the world. Was it, they asked, even possible to understand or describe the complex, irrational, and "unreal" place America had become?

For a few American literature seemed doomed to go into decline. In 1951 the critic John Aldridge, in his study *After the Lost Generation*, argued that American writers had lost the moral capacity to create serious art.

Despite such dire predictions, however, writers in the 1950s did find ways of representing the strange new age in which they found themselves, and the decade would produce some of the century's most original and influential writers as well as some of the United States' most enduring literary classics.

The naturalist tradition

The tradition of naturalism in narrative writing—the attempt to portray society and how it shapes the lives of individuals in a full, rounded, and even scientific or objective way—had been an important strand in American writing since the beginning of the 20th century. In 1900 Theodore Dreiser (1871–1945) published *Sister Carrie*, the story of a young woman who goes to New York City and is "undone" by "forces wholly superhuman"—the economic, political, and social realities

Nelson Algren poses for a photo in about 1951. His most famous novels, *The Man with the Golden Arm* (1949) and *A Walk on the Wild Side* (1956), were both turned into films.

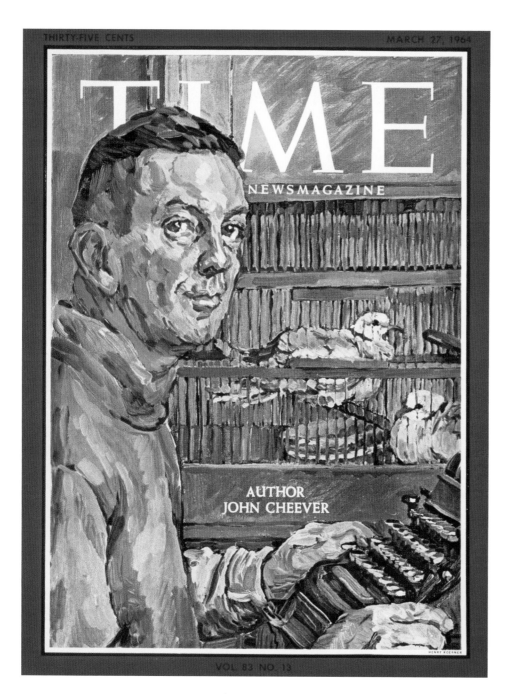

THIRTY-FIVE CENTS

MARCH 27, 1964

TIME

NEWSMAGAZINE

AUTHOR
JOHN CHEEVER

VOL 83 NO. 13

HENRY KOERNER

John Cheever is depicted on the cover of *Time* in 1964. He regularly wrote short stories for *The New Yorker*. *The Wapshot Chronicle* won him the National Book Award in 1958.

and Norman Mailer's (1923–) *The Naked and the Dead* (1948), which ends with the hero's chilling cry of "Long live regimentation!"

Urban alienation

Dreiser's depiction of a merciless, inhuman city whose "cunning wiles" tempt inhabitants to their physical or moral destruction also found resonance. For many writers in the 1950s the modern American city was a nightmarish place of darkness, violence, poverty, loneliness, and alienation, remote indeed from the cosy suburban world of the "American Dream." *The Man with the Golden Arm* (1949) by Nelson Algren (1909–1981) is set in the Chicago slums and is the story of poker dealer Frankie Machine, who yearns to escape his poverty and drug addiction. Algren's was a nightmarish, grimly poetic vision that reverberated throughout 1950s literature in novels such as Ralph Ellison's (1914–1994) *Invisible Man* (1952), which ends with a near hallucinatory depiction of a riot in Harlem, as well as poems such as Allen Ginsberg's (1926–1997) "Howl" (1956), in which New York City is a drug-inflected kaleidoscope of "blind streets," "unshaven rooms," and "neon blinking traffic light."

The compassion for the "dispossessed" and the "outsider" figure found in Algren was shared by many writers of the period, who themselves felt at odds with contemporary society (*see p. 20*). It was often accompanied by a critique of the American Dream and of its latest incarnation: the flourishing culture of suburbia epitomized by the Levittown home and the Buick automobile. In the bestselling *The Man in the Gray Flannel Suit* (1955) Sloan Wilson (1920–2003) portrayed an ex-soldier, Tom Rath, who, in the belief that "the [only] important thing is to make money," sinks into a routine job and lifestyle only to end up realizing that he has sacrificed his inner life. At

(such as money and class) that Dreiser saw as imprisoning modern people.

Dreiser's analysis of the modern condition seemed, if anything, to have even greater relevance in the years after World War II, as novelists continued to show characters in the grip of forces that they could neither control nor fully understand. The war itself was the subject matter for many former soldiers, who had experienced the feeling of being trapped inside a "military machine." In the bestselling novel *From Here to Eternity* (1951), for

example, James Jones (1921–1977) gave a grimly realistic portrayal of army life on Hawaii in the months leading up to the attack on Pearl Harbor and showed how an individual—the rebellious and idealistic Private Robert E. Lee Prewitt—is slowly destroyed by the dehumanizing pressures of the military. Similar concerns with the fate of the individual under the weight of military regimentation can be found in novels such as Herman Wouk's (1915–) *The Caine Mutiny* (1951), J.D. Salinger's (1919–) *Nine Stories* (1953),

Vladimir Nabokov was born in Russia, educated in England, and emigrated to America in 1940. His controversial novel *Lolita* (1955) brought him fame and wealth.

the end of the novel he watches the "bright young men in gray flannel suits rushing around New York in a frantic parade to nowhere." Much subtler dissections of American suburban life were found in the short stories of John Cheever (1912–1982), with their evocation of a world of cocktail parties, Dutch Colonial houses, and domestic crises (*see p. 24*).

The rural world as depicted in 1950s fiction was scarcely less troubled. The vibrant tradition of southern writing that had included in most recent years such major figures as William Faulkner,

Young authors Norman Mailer (left) and Allen Ginsberg (center) appear on a televised discussion program with the English-born writer Ashley Montagu in 1957.

THE *NEW YORKER* SHORT STORY

Many of the novelists of the 1950s also wrote short stories, although a few, notably John Cheever, largely concentrated on the form. It was a flourishing genre, whose most recent heritage included such notable practitioners as Ernest Hemingway, Sherwood Anderson (1876–1941), and John O'Hara (1905–1970), and had a wide readership. Many 1950s short stories were initially published in popular magazines such as *The New Yorker*, *Collier's*, and *The New Republic*, providing writers, especially up-and-coming ones, with a valuable source of income. John Updike (1932–) famously claimed that during the 1950s he could easily have supported his wife and family by selling five or six stories to *The New Yorker* each year.

Many of the short stories published during the decade were of a naturalistic, "slice of life" type that focused not so much on plot but on character and mood. The master of what became known as the "*New Yorker* story" was John Cheever, who published many of his works in that magazine. Cheever's finely crafted, elegantly written stories were acutely observed portrayals of middle-class suburban life that achieved a balance between irony and compassion. Perhaps Cheever's most famous collection of the period was *The Housebreaker of Shady Hill and Other Stories* (1958), set in a fictional town where the "waspish" characters—small businessmen, anxious teenagers, and frustrated housewives—are caught between their dreams and the more prosaic realities of their everyday lives.

John Updike joined the staff of *The New Yorker* in the mid-1950s and contributed short stories to the magazine.

Carson McCullers (1917–1967), and Eudora Welty (1909–2001) continued through the decade in the work of Flannery O'Connor (1925–1964). McCullers's *The Ballad of the Sad Café* (1951), the tale of the love of a lonely storekeeper for her hunchback cousin, is suggestive of the poetic, mythic, or even surreal quality that southern writers often brought to naturalism.

If anything, the works of O'Connor were stranger still. In the bleakly humorous, unsettling *Wise Blood* (1952) a misfit former soldier, Hazel Motes, sets up a new church—the church of the "Unrisen Christ"—and in the process comes into conflict with a grotesque cast of characters, including a con-artist preacher and a man in a gorilla suit.

Experimental writing

Some writers believed that the naturalist tradition could no longer successfully portray the experience of living in modern America. As the novelist Philip Roth (1933–) wrote a little later: "The American writer in the middle of the 20th century has his hands full in trying to understand, describe, and make *credible* much of the

BOOK CENSORSHIP

The politically repressive and socially conservative climate of the early 1950s heightened the debate over the United States' longstanding censorship laws. Most notable was the so-called "Comstock law," which since 1873 had barred the sending through the mail of "any obscene, lewd, or lascivious book, pamphlet, picture, print, or other publication of vulgar and indecent character." For decades books had fallen foul of the Comstock law as well as customs, state governments, the police, and other public and legal bodies. In the prewar period D.H. Lawrence's *Lady Chatterley's Lover* (published privately, 1928) and Henry Miller's *Tropic of Cancer* (published in Paris, 1934) —both novels in which sex was extremely candidly described— were among the most notable books banned in America.

During the 1950s, when many authors tackled contentious issues such as homosexuality, drug-taking, and crime, there were numerous instances of book censorship. In 1957, for example, the San Francisco police seized copies of Allen Ginsberg's *Howl and Other Poems* from the City Lights bookstore, and its owner, Lawrence Ferlinghetti (1919–), was charged with selling "obscene and indecent writings." While those who promoted censorship were seemingly fixated on the supposed sexual immorality of such books, their concerns were often closely allied with anxieties about political subversion, as seen in the widespread association of homosexuality with communism.

The threat of censorship made many publishers wary of putting out anything that might be considered "beyond the pale," and they therefore took part in a kind of "self-

censorship." Nabokov's *Lolita* was turned down by every American publisher it was submitted to and eventually had to be published in Paris by Olympia Press (which was also to publish Burroughs's *The Naked Lunch*). Only in 1958 was the first U.S. edition of *Lolita* brought out, its notoriety ensuring it a place on the bestseller list that year.

There were widespread fears among liberals that America was becoming an authoritarian state. In his 1953 novel *Fahrenheit 451* the science fiction writer Ray Bradbury (1920–) portrayed a society in which all books are banned, and firemen are paid to burn down houses where illegal books have been found. For many who campaigned against censorship at this time, the freedom of speech enshrined in the First Amendment was more or less absolute, allowing of no exceptions.

By the late 1950s the tide was beginning to turn against censorship. In 1957 the Supreme Court ruled in the case *Roth v. United States* that only those materials that had predominantly "prurient" appeal to the average adult and that utterly lacked "redeeming social importance" were not protected by the First Amendment. While such descriptive terms could clearly be open to broad interpretation, the decision heralded an era of more liberal attitudes toward the sexual content of books. The ban on one of the century's greatest *causes célèbres* of censorship—*Lady Chatterley's Lover*—was finally lifted in the United States in 1959.

Ray Bradbury, the science fiction author, published *Fahrenheit 451* in 1953. The novel portrays a society in which all books are banned.

Kerouac's *On the Road* (1957) is a first-person account of a journey into the American West, away from the nightmare of city life toward individualistic freedom. With its blend of drug culture and Zen mysticism *On the Road* was to become the "bible" of the hippie movement in the 1960s.

Other writers chose a different kind of revolt, turning their backs on reality altogether to create novels that were celebrations and examinations of art itself. The key figure here was the Russian-born writer Vladimir Nabokov (1899–1977), who once famously wrote that "Reality is neither the subject nor the object of true art, which creates its own special reality." For Nabokov novels (like abstract paintings) are works that deal primarily with their own substance—that is, words. Thus Nabokov's most famous, not to say notorious, novel of the period, *Lolita* (published in Paris, 1955), is less about its "plot"—the tale of a middle-aged Russian emigrant called Humbert Humbert who falls in love with a young 12-year-old girl called Dolores Haze—than about Nabokov's own "love affair with the English language" and with American literature and culture.

Other voices

While many novelists wrestled with the problems of representing the reality of postwar America, writers belonging to socially and culturally marginalized groups, such as African Americans and women, were still struggling to get their own experience of that reality into print and to gain public recognition. There were, of course, some notable exceptions; for example, Ellison's *Invisible Man* won the 1953 National Book Award, and both the Catholic novelist Frances Parkinson Keyes (1885–1970) and the black historical novelist Frank Yerby (1916–1991) regularly made it into the bestseller lists. However, for the most part the

American reality." America, such writers thought, was too complex, too multidimensional, and too fast-changing to be pinned down in any straightforward, realistic way. The trauma of war, the atomic bomb, and the Holocaust, they further felt, made the traditional plot-novel obsolete.

That sense of having "their hands full" encouraged some writers to try out more experimental and expressionistic forms of writing in order to convey their sense of dismay, confusion, and horror. In the early 1950s Norman Mailer produced two novels, *Barbary Shore* (1951) and *The Deer Park* (1955), that were virtually plotless, but which brimmed with ideas.

Still more anarchic were the novels of William Burroughs (1914–1997). In novels such as *Junkie* (1953) and *The Naked Lunch* (published in Paris, 1959)

Burroughs rejected realistic narrative for a loose progression of "junk"-like and seemingly random fragments drawn both from contemporary American life and culture as well as from Burroughs's own drug-induced experiences. As much as for their free-form spirit as for their frankness about themes such as drugs and homosexuality, Burroughs's novels made for unsettling reading for most readers, although they quickly established themselves as underground classics.

Burroughs's work was an important strand in the counterculture movement known as the Beats that developed toward the end of the decade. For Beats such as Jack Kerouac (1922–1969) and the poet Allen Ginsberg the "outsider" was a new kind of hero whose nonconformity offered a route toward the spiritual regeneration of the nation.

JEWISH AMERICAN LITERATURE

One of the outstanding features of 1950s literature was the massive contribution made by Jewish American writers, including such prominent novelists as Saul Bellow (1915–2005), Nelson Algren, Bernard Malamud (1914–1986), and Norman Mailer and the playwright Arthur Miller (1915–2005). Earlier Jewish American writers had largely addressed other Jewish immigrants, sometimes using English but quite often writing in Yiddish. Their work, born of out of their experience of poverty and racism in American cities such as Chicago and New York, was often left-wing and radical, and largely rejected Judaism, even though it retained a pride in Jewishness itself.

In the postwar period Jewish American writing entered the mainstream (Algren, Bellow, and Malamud all won National Book Awards in the 1950s) and was read much more widely. For this reason it is sometimes viewed by critics as reflecting the assimilation of Jews into American society. In reality, writing by Jewish Americans during this period represented a rather more complex response to both their adopted homeland and their Jewish heritage. Much of their work was still concerned with feelings of alienation (of not quite fitting into American society) as well as with a sense of loss and sometimes nostalgia for the European past. The Holocaust preoccupied many.

The most overtly "Jewish" among these postwar writers was undoubtedly the Polish-born writer Isaac Bashevis Singer (1904–1991), who immigrated to the United States in 1935. In his new home Singer continued to write in Yiddish, although translations of his novels and short stories also appeared. Singer's most famous novel of the 1950s was *The Family Moskat* (1950), a long, realistic chronicle of Jewish life leading up to the German bombardment of Warsaw in 1939. It was widely seen by many as a monument to the millions of Polish Jews who had died in the Holocaust.

Singer exerted a powerful influence on many younger Jewish American writers. Bernard Malamud's works, which in the 1950s included the novel *The Assistant* (1957) and a collection of short stories, *The Magic Barrel* (1958), revealed the struggles of immigrant Jews to make lives for themselves in an alien culture. Saul Bellow's exuberant epic *The Adventures of Augie March* (1953), about a young Jewish boy growing up in Depression-era Chicago, is a celebration of the human spirit in the face of adversity. Both Malamud and Bellow were deeply concerned with human beings' ethical responsibilities: "How should a good man live, what ought he to do?" as the hero of Bellow's first novel, *Dangling Man* (1944), wonders.

A direct confrontation with the Holocaust was found in the work of the American Yiddish poet and writer Chaim Grade (1910–1982), whose wife and mother had both died in the genocide, and who immigrated to the United States in 1948. In the devastating short story "Mayn krig mit Hersh Rasseyner" ("My Fight with Hersh Rasseyner"; 1950), two friends, one atheist and one devout, passionately debate whether it is still possible to believe in God after the murder of six million Jews.

Isaac Bashevis Singer published the novel *The Family Moskat* in 1950. He wrote mostly in Yiddish and personally supervised translations into English.

Isaac Asimov was born in Russia but came to America when he was three. In addition to his successful science fiction stories he also wrote popular nonfiction science books.

literature of the 1950s remained overwhelmingly white and male.

During the 1950s the renewed emphasis on the woman's role as homemaker, wife, and mother made it more difficult than ever for female novelists and poets to make their mark on mainstream writing. Parkinson Keyes's popularity was as much due to her deeply conservative outlook as to the lovingly described settings of her novels, while Flannery O'Connor, one of the most highly regarded female writers of the decade, was herself subtly marginalized by her categorization as an exotic "southern" writer.

Perhaps more typical of the difficulties faced by women writers during the 1950s was the career of Jewish, working-class Tillie Olsen (1913–). Olsen had begun writing her highly personal, feminist fiction back in the 1930s but had succeeded in publishing only short fragments. Not until 1961 did she finally publish her first major work, *Tell Me a Riddle: A Collection*, a volume of three short stories and a novella. By contrast, many women writers were able to flourish in "popular" fiction, in genres such as the thriller and historical romance. Thus Patricia Highsmith (1921–1995) found

considerable acclaim for her series of thrillers about a charming psychopath, the first of which, *The Talented Mr. Ripley*, was published in 1955.

African American writers

African American writers had a rich heritage on which to build, notably the writers of the Harlem Renaissance of the 1920s and the protest novels of Richard Wright (1908–1960), whose most famous work was *Native Son* (1940). However, many among the new generation of black writers, notably James Baldwin (1924–1987) and Ralph Ellison, wanted to go further than Wright in exploring the experience of individual black men and women, free as they now were from the need to use their works as a political platform. Baldwin, in particular, was eager to write fiction from a highly personal viewpoint. His lyrical first novel *Go Tell It on the Mountain* (1953) tells the story of a 14-year-old growing up in an impoverished Pentecostal community in New York's Harlem.

Homosexuality was openly featured as a theme in many novels and short stories of the period—from James Jones's treatment of homosexual tensions between some of the soldiers in *From Here to Eternity* to the more outrageous fantasies of William Burroughs in *The Naked Lunch*. However, a self-consciously "gay" literature written by "out" writers was still a long way off, although its first glimmerings were already discernible. One of the first American novels to portray a homosexual love affair between two "ordinary" men was the brave *The City and the Pillar* (1948) by Gore Vidal (1925–), which was banned from many bookstores at the time.

One persistent problem for many "minority" writers at the time was that there was an expectation that not only would they portray members of their own "community" in their work, but also that they would do so in a positive

Grace Metalious reads at home in 1956. Her novel *Peyton Place*, which was published that same year, was a great success, selling 20 million hardbacks alone.

light. Authors often stoutly resisted this expectation, partly for artistic reasons and partly because they felt that stereotypes of any kind were dehumanizing. Baldwin, for example, wanted to be seen as more than simply a "black" novelist and, accordingly, in his second novel, *Giovanni's Room* (1956), wrote about a subject matter apparently far removed from the concerns of contemporary African Americans—the love affairs of a white American expatriate in Paris. The Jewish writer Isaac Bashevis Singer (1904–1991) almost exclusively portrayed Jews in his work: He was anxious not to idealize them but to show them as fully rounded human beings, with failings as well as virtues (*see p. 27*).

Popular fiction

Popular fiction flourished in the 1950s with the massive expansion of paperback publishing. Popular titles from genres such as thrillers, science fiction, historical romance, and detective fiction were brought out in vast numbers by companies such as Dell, Bantam, and Ace, and sold largely at kiosks, newsstands, and drugstores rather than at traditional bookstores. With their garish covers and sensational subject matter such titles often attracted criticism and even moral outrage. However, many good writers were increasingly attracted to working in these genres—especially in science fiction and the detective novel—and their work accordingly garnered serious critical attention (*see box on p. 30*).

No less than "quality" mainstream literature, "pulp fiction" reflected the anxieties and preoccupations of the age. Science fiction writing, which boomed in the 1950s, provides a clear illustration. Writers such as Robert A. Heinlein (1907–1988) and Isaac Asimov (1920–1992) responded to the rapid changes in technology that took place during the decade, including the

testing of the hydrogen bomb and the beginning of the space race. They imagined the possible developments from these scientific changes and the implications for human society. At the beginning of the decade, for example, Asimov's famous collection of short stories *I, Robot* (1950) examined the ethical implications of a robotic future, while Heinlein's *Starship Troopers* (1959) depicted a future society so dominated by warfare that citizenship could be earned only through military service.

Not all writers or readers of the 1950s, of course, felt compelled to

confront serious issues. Romantic fiction featured heavily on the decade's bestseller lists. The African American Frank Yerby wrote swashbuckling novels set in the antebellum South that somehow sidestepped the issue of racism altogether, while one of the most popular novels of the 1950s was *Peyton Place* (1956) by Grace Metalious (1924–1964), which sold 20 million copies in hardback alone and spawned a sequel, *Return to Peyton Place*, in 1959. Its scandalous subject matter—the sexual secrets of a New England town—shocked America and led to it being banned in many public libraries.

NOIR FICTION

The "hardboiled" or "noir" novel—stories of violent crime set in seamy city settings—had been pioneered in the 1920s and 1930s by writers such as Dashiell Hammett (1894–1961) and Raymond Chandler (1888–1959). After the war the genre's depiction of decaying city life and modern ills such as drug addiction, corruption, and alienation chimed particularly well with the 1950s undercurrent of social malaise. As a result, crime fiction and science fiction flourished. A new generation of writers continued to exploit the genre's trademarks: gun-toting detectives, dangerous "dames," and tough talk, all presented in the slick, slang-ridden style honed to perfection by Chandler.

One of the most popular hardboiled writers of the decade was Mickey Spillane (1918–), whose most famous series of novels, including *My Gun Is Quick* (1950) and *The Big Kill* (1951), featured the detective Mike Hammer. The crime novels of Ross Macdonald (1915–1983), such as *The Way Some People Die* (1951) and *The Ivory Grin* (1952), were more sober and reflective, and thus won praise from the literary establishment. Patricia Highsmith was one of the rare female novelists writing in a genre largely aimed at male readers. She was unusual, too, in that she took as her protagonist a suave amoral murderer, Tom Ripley, who appeared in a series of novels published in the fifties, sixties, and seventies.

Writers of the 1950s sometimes used the "hardboiled" genre as a way of exploring radical themes. William Burroughs's *Junkie: Confessions of an Unredeemed Drug Addict* was first published by Ace in the "noir" format, complete with lurid front cover, while the African American Chester Himes's (1904–1984) series of novels (beginning in 1957 with *For Love of Imabelle*, later retitled *A Rage in Harlem*) about two black New York detectives explored the corrupting influence of racism.

Mickey Spillane tells a story in 1952. Spillane started out writing for pulp magazines and comics. His first novel was *I, The Jury* (1947).

Critics have long debated whether any writer in the 1950s succeeded in creating the "Great American Novel." The works most frequently nominated for that accolade are J.D. Salinger's *The Catcher in the Rye*, Saul Bellow's *The Adventures of Augie March,* and James Jones's *From Here to Eternity*. Even at the time, however, there was a growing feeling among commentators that such a novel—describing a singular, inclusive American experience and appealing to a broad national readership—could no longer be written. Postwar America was an entity too complex, too disjointed, and too racially divided to allow for a new *Huckleberry Finn* or a national literature. A new literary ideal was emerging, one that celebrated diversity and liberation and a plethora of American literatures.

See Also:

Baldwin, James • Beat Movement • Bellow, Saul • Black Writers • Book Publishing • Burroughs, William • Children's Books • Ginsberg, Allen • Hemingway, Ernest • Kerouac, Jack • Malamud, Bernard • Miller, Arthur • O'Connor, Flannery • Poetry • Salinger, J.D. • Science Fiction

LITTLE RICHARD 1932–

Manic piano-pounding, falsetto-voiced singer-songwriter Little Richard wrote many of the classic rock-'n'-roll anthems and inspired generations of musical talent. Despite giving up rock 'n' roll for the church at the height of his career, he later returned to the fold.

The self-proclaimed "architect of rock 'n' roll," Little Richard had an enormous influence as a singer-songwriter on the development of popular music in the 1950s and beyond. Born Richard Wayne Penniman into a family of 12 children in Macon, Georgia, on December 5, 1932, he sang gospel as a boy in the local church choir. He gave himself the name Little Richard when, in his early teens, he began to appear in nightclubs and medicine shows (staged to draw crowds who would then be persuaded to buy medicines). In 1951 he received his first recording contract after winning a talent contest in Atlanta, and over the next few years he made a number of rhythm-'n'-blues (R&B) records with a variety of bands. However, not all were released, and those that were did not sell.

First success

Little Richard's fortunes changed in 1955, when he signed with a new record label, Specialty, and recorded a dozen songs in New Orleans. They included "Tutti Frutti," which became his first R&B and pop hit in the United States and is regarded as one of the great pop classics. His next record was "Long Tall Sally," which became a Top 10 hit. Both songs were "covered" by the popular singer Pat Boone; in fact, Boone's version of "Tutti Frutti" outsold Little Richard's original. Both songs were also big hits in the United Kingdom. Other records that were successful on both sides of the Atlantic included "Rip It Up" (backed with "Ready Teddy"), "The Girl Can't Help It," "Lucille," and "Good Golly, Miss Molly."

Cover versions of Little Richard hits were also recorded by Elvis Presley, Buddy Holly, and many others.

Little Richard's stage act, in which he energetically pounded his piano and sang in a manic falsetto, served as a model for many other popular stars, including Jerry Lee Lewis and James Brown. With his pompadour hairstyle and frequent use of makeup and flamboyant costumes, he was an ideal star for the early rock-'n'-roll films of 1956–1957: *Don't Knock the Rock, The Girl Can't Help It,* and *Mister Rock and Roll.*

It came as a shock to all his fans when Little Richard announced in October 1957, while touring in Australia, that he was giving up rock 'n' roll to become a minister. He entered a seminary in Alabama and in 1961 was ordained a minister of the Seventh Day Adventist Church. Between 1958 and 1962 he recorded only gospel music. However, in late 1962 Little Richard changed direction once again. He embarked on tours of Europe and the United Kingdom—where he was much admired by groups such as the Beatles and the Rolling Stones—and began to make recordings of rock and soul music. His popularity began to wane in the 1970s, and in 1976 he rejoined the church. He became a full-time evangelist until 1986, when he was inducted into the Rock and Roll Hall of Fame in its opening year. In 1993 he performed in the presidential inaugural ceremony for Bill Clinton.

Rock-'n'-roll icon Little Richard followed Elvis Presley's example by appearing in the movies. However, in the great majority of his films he simply played himself.

See Also:

Holly, Buddy • Popular Music
• Presley, Elvis • Rock 'n' Roll
• Teenage Culture

LITTLE ROCK SCHOOL CRISIS

In 1957 President Eisenhower reluctantly used federal troops to enforce a court desegregation order at a school in Little Rock, the capital and largest city in the state of Arkansas. It was a turning point in the civil rights movement.

The seeds of the 1957 Little Rock crisis were sown in the 1954 U.S. Supreme Court decision *Brown v. Board of Education* and the subsequent 1955 Supreme Court order that desegregation of public schools should proceed "with all deliberate speed." Although the Supreme Court had condemned the system of racially segregated schools that predominated in the South, it had given little guidance on how schools were to be integrated. Many state-level officials in the South read—or rather chose to read—the ambiguous phrase "all deliberate speed" as giving them the right to stall and frustrate integration indefinitely. One such official was Arkansas Governor Orval Faubus (1910–1994). A populist who had already refused to use his police powers to enforce desegregation, Faubus had come under pressure from racist groups to prevent the highly symbolic integration of Central High School in the state capital, Little Rock.

The school board in Little Rock had voted in 1954 to comply with the *Brown* decision and had set a target of September 1957 to begin integrating the city's high schools. By that date nine African American students had registered to attend the previously all-white Central High. They would come to be known as the Little Rock Nine: Ernest Green, Elizabeth Eckford, Jefferson Thomas, Terrence Roberts, Carlotta Walls, Minnijean Brown, Gloria Ray, Thelma Mothershed, and Melba Pattillo.

In response Faubus called out the Arkansas National Guard, which was under his command unless or until it was called into federal service, and ordered the guardsmen to prevent the students from entering the building. Faubus also allowed a fierce mob of white citizens to gather at the school to threaten further violence.

Faubus's actions infuriated President Dwight D. Eisenhower (1953–1961), who had largely kept the federal government out of the civil rights question. Eisenhower himself was in part to blame for Faubus's defiance, however. In July 1957 he had declared that he could not "imagine any set of circumstances that would ever induce me to send Federal troops … into any area to enforce the orders of a Federal Court, because I believe that common sense in America will never require it." In Faubus's view such an attitude, coupled with the leeway the court had provided in the phrase "all deliberate speed," meant that in practice a federal court order was just a piece of paper.

The president gets involved

Eisenhower summoned Faubus for a meeting at which the president promised not to send in federal troops, while Faubus agreed to allow desegregation to go ahead. Days later the governor broke the deal, arguing in the U.S. District Court that he would not "concede that the United States in this court or anywhere else can question his discretion and judgment." Faubus explained his change of mind by saying, "Just because I said it, doesn't make it so."

Faubus withdrew the National Guard. Its removal, however, left the

Students outside Central High in 1958 display a banner blaming its closure on the U.S. "goverment." In fact, Governor Faubus ordered the closure of Little Rock's schools.

mob with the upper hand when school opened on Monday, September 23. The mob beat up four black journalists, assuming they were students. In fact, the beatings served as cover for the nine students to make their way into class. Faced with frenzied protests from the mob outside the school—the white students inside remained calm—the mayor of Little Rock had the nine removed under police protection. He telegraphed Eisenhower, warning that the city police could not control the mob and pleading for federal troops. (The violence was not limited to Little Rock: In that same week a new school in Nashville, Tennessee, was partially blown up in order to prevent a single black student from attending.)

Eisenhower brooded overnight on what action to take. In response to what he termed "disgraceful measures," he determined to use "the full power of the United States" to restore order. At lunchtime on September 24 he sent 1,200 paratroops from the Army's 101st Airborne Division to Little Rock, the first time Army troops had been deployed in a police action in American streets in the 20th century. Eisenhower also removed Faubus's control over the Arkansas National Guard by calling it into federal service. The next morning troops armed with bayonets guarded the nine students with minimal opposition. The mob soon dispersed, and the Army and the National Guard continued to provide protection for the nine throughout the school year.

Faubus meanwhile went to the courts to seek backing for his resistance to integration. At the request of the school board a federal judge agreed to suspend desegregation plans for another two and a half years. That judgment was overthrown by the U.S. Supreme Court. In response Faubus closed all public schools in Little Rock for the 1958–1959 school year, arguing that the action was necessary to prevent violence. Students had to attend private schools or study through correspondence courses. When Central High reopened in 1959, four of the original Little Rock Nine reenrolled to continue to study for their diplomas.

Eisenhower and Little Rock

A Gallup poll showed that two-thirds of Americans supported the president's action. However, Eisenhower's motives have been much debated. In a televised address he explained that his intervention was necessary to preserve the rule of law, but he did not take the opportunity to endorse school integration, which he believed was a state rather than a federal matter. In private, meanwhile, he confided to Vice President Richard M. Nixon that he felt betrayed and angered by Faubus's "duplicity."

Eisenhower's actions in Little Rock might have owed as much to foreign-policy considerations as to any commitment to civil rights, which he saw as a threat to the country's social stability. At the same time that black students were being intimidated on the streets of an American city, America's ambassador to the United Nations was criticizing the harsh Soviet repression of a 1956 uprising in Hungary. The Soviets were quick to accuse the United States of hypocrisy. Like President Harry S. Truman a decade before,

The Little Rock Nine meet New York City Mayor Robert Wagner in 1958. The nine rapidly became powerful symbols of the civil rights movement.

Eisenhower concluded that an America that was making progress on civil rights at home would be a more powerful spokesman for democracy against the brutal Soviet system.

In November 1999 the members of the Little Rock Nine were each awarded the Congressional Gold Medal, America's highest civilian honor, for their courage and their contributions to the civil rights movement. The medals were bestowed by Bill Clinton, the first president from Arkansas, who had been an impressionable 12-year-old at the time of the Little Rock crisis.

See Also:

Black Americans • *Brown v. Board of Education* • Civil Rights • Eisenhower, Dwight D. • Schools and Universities • Segregation and Desegregation

LOS ALAMOS

The Los Alamos National Laboratory is the U.S. government's top nuclear weapons research center. During the 1950s some of the world's leading physicists developed the hydrogen bomb in its laboratories under conditions of great secrecy and professional tension.

Situated on a remote plateau in the heart of New Mexico, Los Alamos is the site of the U.S. government's top nuclear weapons research center. During World War II (1939–1945) it was scientists at the Los Alamos laboratory who developed the atomic bomb. The use of this bomb on the Japanese cities of Hiroshima and Nagasaki in August 1945 led to immediate surrender negotiations and the end of the conflict. Los Alamos researchers also developed and built the hydrogen bomb in the years following the war. The first H-bomb test, Mike, on November 1, 1952, had an explosive force more than 500 times more powerful than the earlier atom bombs.

The U.S. government chose the Los Alamos site in 1942 for it remoteness. The nearest town is Santa Fe, New Mexico, more than 35 miles (56km) distant. Such an isolated location was seen as desirable not just for security and secrecy but also to ensure that an accidental explosion would not harm the local population. Scientific director of the atom-bomb project J. Robert Oppenheimer (1904–1967) selected the former Los Alamos Ranch School to be the site of the most important weapons program in world history. Its name is Spanish for "the poplars."

H-bomb development

In the 1950s Los Alamos remained one of the world's leading scientific centers, attracting numerous outstanding scientists. Its main role was to develop the H-bomb. These weapons fuse hydrogen atomic nuclei into helium nuclei, thereby releasing immense energies that are similar to the thermonuclear reactions that take place inside the sun. Los Alamos scientists were initially unsure whether the H-bomb could actually be built. Even if it were possible, others wondered whether humans should create such a weapon. In particular, Oppenheimer, who resigned in 1945, argued it might become a "weapon of genocide."

President Harry S. Truman (1945–1953) ordered Los Alamos to start construction of the H-bomb on January 31, 1950. His decision was a direct response to a perceived potential threat from the Soviet Union. By the end of August 1949 the Soviets had developed and tested their own atomic bomb. The U.S. government and its military advisers reacted with shock to the news. Physicist Edward Teller (1908–2003) had for some time been lobbying the government to begin work on the H-bomb. After the Soviet A-bomb test many top military advisers

Edward Teller, the "father of the hydrogen bomb," had a difficult relationship with his colleagues at Los Alamos and ultimately quit the laboratory before the bomb was tested.

SECRECY AT LOS ALAMOS

When Los Alamos scientists were developing the atom bomb during World War II, secrecy was so great that the town had no name. It was instead known for mailing purposes only as PO Box 1663. The military headquarters were simply called "Project Y." The roads in the town had no names, while a single letter designated each research building. Scientists traveling to Los Alamos were advised to buy their tickets from different rail stations than usual to avoid arousing suspicion.

In the early 1950s secrecy concerns led to the removal of the security clearance of former Los Alamos Scientific Director J. Robert Oppenheimer, who was a leading spokesman against the H-bomb. Fellow nuclear physicist Edward Teller claimed that Oppenheimer had slowed the development of the H-bomb and could not therefore be trusted. Although Teller was the only scientist who publicly spoke against his former boss, the military establishment revoked Oppenheimer's clearance, thereby effectively ending his career. The scientific community responded by making Teller an outcast in academic circles.

A policeman stands guard at Los Alamos in 1951. Nuclear weapons development was considered a prime target of Soviet espionage.

came to see Teller's proposed bomb as a way to return to nuclear superiority.

Los Alamos scientists created a working design for the hydrogen bomb by June 1952. This was quite a feat, given that the H-bomb was far more complicated than the atomic bomb. In a conventional A-bomb high explosives compress a core of uranium or plutonium to a critical mass that undergoes a nuclear chain reaction. An H-bomb, on the other hand, must be capable of heating a mass of hydrogen to the temperature of the sun to ignite its nuclear material. Such extreme conditions can only be achieved by using an atomic-bomb detonator. The bomb must also be precisely shaped to ensure that the hydrogen is compressed into hot plasma rather than just simply blown away.

A troubled development

The 1950s work on the H-bomb at Los Alamos was marred by a series of political squabbles between Teller and other staff. Teller is considered the "father of the H-bomb." Even during the 1940s, when Los Alamos had been developing the atomic bomb, he had kept returning to his plans for what was then called the Super. Because the H-bomb itself would need an A-bomb to act as a detonator, other scientists did not consider it a high priority. This preoccupation created a tension between Teller and other scientists that continued into the next decade.

After Truman authorized the H-bomb, a large proportion of the Los Alamos scientists worked on the project. Some individuals, such as Oppenheimer, objected in principle to the catastrophic power such a weapon would possess. Others thought that the original design for the bomb was flawed. Their misgivings proved correct in June 1950, when mathematician Stanislaw Ulam (1909–1984) found serious errors in Teller's calculations. It took until mid-1951 for scientists to come up with a new design for the bomb. These difficulties led to Teller quitting Los Alamos before the bomb was successfully tested in 1952. In 1954 he also testified in a government hearing about whether Oppenheimer was a security risk. Teller argued, "I would feel personally more secure if public matters would rest in other hands." The hearing effectively ended Oppenheimer's career.

In 1957 the city and some laboratory areas were opened and made accessible to the public. Today, in addition to nuclear weapons research the laboratory has divisions focusing on biology, theoretical physics, solar research, lasers, and computing. There are still many secure areas where national security work is performed.

See Also:

Arms Industry • Civil Defense • H-bomb Tests • Oppenheimer, J. Robert • Science and Technology • Teller, Edward

CLARE BOOTHE LUCE 1903–1987

Clare Boothe Luce enjoyed a varied career as a magazine editor, playwright, war correspondent, and politician. In the 1950s she became the first American woman to hold a major diplomatic post.

Ann Clare Boothe was born in New York City on April 10, 1903. As a child she wanted to be an actress, and she briefly attended theater school after graduating in 1919. She married a clothing manufacturer in 1923, but the marriage ended in divorce six years later. She began a career in publishing in 1930, working first for the fashion magazine *Vogue*. Her short satirical sketches about New York society were published as *Stuffed Shirts* in 1933, the same year she became managing editor of *Vanity Fair*. She soon resigned in order to devote time to writing plays. In 1935 she met and married Henry R. Luce (1898–1967), the founder of *Time* magazine and later of *Life* and *Sports Illustrated*, and saw the opening on Broadway of *Abide with Me*, the first of several plays she wrote during that period. *The Women* (1936), *Kiss the Boys Goodbye* (1938), and *Margin for Error* (1939) were popular with the public—if not always with the critics—and by the end of the decade Luce was regarded as a leading American playwright.

War correspondent and politician

Following the outbreak of World War II (1939–1945) Luce traveled through Western Europe as a journalist for *Life*. In 1941 and 1942 she toured Asia and Africa, interviewing military and political leaders. On the basis of her experiences as a war correspondent Luce ran for election to Congress as a Republican representing Connecticut in 1942 and won by a large majority. In 1944 she was elected to a second term.

Clare Boothe Luce had a way with words, successfully working as a magazine editor, a playwright, and a screenwriter, for which she earned an Academy Award nomination.

Following the death of her daughter from her first marriage and her conversion to Roman Catholicism, Luce decided not to run for reelection in 1946. She returned to writing, producing the screenplay for the movie *Come to the Stable*—which won her an Oscar nomination—and, in 1951, a play entitled *Child of the Morning*. In 1952 she took to the campaign trail again on behalf of the Republican presidential candidate, Dwight D. Eisenhower. After Eisenhower's election Luce was appointed ambassador to Italy, becoming the first American woman ambassador to a major country. A fervent anticommunist, Luce was concerned by leftist elements in the Italian labor movement. However, her main achievement was helping produce the settlement in 1954 of an international dispute under which Italy received the city of Trieste, while Yugoslavia received the surrounding territory.

Life after Italy

In 1956 Luce became seriously ill and had to resign. In 1959 Eisenhower appointed her ambassador to Brazil. The appointment was bitterly opposed by Democratic Senator Wayne Morse from Oregon; and when Luce said that he appeared to have been "kicked in the head by a horse," there was such an uproar that she resigned. This did not mark the end of her political activity, however; over the next few years she gave much public support to the ultraconservative wing of the Republican Party. In 1964 she retired with her husband to Phoenix, Arizona.

During the following two decades Luce maintained her political contacts. She served as a member of the President's Foreign Intelligence Advisory Board in the seventies and eighties. In 1983 President Ronald Reagan awarded her the Presidential Medal of Freedom. Luce died on October 9, 1987.

> **See Also:**
> Eisenhower, Dwight D. • Magazines • Politics and Government • Republican Party

DOUGLAS MACARTHUR 1880–1964

Douglas MacArthur was one of the most influential American military leaders of the 20th century. However, having distinguished himself during both world wars, his career came crashing down in the 1950s during the Korean War.

The son of a senior military officer, Douglas MacArthur was born in Little Rock, Arkansas, on January 26, 1880. Having performed poorly at school, as a young adult MacArthur excelled at the U.S. Military Academy, West Point, where he achieved the top marks out of 93 students. He then entered the Army in the Corps of Engineers and was sent to serve in the Philippines, becoming a first lieutenant in 1904.

War service

When the United States entered World War I in 1917, MacArthur was sent to command the U.S. 42nd Division. By the end of the war in 1918 he had received 13 decorations and risen to the rank of brigadier general in command of the 84th Infantry Brigade.

Between the world wars MacArthur maintained his meteoric rise. In 1919 he was appointed the youngest-ever superintendent of West Point. He returned to the Philippines in 1922 to command the Military District of Manila, was promoted to general in 1930, and served as Army chief of staff until 1935. He then went back to the Philippines as military adviser and in 1936 was made a field marshal (the highest army rank) in the Philippine Army. The following year MacArthur retired from the U.S. Army; but when war broke out between the United States and Japan in 1941, President Franklin D. Roosevelt (1939–1945) recalled him to serve as the commander of the U.S. Army Forces, Far East.

It was World War II that made MacArthur. Having lost the Philippines to the Japanese in 1942, he famously vowed: "I shall return." He was promoted to supreme commander of the Southwest Pacific Theater,

heading not only U.S. forces in the region but all Allied troops. Over the next four years MacArthur relentlessly and steadily stripped the Japanese of their conquests. He secured the Solomon Islands and New Guinea before, in 1944, fulfilling his promise of returning to the Philippines. MacArthur's Philippine campaign was among the bloodiest in U.S. military history, and he followed it up with the invasion of the Japanese island of Okinawa in April 1945. It was MacArthur who formally received the final Japanese surrender the following September.

Japan and Korea

Although MacArthur's costly battle tactics in World War II had been controversial, the war ended with his achieving almost legendary status among the American people. He was appointed Supreme Commander Allied Powers (SCAP) and took effective control of the occupation and reconstruction of Japan as its military governor. He remained in the country until 1950, when he faced a fresh military challenge—the Korean War.

The conflict in Korea broke out in June 1950, when the forces of Communist North Korea invaded the territory of U.S.-backed South Korea. The United Nations raised a multi-national force dominated by the United States, and MacArthur's SCAP status made him its commander. For the next three months MacArthur presided over a disastrous Allied retreat that nearly saw the Communists take the whole of

the Korean Peninsula. In September 1950, however, MacArthur showed true military brilliance by landing a large force of U.S. infantry and Marines at the port of Inchon, deep behind the enemy lines, and forcing the now-exhausted North Korean Army back out of the South, into the North, and right up to the Yalu River on the border with China by October.

MacArthur now began to sow the seeds of his downfall. He argued with President Harry S. Truman (1945–1953)—whom MacArthur held in scarcely concealed contempt—and

Douglas MacArthur came out of retirement at the outbreak of World War II at the request of President Roosevelt, who placed him in charge of U.S. Army Forces, Far East.

Secretary of State Dean Acheson that the war should be expanded to liberate North Korea, despite warnings passed from Communist China via India that any U.S. action north of the 38th parallel would result in Chinese intervention in the war. MacArthur wrongly believed that the Chinese were not ready to fight such a war, and that they would be easy to defeat. In late October 1950 hundreds of thousands of Chinese troops crossed the border and forced U.S. and UN forces to retreat. MacArthur publicly blamed U.S. government policy for his own misjudgment. He also advocated the use of atomic weapons and in December 1950 presented the president with a list of 24 targets for atomic weapons across China and North Korea.

Fading away

By spring 1951 Truman had had enough of MacArthur's complaints about the conduct of the war; he

---

During the Korean War MacArthur advocated the use of atomic weapons to stop the spread of communism in Asia. This aggressive stance, however, proved to be his downfall.

MacARTHUR'S FINAL ADDRESS

On April 19, 1951, MacArthur delivered a final address to a joint session of Congress in which he defended his conduct during the Korean War. This is how he closed his speech:

I have just left your fighting sons in Korea. They have met all tests there, and I can report to you without reservation that they are splendid in every way. It was my constant effort to preserve them and end this savage conflict honorably and with the least loss of time and a minimum sacrifice of life. Its growing bloodshed has caused me the deepest anguish and anxiety. Those gallant men will remain often in my thoughts and in my prayers always. I am closing my 52 years of military service. When I joined the Army, even before the turn of the century, it was the fulfillment of all my boyish hopes and dreams. The world has turned over many times since I took the oath on the plain at West Point, and the hopes and dreams have long since vanished, but I still remember the refrain of one of the most popular barracks ballads of that day, which proclaimed most proudly that old soldiers never die; they just fade away. And like the old soldier of that ballad, I now close my military career and just fade away, an old soldier who tried to do his duty as God gave him the light to see that duty. Good-bye.

---

relieved MacArthur of his command on April 11, replacing him with General Matthew B. Ridgway (1895–1993). It was a sad end to MacArthur's military career, and on returning to Washington, D.C. (his first visit to the continental United States in 11 years), he campaigned against Truman and made a final address to Congress that received 30 ovations (*see box*). Dwight D. Eisenhower won the 1952 election (MacArthur himself had tried to run for the presidency) and consulted MacArthur about ending the war. MacArthur reiterated his views on atomic weapons, which Eisenhower ignored.

MacArthur fulfilled his own observation in his final speech to Congress, "old soldiers never die; they just fade away." He became chairman of the board of the Remington Rand Corporation in 1952 but spent much of the rest of his life living fairly anonymously in New York City. He died on April 5, 1964, and was buried in Norfolk, West Virginia.

See Also:

Acheson, Dean • Armed Forces • China • Eisenhower, Dwight D. • Election of 1952 • Foreign Policy • Japan • Korean War • Soviet Union • Truman, Harry S.

JOSEPH McCARTHY 1908–1957

Republican Senator Joseph McCarthy was not the first promoter of the postwar "Red Scare," but by becoming its most famous scaremonger, he lent his name to it. "McCarthyism" entered the language as a term for the smearing of political opponents by lies and innuendos.

Born into an Irish Wisconsin family on November 14, 1908, Joseph Raymond McCarthy tried his hand at various vocations before becoming a lawyer in 1935. He served as a circuit judge for three years then joined the Marines during World War II (1939–1945). In 1946 he won election to the U.S. Senate after an upset primary victory against Robert La Follette, Jr. McCarthy's first few years as a senator were undistinguished. In 1950 he sought advice from dinner companions about how he could further his career. They suggested he take an anticommunist stance. In a speech given in West Virginia, McCarthy claimed that he had a list of 205 State Department employees who were card-carrying communists. He was actually holding a State Department document from 1946, but he was careful not to show it to anyone. He immediately captured national attention.

McCarthy's rise and fall

For four years McCarthy flung wild charges against various targets in the federal government. He gained a large public following; but President Harry S. Truman shrank from facing him down, and the Senate did nothing to disown him. The Senate Foreign Relations Subcommittee investigating McCarthy's charges found evidence for none of them but still did not censure him. McCarthy led a campaign against Senator Millard Tydings, chairman of the subcommittee, who was running for reelection in 1950. The smears cost Tydings his seat. "After nearly two years of tramping the nation," *Time* magazine wrote in 1951, "shouting that he is 'rooting out the skunks,' just how many communists has Joe rooted out? The answer is none."

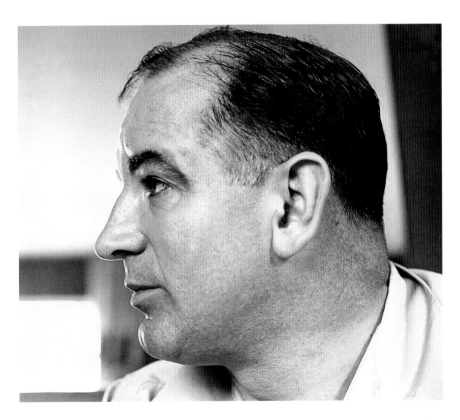

Burly, with a boyish grin and a thirst for publicity, Senator Joseph McCarthy was the most vociferous representative of the postwar communist scare.

After winning reelection to the Senate in 1952, McCarthy became chairman of the Senate Committee on Government Operations and its Permanent Subcommittee on Investigations. He led hearings into communist influence within government institutions and agencies. Although President Dwight D. Eisenhower chose not to speak out against a fellow Republican, he was angered by McCarthy's behavior. In the end McCarthy brought himself down. In 1953 he turned his fire on communists in the Army. It was a step too far. The Army countered that McCarthy was

seeking preferential treatment for David Schine, a consultant of McCarthy's who had been drafted into the Army. Hearings into the matter were televised in spring 1954. The public saw McCarthy for what he was, and his bubble burst. In December 1954 the Senate voted to censure McCarthy for his conduct. The media lost interest in the idea of a communist conspiracy, and McCarthy, increasingly isolated politically, fell victim to alcoholism and died of liver disease on May 2, 1957.

See Also:
House Un-American Activities Committee • McCarthy Hearings • Politics and Government • Republican Party

McCARTHY HEARINGS

The hearings into communist activity conducted by Wisconsin Senator Joseph R. McCarthy between 1953 and 1954 were a high-water mark of anticommunist fever in the United States. McCarthy's relentless witch hunt gave the language a new word, "McCarthyism."

Republican Senator Joseph R. McCarthy (1908–1957) stepped into the national limelight in 1950 when he mounted a fierce attack on the State Department, which he accused of harboring communists. His remarks fit well with the suspicions, if not outright paranoia, about communist influence in Cold War America.

That suspicion had been fired in the late 1940s by a series of political and military setbacks. In 1949 the Soviet Union exploded its first atomic bomb. That same year the culmination of

China's civil war in victory for Mao Zedong vastly increased the area of the world under communist control.

The atmosphere of fear in the United States led to hearings into communist influence by the House Un-American Activities Committee (HUAC), a body originally created to investigate communist and Nazi influence in the late 1930s. In 1947 HUAC began investigations into the role of communists in Hollywood, and many implicated individuals were subsequently blacklisted. In 1948 HUAC

investigated accusations that former State Department official Alger Hiss (1904–1996) had passed classified documents to the Soviet Union; Hiss was convicted of perjury and sent to prison for five years in 1950. The committee also examined the role of communists in the education system, seeking declarations of loyalty from individuals and institutions.

The Korean War (1950–1953) between Communist North Korea and the South, which was supported by U.S.-led United Nations forces, increased the mood of anticommunism. In 1953, for example, Julius and Ethel Rosenberg were executed for espionage on behalf of the Soviet Union on evidence that many observers found unconvincing. Meanwhile, politicians began to blame the "enemy within" for the setbacks in the Cold War.

The hearings

McCarthy launched his campaign with a statement made before the Women's Republican Club of Wheeling, West Virginia, on February 9, 1950: "While I cannot take the time to name all the men in the State Department who have been named as members of the Communist Party and members of a spy ring, I have here in my hand a list of 205 that were known to the Secretary of State as being members of the Communist Party and who nevertheless are still working and shaping the policy of the State Department." The next day McCarthy told reporters that the list of names was in a suit he had left on a plane. When he

Lawyer Dorothy Kenyon appears before the Senate's Tydings Committee in 1950 to answer McCarthy's charges that she supported a communist organization.

THE CRUCIBLE

Arthur Miller's play *The Crucible* (1953) is a fictional retelling of events surrounding the Salem witch trials, which took place in Massachusetts in 1692. During the trials and the surrounding witch hunts 19 men and women were hanged for witchcraft, while another man, Giles Corey, was pressed to death for refusing to stand trial. Hundreds of other people faced accusations of witchcraft, and dozens more were put in jail without trial. A new court was created to oversee the witchcraft cases, under Chief Justice William Stoughton, an avid witch hunter who allowed many deviations from normal courtroom procedure, including the admission of private conversations between accusers and judges.

It was clear from the play's debut that Miller did not intend it as a straightforward retelling of historical fact but as an elaborate parable of the McCarthy era, with its anticommunist witch hunts, its pervasive atmosphere of paranoia and betrayal, and its blatantly unconstitutional legal practices. McCarthy was only one manifestation of the national paranoia. The House Un-American Activities Committee (HUAC) had earlier taken the lead in investigating communism within Hollywood. It summoned a number of playwrights, directors, and actors known for left-wing views to testify to their own beliefs and to implicate others. A group known as the Hollywood Ten refused to testify before HUAC; they were convicted of contempt and sentenced to up to one year in prison. Several hundred other entertainers, including Miller himself, were placed on a blacklist for their suspected communist views. They found themselves barred from working for major Hollywood studios or receiving screen credit for any work they did do.

Actors perform in *The Crucible*, Arthur Miller's parable written at the height of McCarthyism in the early 1950s.

was called before a subcommittee of the Senate Committee on Foreign Relations that was investigating his charges (the Tydings Committee), McCarthy was unable to produce any names of communists currently working in any government department. His charges were dismissed by the Tydings Committee report as "a fraud and a hoax." Nevertheless, the senator split the nation into supporters who saw him as a dedicated American patriot and critics who saw him as a publicity-hungry witch hunter.

Among McCarthy's major targets were Secretary of State Dean Acheson (1893–1971) and his predecessor George C. Marshall (1880–1959). McCarthy accused the two of "a conspiracy on a scale so immense as to dwarf any previous such venture in the history of man." The senator, however, never produced any evidence to support his charge.

McCarthy was reelected in the midterm elections of 1952. He became chairman of the somewhat obscure Senate Committee on Government Operations and its Permanent Subcommittee on Investigations. The subcommittee had almost unlimited powers to investigate alleged communist subversion in government, a role it gradually took over from HUAC.

The subcommittee at work

Over the next two years McCarthy's subcommittee called more than 500 witnesses to testify about possible communist infiltration of institutions ranging from the State Department to broadcasters such as Voice of America, the U.S. Information Libraries, and the Government Printing Office.

The subcommittee's hearings were held in public, but only after closed executive sessions at which McCarthy was often the only senator present. The hearings were bullying. McCarthy's chief counsel, Roy Cohn (1927–1986), launched tirades against witnesses and probed them about their beliefs,

Joseph McCarthy (left) confers with Roy Cohn during hearings in 1954. The pair seemed to relish bullying witnesses called before the subcommittee.

associations, families, and colleagues. When witnesses took the Fifth Amendment, refusing to testify on the grounds that they might incriminate themselves, McCarthy threatened to prosecute them for contempt.

McCarthy's targets ranged from the Girl Scouts—accused of being a communist front—to students, academics, and musicians. The State Department banned some 400 writers on suspicion of communism. Many Americans became afraid to voice opinions that could lay them open to accusations of communism. McCarthy's attacks came to include President Dwight D. Eisenhower (1953–1961) himself, along with numerous other senior figures from both political parties.

The downfall

In 1953 McCarthy began investigating the U.S. Army. With Eisenhower's support the Army mounted a counterattack. It emerged that Roy Cohn had put pressure on the Army to stop it from drafting his friend, subcommittee "consultant" David Schine; when he failed, Cohn threatened to ruin Army Secretary Robert T. Stevens if Schine was posted overseas.

When the news broke, McCarthy was condemned in the Senate and in the media, where broadcaster Ed Murrow launched the first full-scale attack on McCarthyism on his show *See It Now*. McCarthy and Cohn attempted a coverup, but the Senate convened an investigation that was broadcast live on television between April and June 1954 and watched by some 20 million Americans. McCarthy finally met his match in Army counsel Joseph N. Welch. Gradually the con-

summate bully became the victim. The culminating exchange came when McCarthy was interrupted by Welch while attacking a member of Welch's law firm who was not even on the Army legal team: "Until this moment, Senator, I think I never really gauged your cruelty or your recklessness. Let us not assassinate this lad further, Senator, You have done enough. Have you no sense of decency, sir, at long last? Have you no sense of decency?" The audience broke into applause at Welch's comments, and the chairman adjourned the hearing. The exchange marked the end of McCarthy's time in the national spotlight.

The suggestion that the Army hearings had been provoked by the drafting of Schine, and the exposure of McCarthy's bullying tactics, discredited him. His allies in the Senate and the media deserted him. On December 2, 1954, the Senate voted 67 to 22 to censure McCarthy for "conduct contrary to senatorial traditions." Largely ignored, he lapsed into alcoholism, from which he died three years later.

McCarthy is now seen by many people to represent much that was wrong with America in the 1950s, although some people on the right still believe that his reputation should be rehabilitated. The hearings promoted fear and conformity, and normalized a pervasive violation of civil rights by the government that lasted throughout the fifties and sixties, when the FBI and CIA opened mail, monitored political groups, and tried to "neutralize" Americans who did not toe the Cold War line. Not least, the hearings also showed a generation of television viewers the specter of a politician intoxicated with his own power in what *Collier's* magazine described as "a carnival, a sprawling, brawling travesty."

See Also:

Acheson, Dean • Armed Forces • Cold War • House Un-American Activities Committee • McCarthy, Joseph • Miller, Arthur • Murrow, Ed • Spies and Spying • Television

MAGAZINES

Despite the growth of television, magazines continued to be very popular during the 1950s. The digest format, and in particular Reader's Digest, *sold millions of copies, while many established glossy publications such as* Time, Life, *and* Esquire *were also widely read.*

By the 1950s the popular magazine had a long, established history in the United States. Although popular magazines were first published in America as early as the 1740s, it was not until the 19th century that they really took off. The 1850s witnessed the birth of *Harper's New Monthly Magazine*, which popularized the general-interest illustrated magazine, while in the 1890s there was a revolution in the magazine industry when publisher Frank A. Munsey and others lowered the price of the popular monthlies to ten cents and generated an advertising boom. In fact, by the mid-20th century the heyday of the traditional general-interest magazine was arguably coming to an end. The 1950s were a decade of transition, when the old guard magazines disappeared and were replaced by multiple new titles.

Types of magazine
During the 1950s certain types of books came to be seen as magazines. The considerable growth of the paperback in the late forties and throughout the fifties saw the emergence of regular anthologies in digest or pocketbook format, such as *New World Writing*, which was published between 1952 and 1964. The term "magabook" was used to describe these and similar publications, although it has since gone out of fashion.

There were various other types of magazines. The leading general-interest titles, such as *Cosmopolitan* and *Life*, were almost all published in large,

flat format, printed on coated ("glossy") paper to carry photographs and advertisements and were referred to generically as the "slicks." The production costs of these magazines were high, and they relied heavily on advertising revenue for their profits. Many of what were regarded as women's magazines, such as *Good Housekeeping* or *Woman's Home Companion,* were "slicks."

At the start of the decade the "pulps" still survived, although their days were numbered. These magazines were so-called because they were printed on coarse paper derived from woodpulp. The pulps had emerged in the late 1890s and had their heyday in the 1920s. They predominantly featured fiction and specialized in popular subjects such as science fiction, mystery, westerns, sports, and romance.

A teenage fan of James Dean reads magazines in her bedroom in 1957. The celebrity magazine was a new phenomenon, and publishers competed for exclusive stories.

TIME MAGAZINE

The cover of *Time* magazine from September 7, 1959, shows the "Man of the Year," President Dwight D. Eisenhower.

The most celebrated publication in its field, *Time* was founded in 1923 by Henry R. Luce (1898–1967) and Briton Hadden (1898–1929) as a weekly news magazine. Their intention was to present news in an organized and simplified form so that it could be easily assimilated by the busy reader. They particularly wanted to demystify the people who made the news. Hadden had a sense of humor and thus often treated his subjects lightheartedly, an approach that continued under Luce after Hadden's death. Luce remained editor-in-chief until 1964. During the 1950s *Time* not only covered every major news story but also developed more insightful articles on key matters. These included issues on the Cold War (1954) and civil rights (1957). Luce was a Republican, but he strove to keep *Time* impartial, and by the 1950s it was generally regarded as representing the pulse of the nation. To appear on the cover of *Time* became the ultimate accolade. Each year from 1927 *Time* nominated a "Man of the Year," although this could also be a woman, animal, or object. The choices for the 1950s were:

1950 American Fighting Man (a choice repeated in 2003)
1951 Mohammad Mosaddeq
1952 Queen Elizabeth II
1953 Konrad Adenauer
1954 John Foster Dulles
1955 Harlow Herbert Curtice
1956 Hungarian Freedom Fighter
1957 Nikita Khrushchev
1958 Charles de Gaulle
1959 Dwight D. Eisenhower

In 1950 Winston Churchill was "Man of the Half-Century."

The more specialized magazines—which were often scientific—tended to be called journals. Such magazines were usually published monthly or quarterly. Literary and academic magazines, which were usually published quarterly or biannually, were known as reviews. Many literary magazines were aimed at an elite readership and, because their paid circulation was low, were called "little magazines" (*see box on p. 46*).

The slicks

At the start of the 1950s there were approximately 6,800 magazines published in the United States, excluding comic books, with circulations varying from just a few thousand to over 10 million. The leading magazines were, with one exception (*Reader's Digest*), all slicks. They were all family magazines aimed primarily at women and included *Ladies' Home Journal*, *Woman's Home Companion*, *Better Homes and Gardens*, *McCall's*, and *The Saturday Evening Post*. While all except *Better Homes and Gardens* carried fiction, the emphasis in the first three, and increasingly in *McCall's*, was on lifestyle, which would come to dominate most of the glossy magazines as the decade went on. More leisure time and increased prosperity meant that women used magazines as their window on the world, and the magazines responded with what became a consumer revolution.

Previously lifestyle magazines had targeted higher income families. Now magazines such as Curtis's *Country Gentleman* attempted to broaden their market by appealing to a larger and increasingly aspirational readership. Almost all of the leading magazines, including *Good Housekeeping*, *Vogue*, *Today's Woman*, and *Woman's Day*, emphasized consumerism. Within this group were several magazines produced for and distributed specifically within supermarket chains. The leader in this group had been *Family Circle*, launched in 1932 as a freely distributed weekly magazine, but by 1946 it had converted into a monthly women's magazine. There were plenty of others, however, including *American Family*, launched in 1948, and *Everywoman's* and *Better Living*, both of which began supermarket distribution in 1951.

Traditional magazines

These new magazines attracted huge shares of advertising revenue, diverting it from more traditional magazines such as *The Atlantic Monthly, Harper's Monthly, Collier's Weekly, The American Magazine,* and the market leader, *The Saturday Evening Post*. All of them were long-lived magazines that had either originated in the 19th century or had succeeded magazines from that era. They clung to the old model that had proved very successful in the twenties and thirties but was suffering by the fifties. This model, established by *Harper's* and *The Century,* had been improved on by George H. Lorimer, who had served as editor of *The Saturday Evening Post* from 1899 to 1936 and had made it the dominant magazine of its kind. While *The Saturday Evening Post* was a general-interest magazine, it placed strong emphasis on fiction, paying very high fees to major authors.

The great days of the fiction magazines, however, were coming to an end. Several factors contributed to their demise, including the postwar rise in paperbacks. Unlike the unwieldy slicks—which were designed more for the coffee table—paperbacks could easily be carried in a pocket. One of the first of the leading slicks to disappear was *Liberty*, established in 1924 as a competitor to *The Saturday Evening Post*. Its last issue was July 1950.

Fiction, however, still dominated magazine publishing in the early years

of the 1950s. Its selling power was apparent when even *Life*, not noted for running fiction, made an exception and ran the complete text of Ernest Hemingway's (1899–1961) novella *The Old Man and the Sea* in its issue for September 1, 1952. Among *The Saturday Evening Post*'s serials at the start of the 1950s were two Horatio Hornblower novels by C.S. Forester (1899–1966), while *Collier's* serialized John Wyndham's (1903–1969) *Revolt of the Triffids* in 1951. Magazines were still the primary route for new authors to learn their craft and build their reputations. Kurt Vonnegut's (1922–) early stories appeared in *Collier's* from 1950 to 1952 and then in *The Saturday Evening Post*. Sylvia Plath's (1932–1963) first story won a contest for new college fiction run by *Mademoiselle* in 1952. In 1954 John Updike (1932–) sold his first story to *The New Yorker*, where he then worked as a staff writer for several years.

However, by the mid-1950s television was having a serious effect on magazine sales. This was not so much because it diverted readers—although it certainly cut into leisure time and thus reduced reading time—but rather

because it diverted advertising revenues away from print publishing. The slicks found their revenues significantly reduced, and that loss could not be replaced by increased circulation. In addition, rises in postal costs meant that subscriptions had to be increased, which led to a further fall in readership, while increases in printing and paper costs also cut into profits.

At the end of 1956 Crowell-Collier was forced to axe its three main popular titles: *The American Magazine, Woman's Home Companion,* and *Collier's*. This was not because of dwindling circulation but because of rising costs and reduced advertising revenue. The McCall Corporation also tightened its belt and, in order to further bolster *Redbook* and *McCall's*, sold its men's magazine *Bluebook*.

Pulps and comics

The middle of the decade also saw the death of the pulp magazines. The warning bell had sounded in 1949, when Street and Smith closed down all its remaining pulps, including *The Shadow* and *Doc Savage*, in order to concentrate on its slicks *Charm, Mademoiselle,* and *Seventeen*. Of its

A *Vogue* fashion model poses in front of a dinosaur in a New York museum in 1952. *Vogue* was one of the most successful lifestyle magazines of the period.

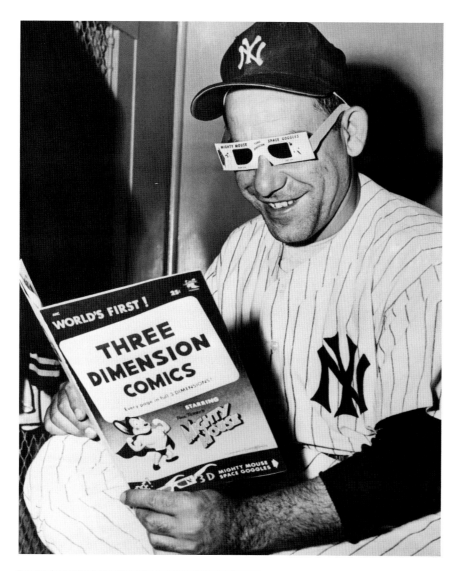

former pulps only *Astounding Science Fiction* survived, and it had been issued in the smaller digest format since 1943. However, the end of the pulps primarily came about because of their close association with the comic-book genre. Many pulp publishers also published comic books, often featuring the same characters and appealing to the same readership (predominantly young males). Sales of comic books flourished, often supporting the companion pulp but, in time, superseding it. The comic book became linked to the growing perceived problem of juvenile delinquency. Psychiatrist Dr. Fredric Wertham published a notorious book, *Seduction of the Innocent*, in 1954, which made a connection between the violent images in comic books and juvenile crime. As a result a Senate sub-committee considered the problem, and publishers introduced a self-regulatory Comics Code. There was a significant backlash against the publishers from parents and educators. Comic sales plummeted because retailers stopped stocking them, and parents chose not to buy them. One of

The baseball player Yogi Berra of the New York Yankees wears a pair of 3-D glasses to read a comic book in 1953. The cartoon character Yogi Bear was later named for him.

LITERARY AND LITTLE MAGAZINES

Often overshadowed by the major commercial magazines are literary magazines and reviews, sometimes published by universities or other institutions but frequently produced as individual labors of love. They push the barriers of experimental fiction and criticism and launch innovative new writers. Philip Roth's (1933–) first story appeared in Bucknell University's *Et Cetera* in 1954, and Ken Kesey's (1935–2001) in *Northwest Review* in 1957. The oldest surviving such magazine in America is the *Sewanee Review*, which began in 1892.

In the 1950s these "little magazines" helped launch the Beat generation of writers. Among the advance guard was *The Paris Review* (founded 1953), the first to publish Jack Kerouac (1922–1969), and the anthology magazine *New World Writing* (founded 1952), edited by Vance

Bourjaily. The seventh volume (1955) ran excerpts from the as-yet unpublished *On the Road* by Kerouac (as "Jazz of the Beat Generation") and *Catch-22* (as "Catch-18") by Joseph Heller (1923–1999). The market leader was *Evergreen Review*, founded in 1957 by Donald Allen and Barney Rosset. It published Kerouac, William S. Burroughs (1914–1997), and Henry Miller (1891–1980) and in its second issue, devoted to the San Francisco scene, ran the full text of Allen Ginsberg's (1926–1997) poem "Howl." The second issue of Doubleday's *Anchor Review* (June 1957) published an excerpt from Vladimir Nabokov's (1899–1977) *Lolita*, then unpublished in America. Other important reviews founded in the 1950s included *Chelsea Review, December, Massachusetts Review, Transatlantic Review*, and *Literary Review*.

MAD MAGAZINE

One of the most popular magazines of the 1950s, *MAD* originated as the comic book *Tales Calculated to Drive You MAD* in October 1952. It was published by William Gaines (1922–1992) of EC Comics but was devised, edited, and predominantly written by Harvey Kurtzman (1924–1993), who also illustrated much of it, along with Jack Davis, Will Elder, and Wallace Wood. It was sufficiently well established after its first year for Kurtzman to sell a compilation from the magazine, *The MAD Reader* (1954), to Ballantine Books. By then Gaines had fallen foul of the Senate inquiry into comic books and pulled out of the comic field, concentrating instead on lampooning it all in *MAD*. The magazine ran such strips as "Superduperman," "Melvin of the Apes," "Shermlock Shomes," and "Flesh Garden." The first issue retitled *MAD* was #24 (July 1955), when the magazine was relaunched as a full-size semislick. It continued to run the spoof strips but also created the carefree, iconic character of Alfred E. Neuman, who first appeared in *The MAD Reader* and then in the magazine from the January 1955 issue. *MAD*'s success led to many imitators, including *Cracked* (1958), the longest surviving rival.

The cover of issue 8 of *Tales Calculated to Drive You MAD* magazine, from 1953, shows a cartoon by Harvey Kurtzman. The magazine was renamed *MAD* in 1955.

the comic-book publishers whose business had suffered as a result of the Senate inquiry was William Gaines. Gaines's magazines, which included *Vault of Horror, Weird Science,* and *Tales from the Crypt,* were in fact designed to appeal to adults as much as children and included superior comic-strip adaptations of serious stories. Gaines folded his comics and instead established *MAD* magazine (*see box*).

The pulps, often distributed alongside comic books, suffered the same fate. By 1955 most of the few remaining publishers of pulps had either dropped their magazines or converted them to the more acceptable digest format. A strike at the main pulps distributor, the American News Company, further damaged sales, and in 1957 the company pulled out of the magazine business entirely. Two-thirds of the existing pulps and digest magazines vanished overnight.

Digests

The digest format, however, remained the preferred format for the surviving genre magazines. *Ellery Queen's Mystery Magazine* had been in digest form since it first appeared in 1941. Likewise, *Zane Grey's Western Magazine* had been in digest form since its launch in 1946. In fact, the leading new magazines were all digests. They included *Galaxy Science Fiction,* launched in 1950, and *Manhunt,* which premiered in late 1952 and soon dominated the hardboiled crime-fiction field (the famous *Black Mask* having folded in 1951). The digest had a veneer of respectability as well as being more

portable. The description had come from the leading magazine in the field, *Reader's Digest,* which was founded in 1922 and by 1955 was selling over 10 million copies each issue.

Reader's Digest defied the trend in the mid-1950s. Previously it had not run any advertising, but rising costs forced its publishers to change their policy in 1954. The scale of the magazine's circulation meant that it was able to attract advertisers at a time when other publications were losing them. The enormous success of *Reader's Digest* also meant that its format was adopted by others and came to be called "digest-size," even though the new magazines did not follow the policy of the *Reader's Digest,* which was to publish condensed versions of books or articles from other sources.

Not all comic books floundered, and indeed the genre soon recovered from the Comics Code episode to become a $150 million-a-year industry by 1955. The popularity of comic books had a detrimental effect on other magazines aimed at young readers. What was once a flourishing field was now struggling. Always popular were the high school weeklies *Senior Scholastic* and *Junior Scholastic*, which had both begun as *Scholastic Magazine* in 1920 and had been published separately since 1943. *The Open Road for Boys*, which had first appeared in 1919, suspended publication in 1954 and was never revived. The scouting magazine *Boys' Life*, however, survived and continues to be published today.

Both *Open Road* and *Boys' Life* championed the outdoor life, travel, and sports, and the decade saw a profusion of magazines that were devoted to such subjects and aimed at the widest range of age groups. *National Geographic* continued to grow in popularity during the 1950s, and other long-surviving titles, including *Outdoor Life*, *Field and Stream*, and *Sports Afield*, as well as the new *Sports Illustrated*, sold well. These outdoor lifestyle magazines succeeded in appealing to both the new teenage readers and to the growing readership for men's magazines.

Men's magazines

Although partly a response to the profusion of women's magazines, the growth in men's magazines came about largely as a result of the demise of the more adult adventure pulps, which left a gap in the market. For example, the adventure pulp *Argosy* converted into a men's magazine in 1944. Men's magazines had existed before the forties. At the one extreme was the slick *Esquire*, which had first appeared in 1933 as the men's equivalent of *Cosmopolitan* or *Vogue*, with high-class fiction and an emphasis on fashion, cars, and elitist sports. By the late 1940s *Esquire* had recognized the need for a wider range of men's fiction and had expanded its coverage to include westerns and crime fiction. It was deliberately trying to appeal to the men of the armed forces who, on returning from the war, needed more excitement and sensation in their reading matter to reflect their experiences. By the 1950s the magazine was thriving, with a circulation of just under one million.

The real forerunner to the men's magazine was *True*, which had been launched by Fawcett Publications as a pulp in 1937 and then converted to a slick in 1944. It phased out fiction in favor of daring factual stories and macho adventures. Sales exceeded one million copies in 1947. *Argosy* also broke the million barrier in the early 1950s. Other new titles followed, including *Male* (1950), *Man's Life* (1952), *Cavalier* (1953), and *For Men Only* (1954). From 1955 onward the market erupted with men's adventure magazines, each one becoming increasingly more lurid and violent, frequently featuring torture and sadism on the cover.

Parallel to this development came the emergence of what has become known as the "girlie" or "pin-up" magazine. Although under-the-counter magazines of erotic and risqué fiction had existed before World War II (1939–1945), they had faded away during the war. Among the more tasteful above-the-counter items were *Swank*, launched in 1941, and *Sir!*, launched in 1942, both imitations of *Esquire* blended with the humor magazine *Ballyhoo*. However, by the start of the 1950s, following the success of *True* and *Argosy*, they had switched to printing macho adventures stories and "pin-ups." Both would soon go much further but only after the success of *Playboy*, which was launched in late 1953. *Playboy* managed to merge the sophisticated elements of *Esquire* with the raunchier elements of the more risqué magazines in a formula that has kept it a market leader ever since. From 1955 onward the market became filled with *Playboy* imitations, including *Rogue*, *Nugget*, *Escapade*, *Gent*, *Dude*, *Adam*, and *Knave*.

TV and movie magazines

The rapid growth in television led to a range of TV magazines. *TV Guide* soon established itself as the field leader. Launched in New York in 1948, it was revamped in 1953 as a national magazine but with some 26 different regional editions. It was the first such magazine to do this, and its popularity grew quickly: In 1953 it already had a circulation of around 2 million (today

This picture shows Lila Acheson Wallace and DeWitt Wallace, coeditor and copublisher of *Reader's Digest*, in 1954. The magazine had a circulation of over 10 million in the 1950s.

This *Look* magazine from 1956 shows the actors Lucille Ball, Desi Arnaz, and Keith Thibodeaux. Magazines used celebrities on their covers to help boost circulation.

that figure is over 10 million). Before *TV Guide* existed, there was a wide range of movie magazines on the market, most of which had been around since the twenties and thirties, and continued to thrive during the fifties. Among the most popular were *Photoplay*, *Screen Stories*, and *Modern Screen*, while a new breed of publication appeared in 1958 with *Famous Monsters of Filmland*. The latter spawned a new genre of monster magazine, including *Monster Parade* and *Monsters and Things*. It also encouraged a new generation of young horror writers, including Stephen King (1947–), and influenced publishing in the sixties and seventies.

Celebrity magazines

The movie magazine relied on the public's fascination with celebrities. That factor came strongly to the fore during the fifties, particularly through news-related magazines that began to popularize the "instant" celebrity. The field leader, since its debut in 1936, was *Life*, the companion to *Time*, which reflected life and the news through pictures. It soon had a rival when *Look* was launched in 1937. These magazines continued to dominate the publishing scene in the fifties and were the bestselling magazines after *Reader's Digest*. *Life* did not rely solely on stories through pictures. During the decade it acquired several major scoops, including the war memoirs of Sir Winston Churchill (1950) and Churchill's *A History of the English-Speaking People* (1956). In 1950 *Life* published the Duke of Windsor's memoirs, *A King's Story*. *Look* was able to compete a few years later by acquiring the Duchess of Windsor's account of the couple's life together (1956). The covers of both magazines reflected the glamorous lives of movie stars and royalty: Marilyn Monroe and Anita Ekberg, for example, were frequently photographed and discussed

along with the European royal families. A typical and popular story was the romance between movie star Grace Kelly and Prince Rainier of Monaco. Both magazines vied for exclusive photographs and stories of major events, with *Life* scooping pictures of the conquest of Mount Everest in 1953 and the exploration of space in 1957.

These types of magazine—along with confession magazines—became the most popular general-interest titles of the fifties. They required little concentration and could be flicked through during a coffee break or at the hairdresser. Although the dominant force in the genre, *The Saturday Evening Post*, survived the decade and even increased its circulation, it did so chiefly at the expense of reducing its quota of fiction, focusing instead on

current affairs. The end of the pulps and the rise of men's magazines and comic books meant that by the end of the decade magazines were catering largely to a readership with a short attention span and an interest only in the here-and-now, a factor that would increase with the growth of television. While magazine publishing continued to flourish, by the mid-1950s the golden age of magazines had ended.

See Also:

Advertising Industry • Book Publishing • Cartoons and Animation • Communications • Hemingway, Ernest • Kerouac, Jack • Literature • Movie Industry • Newspapers • *Playboy Magazine* • Science Fiction • Television

BERNARD MALAMUD 1914–1986

The Jewish American author Bernard Malamud first won acclaim in the 1950s with his baseball novel The Natural, *but most of his works focused on the situation of ordinary working-class Jews in urban American society.*

Bernard Malamud was born in Brooklyn, New York, on April 26, 1914. His parents were Russian Jewish immigrants who eked out a living from a small grocery business. Malamud attended Erasmus Hall High School and graduated from the City College of New York in 1936. For the next four years he worked in various jobs, including teaching at evening high schools. He began to write short stories in the early 1940s while studying for a masters degree at Columbia University. After graduating from Columbia in 1942, he taught at high schools in New York City and, from 1949, at Oregon State University.

Malamud's short stories of the early 1940s had been aimed at young readers, but by 1950

Bernard Malamud was often categorized, along with Saul Bellow and Philip Roth, as a "Jewish writer." He rejected this label, claiming that he wrote for all readers.

he was writing for an older readership, producing stories that appeared in magazines such as *Harper's Bazaar*, *Commentary*, and *Partisan Review*. His first novel, *The Natural*—a parable about an injured baseball player granted miraculous powers—was published in 1952. In 1957 his second novel and the one often considered to be his best, *The Assistant*, was published. The book tells the story of a poor Jewish grocer and his young gentile assistant, who has robbed him. Eventually, the assistant inherits the business and is converted to Judaism. The novel contains many of the features that characterize Malamud's work, most notably the portrayal of the speech and manners of immigrant working-class Jews, the relationship between victim and victimizer, and the notion that good can come out of suffering.

During his time in Oregon—later recalled in his 1961 novel set at Oregon State, *A New Life*—Malamud followed a rigid schedule, teaching composition at the college three days a week and writing in the seclusion of his office on the other days. In 1956 he was rewarded with a *Partisan Review* fellowship, and he spent some time traveling around Europe and living in Rome. In 1958 his first collection of short stories, *The Magic Barrel*, was published and subsequently earned him the National Book Award. He was also given a literary prize for *The Assistant*.

Pulitzer Prize

In 1961 Malamud moved to Vermont, taking up the offer of a job to teach creative writing at Bennington College. More short stories and novels followed, and in 1966 he reached the height of his fame with the publication of *The Fixer*, a novel set in czarist Russia that recounts the story of a Jew accused of the murder of a Christian child. It earned Malamud a second National Book Award and the Pulitzer Prize.

Malamud's later books were less successful. His 1971 novel *The Tenants*, which examined the relationship between an African American and a white writer, received mixed reviews. His last novel, *God's Grace*, was published in 1982. A collection of his short stories—thought by some commentators to be a truer reflection of his genius than his novels—was published in 1983. Malamud died of a heart attack in 1986.

> **See Also:**
>
> **Bellow, Saul • Literature • Pulitzer Prize**

MICKEY MANTLE 1931–1995

Given the unenviable task of replacing Joe DiMaggio at the age of just 19, Mickey Mantle quickly earned his rightful place in American sports history and went on to become one of baseball's all-time greats.

Born the son of a miner in Spavinaw, Oklahoma, on October 20, 1931, Mickey Charles Mantle was a promising football player in high school but only ever wanted to be a baseball player. He came up to the big leagues to play for the New York Yankees in 1951, age just 19, facing one of the most daunting tasks in baseball. The immortal Joe DiMaggio (1914–1999) was in his last year as the Yankees' center fielder, and Mantle was being groomed to replace him. The chunky, shy, baby-faced kid with a blond crew cut made for a sharp contrast with the suave DiMaggio. But Mantle won the hearts of baseball fans, and in a starry career that lasted until 1968 he became one of the enduring icons of the game.

Mantle's opening season was less than remarkable. He played in 96 games and hit .267 with 13 home runs. The Rookie of the Year award went to his teammate, third baseman Gil McDougald. In the 1951 World Series Mantle injured his right knee chasing down a fly ball from Willie Mays—it was a defining moment. Mantle made his name as a slugger, but he was also very fast around the bases and frequently beat out bunts for base hits. His knee never fully recovered, and for the rest of his career Mantle played in pain, with a cumbersome metal brace. We will never know how good an outfielder a fit Mantle might have been.

As it was, Mantle's reputation rested chiefly with his bat. From an early age Mantle was taught by his father to be a switch-hitter, and he was equally powerful from either side of the plate— one of the landmark hitters, like Babe Ruth and Ted Williams, who could blast the ball a long way. Few right-handed batters could land a ball in the left-field upper deck in Ebbets Field, the field of the old Brooklyn Dodgers. In 1953 Mantle became only the fourth player in history to hit a grand-slam home run in the World Series, hitting a low curve ball there left-handed.

Record-breaking hitter

During his career Mantle hit 536 home runs, and his total of 18 in World Series games remains a record. His lifetime batting average was only .298, but he finished 10 seasons above .300. Perhaps his greatest disappointment was to see his teammate Roger Maris break Ruth's record of 60 home runs in a season—a target that Mantle chased throughout the 1950s. His outstanding year was 1956, when he won the Triple Crown with an average of .353, 52 home runs, and 130 RBIs (runs batted in). That year he won the Most Valuable Player award, an achievement that he repeated in 1957 and 1962. No American League player has ever won the award more than three times. When he retired in 1968, Mantle had played more games in a Yankee uniform— 2,401—than any other player.

Throughout his career Mantle was a heavy drinker, and he paid the price. Just weeks after a controversial liver transplant (given to him despite his alcoholism, critics said, simply because he was a modern American hero) he died of cancer on August 13, 1995.

Seen here wearing the number 7 jersey with which he is inextricably linked, Mickey Mantle broke many records despite a career-long knee injury.

See Also:

Baseball • Mays, Willie • Robinson, Jackie • Sports • Williams, Ted

MAO ZEDONG 1893–1976

Mao Zedong founded the People's Republic of China in 1949 and remained as its ruler for almost 30 years. During the 1950s his policies of collectivization and centralization transformed Chinese society.

Mao Zedong was born into a peasant family in Hunan Province on December 26, 1893. He developed an interest in communism while working as a library assistant at Peking University and attended the First Congress of the Chinese Communist Party in 1921. In the late 1920s the party came under attack from the Kuomintang (Nationalist Party), led by Chiang Kai-shek (1887–1975). From 1931 to 1934 Mao helped establish the Chinese Soviet Republic in southeastern China and was elected its chairman. In October 1934, under growing pressure from the Kuomintang, he started out with his supporters on the "Long March"—a withdrawal to northwestern China, where they founded a Communist base.

Chairman Mao

In 1937 Mao agreed to a truce with Chiang so that they could focus on fighting their common enemy, the Japanese. The Communists took the lead in the war with Japan, and when it ended in 1945, the civil war was resumed. The Kuomintang forces were finally overwhelmed in the second half of 1948, giving the Communists control of mainland China. Chiang fled to Formosa (Taiwan), and in October 1949 the People's Republic of China was established with Mao as leader and chairman of the Communist Party. Zhou Enlai (1898–1976), Mao's long-standing colleague, became prime minister and foreign minister.

Mao was ideologically committed to improving life for China's peasants,

Largely through the support of his country's peasantry Mao Zedong changed the face of China, transforming it into one of the world's great powers.

particularly after their support during the civil war, and in 1950 an agrarian reform law was introduced under which land, animals, surplus grain, and machinery were confiscated from landlords and redistributed among the peasants. Mao's domestic plans were interrupted by the Korean War (1950–1953), in which many Chinese soldiers lost their lives. But after the conflict he pursued a program to collectivize farms, which accelerated during the decade. By 1957 around 90 percent of peasants worked on collective farms owned by the state.

Mao was also determined that China should become an industrial nation, and in 1953 he instigated the First Five-Year Plan, under which some 100 industrial projects were set up with support from the Soviet Union. In 1958 Mao introduced the Second Five-Year Plan, or the Great Leap Forward, which took a very different approach. Peasant collectives were to be united to form communes that would then build and run small-scale iron and steel foundries. The plan had disastrous results. Labor was diverted from agriculture, and the resulting drop in food production caused a nationwide famine that claimed the lives of an estimated 20 million people.

The cult of Mao

In 1959 Mao stepped down as head of state. He remained, however, chairman of the party, and in 1966 he launched the Cultural Revolution to purge the party of his opponents and increase his power. Over a 10-year period anyone in a position of authority was liable to be sent to work in labor camps, attacked, or even murdered. The cult of Mao was encouraged with propaganda devices such as the publication in 1967 of *Quotations from Chairman Mao Zedong* (popularly known as "The Little Red Book"). Mao's death in 1976 was followed by a bitter succession struggle.

See Also:

China • Cold War • Foreign Policy • Formosa/Taiwan • Zhou Enlai

ROCKY MARCIANO 1923–1969

The world heavyweight boxing champion for four years in the 1950s, Rocky Marciano never lost a fight in his professional career. With a devotion to training and fitness unmatched in the sport's history, Marciano displayed awe-inspiring stamina and punching power.

Born Rocco Francis Marchegiano on September 1, 1923, in Brockton, Massachusetts, Rocky Marciano came to national attention in October 1951, when he ended the comeback of Joe Louis (1914–1981) by knocking him out in the eighth round at New York City's Madison Square Garden. A year later he was world heavyweight champion, a title he held undefeated until his retirement from the ring in 1956.

As a boy Marciano dreamed of playing pro football or major league baseball, but he took up boxing while serving in the Army from 1943 to 1946 and turned professional in 1947 after a short amateur career. Marciano was small for a heavyweight, at 5 feet 10 inches (1.78m) the second-shortest world heavyweight champion in history (after Tommy Burns), and with the shortest reach—just 68 inches (1.73m)—of any world champion. At the outset of his career the boxing world thought that he had to take too many punches to make it to the top.

The will to win

The turning point in Marciano's career was his demolition of Rex Layne in July 1951. Layne was a bruising puncher, the strongest man, Marciano said, that he ever faced in the ring. Marciano later said that it was after this fight, which he considered the best of his career, that people first began to take him seriously. Marciano had, in boxing parlance, a "solid chin"—the ability to take a punch to the head without being knocked out—and he could absorb a punch on the rest of his body in the same way. He was also a devastating puncher on both wings. In 1949 he nearly killed Carmine Vingo with a savage left hook (Vingo spent 10 days

in a coma and was given the last rites before recovering), and Marciano rated the thundering right that brought him the championship against Jersey Joe Walcott in 1952 as the best punch he ever unloaded.

Above all, Marciano had an intense will to win. He was also a workaholic in the gym, isolating himself from family and friends in a remote farmhouse in upstate New York for the three months leading up to a title bout. Shortly after beating Walcott, he summed up the secret of his success: "If anyone wants

Marciano is pictured here in 1952 after a workout at his training camp at Grossinger's in the Catskill Mountains of upstate New York. He went there for months at a time to train.

my title, they have to figure on chopping me in two halves. Even then, it would be pretty tough, because I figure both those halves would get up fighting." The image this gave him of a street fighter who never gives up was the key to his popularity with his fans.

Marciano became world heavy-weight champion on September 23,

MARCIANO VS. LaSTARZA

In March 1950 Marciano, with 25 wins in his 25 professional fights, came up against the cultured Roland LaStarza (1927–), also then unbeaten after 37 wins. Marciano won a controversial points decision after 10 rounds. LaStarza claimed he should have won and called for a rematch. He got it in September 1953, when he again used his great agility and technical skills to avoid Marciano's punches, trying to tire him out and entice him into dropping his guard—skills that many considered made LaStarza the best defensive boxer of his time.

After several rounds without making progress, Marciano changed tactics and began to aim his blows at LaStarza's arms. By the 10th round LaStarza could barely raise his hands above his shoulders, laying himself open to Marciano's punishing punches to the head and body. When LaStarza was knocked through the ropes in the 11th round, the fight was over.

Marciano (left) fights LaStarza for the heavyweight title at the Polo Grounds, New York City, in September 1953. Marciano won in the 11th round.

1952, by knocking out Walcott in the 13th round in a fight in Philadelphia. He retained the title by knocking out Walcott in a return match in May 1953 in Chicago—this time in the very first round—and went on to defend it successfully five more times, all but one of them (the first fight against Ezzard Charles, in June 1954) ending in a knockout. Seven months after knocking out Archie Moore on September 21, 1955, however, Marciano took the boxing world by surprise by announcing his retirement from the ring. Citing concern about the cuts around his eyes and their effect on his vision, as well as chronic back pain, he said that he did not want to make the mistake that many good fighters had made, of "hanging in there too long, having that one fight too many." He turned down repeated offers to make a comeback—one of them for $2

million. Unlike many prizefighters, Marciano had looked after the $6 million he had earned.

Undefeated champion

Marciano was portrayed to the public by sports reporters as a man of great gentleness, kindness, and compassion. His brother, Peter, disagreed, saying that if Rocky had never become angry, he would never have become champion because "he never would have hit anyone." Although famous as a miser (he hid money in unusual places, and about $2 million remained hidden at his death, never since discovered), he paid for Vingo's hospital expenses.

Less powerful than Joe Louis and less graceful than Gene Tunney or Muhammad Ali, Marciano is nevertheless regarded as one of the greatest heavyweights of all time. He is particularly renowned for keeping

himself in peak physical condition, running many miles a day and spending hours in the gym even when no fight was scheduled. This gave him the remarkable stamina in the later rounds of a match that was the key to many of his wins. When he retired, Marciano had won all of his 49 professional fights—he remains the only undefeated heavyweight champion in history—and he won 43 of them by knockouts, 11 of those coming in the first round.

Marciano died in August 1969, when the private plane in which he was traveling from Chicago to Des Moines crashed near Newton, Iowa.

See Also:
Boxing • Robinson, Sugar Ray • Sports • Sports and TV

THURGOOD MARSHALL 1908–1993

Thurgood Marshall was a skilled attorney who won several high-profile cases defending the rights of black Americans against racial discrimination. He went on to become the first African American Supreme Court justice.

Thurgood Marshall was born on July 2, 1908, in Baltimore, Maryland. After completing high school in 1925, Marshall went to the historically black Lincoln University in Chester, Pennsylvania. In 1930 he was denied a place to study law at the all-white University of Maryland; instead, he attended Howard University, where he graduated top of his class in 1933. He determined to use his admission to the bar to pursue African American rights in the courts.

Fighting discrimination

Marshall's first major civil rights case was *Murray v. Pearson* (1935). He acted for Donald Murray, a young black who successfully sued the University of Maryland for refusing him admission to its law school. Marshall worked on the case with Charles Hamilton Houston (1895–1950) of the Baltimore branch of the National Association for the Advancement of Colored People (NAACP). Marshall joined the NAACP in 1936 and became its chief counsel in 1938. Two years later he won his first Supreme Court case and became director of the NAACP's Legal Defense and Educational Fund.

In total, Marshall won 29 of the 32 cases he argued before the Supreme Court—more than any other American. In 1950 he won two cases relating to segregated graduate education: *Sweatt v. Painter* and *McLaurin v. Oklahoma State Regents*. Marshall's most important victory came

Thurgood Marshall made his name defending the rights of African Americans after having been denied admission himself to study at the all-white University of Maryland.

in 1954, when the Supreme Court ruled in the case *Brown v. Board of Education* that segregated public schools were unconstitutional. The decision overturned the "separate but equal" doctrine established by the 1896 case *Plessy v. Ferguson*, which ruled that separate public facilities for blacks were legal as long as they were equal to those used by whites.

Marshall won several other Supreme Court cases in the 1950s that led to further desegregation of public facilities. In 1958 he persuaded the

Supreme Court to rule that Governor Orval Faubus's refusal to integrate schools in Little Rock, Arkansas, was both unconstitutional and a danger to the rule of law. By then Marshall had become disquieted by the rising tide of black militancy and the Nation of Islam. He infuriated Malcolm X, the national spokesman for the Nation of Islam, by declaring that "the Muslims are run by a bunch of thugs organized from prisons and jails."

In 1961 President John F. Kennedy (1961–1963) nominated Marshall to the U.S. Court of Appeals for the Second Circuit in New York. Marshall was appointed solicitor general by President Lyndon Baines Johnson (1963–1969) in 1965 and served for two years before becoming the first African American appointed to the Supreme Court. Marshall had a liberal voting record on the court and was associated with dissenting decisions, especially in cases involving freedom of expression and equal protection of the laws for minorities. He was also an outspoken opponent of capital punishment. He retired in 1991 and died in 1993.

See Also:

Black Americans • *Brown v. Board of Education* • Civil Rights • Little Rock School Crisis • National Association for the Advancement of Colored People • Segregation and Desegregation • Supreme Court

WILLIE MAYS 1931–

African American players were still a rarity in the major leagues when Willie Mays joined the New York Giants in 1951. An all-rounder, equally skilled at hitting, running, fielding, and throwing, Mays played with easy, infectious exuberance.

Born in Westfield, Alabama, on May 6, 1931, Willie Howard Mays was catching a ball before he could walk and by the age of 14 was playing on the baseball team run by his father's employers, the local steel mill. At age 16 Mays turned professional, playing in the segregated Negro Southern League. He was scouted by the New York Giants and sent to play outfield at a Giants' "farm team," Triple A Minneapolis. The Giants, who were leading the way in integrating major-league baseball, received reports that Mays was an outstanding player who hit to all fields and made the most spectacular catches. In 22 years in the big leagues Mays more than lived up to his advance notices.

A giant talent

Mays joined the Giants in May 1951 and provided the extra ammunition to carry the team into the World Series in the most dramatic pennant race in baseball history. In his first season, playing against Pittsburgh, he raced across the field to stop a 475-foot (145-m) drive with his bare hand. Playing in 121 games, he won the Rookie of the Year award. His broad grin and his habit of playing stickball in the streets of Harlem made him a crowd favorite. He was known as the "Say Hey Kid."

Mays played with an easy athleticism that gave him deceptive speed in the outfield and deceptive power at the plate. Generally considered to be the best fielding center fielder of all time, he introduced the "belt-buckle" or

Willie Mays's enthusiasm and talent made him one of America's most enduring baseball stars. He won the National League batting title in 1954 while playing for the New York Giants.

"basket" catch, made with the glove facing upward at belt level. "I don't think there was ever a center fielder," wrote his teammate, Monte Irvin, "who was better than Willie in going and getting a ball." No catch has been replayed as often as the one Mays made in the first game of the 1954 World

Series against the Cleveland Indians. Tracking down a line drive from Vic Wertz that was headed for the far distance of the Polo Grounds center field, he caught the ball over his shoulder at the wall and turned to drill a throw into second base, holding the Indians' base runner to first. "Willie's glove," said the announcer Vin Scully, "is where triples go to die."

Baseball superhero

In 1958 the Giants moved from New York to San Francisco. Mays led them to another pennant victory in 1962 and became team captain in 1964. There was nothing Mays could not do. He won the National League batting title only once—with a .345 average in 1954—but he was generally considered to be the best clutch hitter of his era, and his lifetime average was .302. He also stole 338 bases, more than double the total of his rival Mickey Mantle. He led the league in home runs four times (1955, 1962, 1964, and 1965), and he was twice voted the Most Valuable Player (1954 and 1965). At his retirement in 1973 he had hit 660 home runs, more than anyone else except Babe Ruth, Hank Aaron, and Barry Bonds. In 2000 sportswriters voted him the second greatest player ever behind Ruth.

See Also:

Baseball • Black Americans • Mantle, Mickey • Robinson, Jackie • Sports • Williams, Ted

MEDICINE

The 1950s were a period of huge medical advances, particularly in the development of revolutionary new drugs and surgical techniques. New vaccines and antibiotics transformed the treatment of infectious diseases such as polio and tuberculosis.

Penicillin, a drug that had been tried and tested by the end of World War II (1939–1945), was a vital weapon in the fight against disease in the 1950s. The ability of penicillin to destroy bacteria had been discovered by Alexander Fleming in 1928. However, it did not get beyond the laboratory until 11 years later, when Ernst Chain and Howard Florey, working at Oxford University, England, isolated the bacteria-killing substance. In 1940 they discovered that penicillin remained effective even when diluted half a million times.

The race was now on to produce penicillin in sufficient quantities to treat human beings and ultimately save the lives of Allied troops injured during the fighting. Penicillin was to prove highly effective against pus-forming bacteria and those responsible for a range of diseases that include pneumonia, diphtheria, anthrax, tetanus, and syphilis. In the postwar years it reduced the rate of death from pneumonia, for example, from around 30 percent to 6 percent.

Meanwhile, the search had begun for other antibiotics—substances that would destroy bacteria. In 1944 an American research team discovered a new antibiotic, named streptomycin. Tests on the antibiotic indicated that it was active against a number of bacterial disease organisms that were not affected by penicillin, including the tubercle bacillus, the cause of tuberculosis. The breakthrough, however, would not prove to be the end of the hunt for a cure for this lethal infectious disease.

Dr. Ruth Gordon of Rutgers University, New Jersey, works on antibiotics research in the laboratory of the department of microbiology in 1951.

The fight against tuberculosis

The general decline in infectious diseases in the Western world between the mid-19th and mid-20th centuries was partly due to improvements in the urban environment, such as the installation of sewage and water systems, regular garbage collection, and the clearance of some of the worst slums. The development of vaccines also helped reduce the number of deaths. Diphtheria, for example, practically disappeared with the mass vaccination of children from the 1930s onward. However, although a vaccine called BCG had been developed in France to combat tuberculosis and had been used in several European countries since the 1920s, it had not been taken up in the English-speaking world because of fears about its safety. Consequently, in the 1940s tuberculosis was still a major disease in the United States, even if it was only the eleventh most frequent cause of death in cities such as New York.

Anyone could catch tuberculosis. The first symptom of the disease was usually a light, dry cough. After a period of time, which varied from person to person, the cough became more persistent and was accompanied by symptoms that included shortness of breath; loss of appetite, weight, and strength; a high temperature; and the spitting of blood. Once the disease had been diagnosed, an X-ray of the lungs was taken to reveal the extent to which

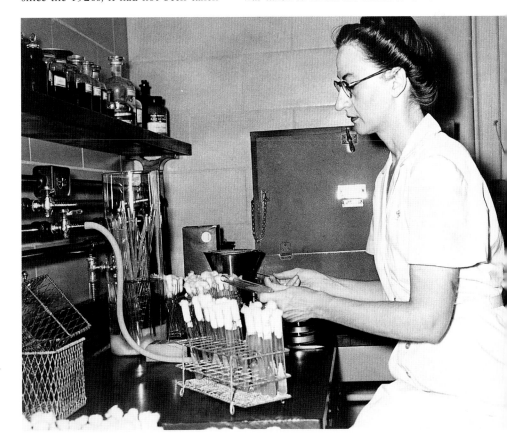

they were damaged, at which point the patient would be sent off to a sanatorium in the country—provided that he or she could afford it. Even in a sanatorium there was a good chance that the patient would die in anything from a few weeks to a few years. Death was certain if the disease spread to the brain to cause tuberculosis meningitis. It was essential for a cure to be found.

The discovery of the antibiotic streptomycin, which killed the tubercle bacillus, began with the work of Selman Waksman (1888–1973) in the United States. In the 1930s he carried out detailed research on the effects of fungi and bacteria on the fertility of soil. He was convinced that soil was capable of generating antibiotic-producing organisms and started a

screening program to find them. Between 1940 and 1952 his lab isolated more than 10 antibiotics produced by actinomycetes, a group of soil organisms capable of inhibiting the growth of bacteria and fungi. In 1943 Waksman was joined by a graduate student, Albert Schatz (1920–2005), who threw himself into the search for an antibiotic that would be effective against the tubercle bacillus. Within a few months Schatz had isolated two highly active strains of actinomycetes (subsequently renamed *Streptomyces griseus*), which stopped the growth of several virulent bacteria known to resist penicillin, including the tubercle bacillus.

A woman with tuberculosis was treated with the antibiotic, named streptomycin, between November 1944 and April 1945. After receiving five courses of injections over 10 to 18 days, the woman fully recovered. There was, however, some concern over the fact that the treatment had taken several months to be effective. When, in 1946, the U.S. government offered to give Britain enough streptomycin to treat 100 patients, the British decided to carry out clinical trials on the drug (*see box opposite*). There was little point in investing money—of which there was a severe shortage in postwar Britain—in a drug that was not the wonder cure that people were so desperate to find.

PAS and isoniazid

Meanwhile, a second drug for the treatment of tuberculosis had been developed. It was para-aminosalicylic acid (PAS), a chemical variant of salicylic acid (aspirin). In 1940 the Danish doctor Jorgen Lehmann (1898–1989), while working in Sweden, was told about an experiment in which aspirin had been added to a culture of tuberculous bacilli, increasing the amount of oxygen they consumed by 100 percent. Lehmann then suggested to a pharmaceuticals company that if it made a chemical variant of aspirin—

This poster warns against the dangers of transmitting tuberculosis by kissing children. Tuberculosis is a highly communicable disease caused by the tubercle bacillus.

RANDOMIZED TRIALS IN MEDICINE

The use of randomized trials was an important development in medicine in the 20th century. It would end the practice of hailing new treatments as great saviors only to discover later that they were not so wonderful. Such trials, which require the use of statistical skills, date back to the 1920s, when they were used to compare different strains of wheat. However, the pioneer in applying statistics to medical trials was Austin Bradford Hill (1897–1991), professor of medical statistics at the London School of Hygiene and Tropical Medicine.

In 1946 the U.S. government offered the United Kingdom enough streptomycin to treat 100 patients. With around 70,000 people dying from tuberculosis in that country every year, and over four times that number suffering from the disease, experts considered how to select 100 patients. Bradford Hill persuaded the Tuberculosis Trials Committee that the obvious thing to do in such a situation was to test the new drug in a randomized trial using two groups of patients. The composition of each group was based on a complicated formula that he devised under which those who were given the drug and those who were not—and so acted as the "control" group—was determined at random.

In 1947 three London hospitals took part in trials in which 55 patients were given streptomycin for four months, and 52 "controls" were given the traditional bedrest. After six months four of those who had been given streptomycin had died, but 28 were much better. In comparison, there had been 14 deaths in the control group. Those on streptomycin had obviously done better, but not in the dramatic way that had been hoped for. In fact, within three years a total of 32 of the 55 treated with streptomycin had died, compared with 35 of the original 52 controls. In short, the fact that the treatment had taken several months to work (because tubercle bacilli have hard, waxy shells) meant that some of the tubercle bacilli had become resistant to streptomycin, causing the patient's health to deteriorate again.

The next step for the trial committee was to repeat the trial, but combine it with a second drug, Jorgen Lehmann's PAS. The trial began in December 1948 and was so successful that one year later it was announced that "the combination of PAS with streptomycin considerably reduces the risk of the development of streptomycin-resistant strains of tubercle bacilli." The full results, which were published in November 1950, revealed that only five participants in the second trial had become resistant to streptomycin, and that a combination of the two drugs produced a survival rate of 80 percent.

Thus began the procedure of conducting randomized trials for all new antibiotics and vaccines—a practice that continues to this day.

PAS—it might act as a "competitive inhibitor" that blocked the bacilli's consumption of oxygen so that they could not survive. It took Lehmann a long time to convince anyone that this was worth trying, and it was only in 1946 that he was able to report on two cases in which PAS had led to a fall in temperature and increased appetite in two patients suffering from tuberculosis. This, however, was not evidence that PAS could cure tuberculosis. As a result, when the clinical trials began in Britain in 1946, only streptomycin was investigated initially. When it was discovered that streptomycin stopped working effectively after a limited time period,

A nurse dispenses para-aminosalicylic acid and isoniazid to a tuberculosis sufferer. Such treatments were used to supplement a course of streptomycin injections.

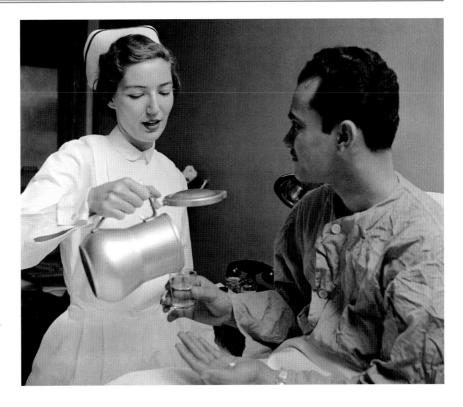

Two children with polio make donations to help an airline stewardess launch a "flying vaccine bank" in the shape of a polio vaccine bottle in 1955.

tuberculosis were found to have tubercle bacilli that were resistant to all known drugs.

Search for a polio vaccine

Poliomyelitis, or polio, was another terrible disease that was still afflicting large numbers of people in the United States at the beginning of the 1950s. Known as "the summer plague" because of its seasonal prevalence, its victims were mainly children. It was caused by a virus that was taken into the body in food or water and then spread to the nerves in the spinal cord that control the movement of muscles. This resulted in one or more limbs becoming paralyzed or—far worse—the muscles that control breathing struggling and then ceasing to function, causing enormous suffering for the victim.

The National Foundation for Infantile Paralysis was set up in the United States in the 1930s to raise funds for research into an effective vaccine. It would, however, take many years for such a vaccine to be found. One was tested in 1935; but of 17,000 children who were vaccinated, 12 developed polio and six died, causing the vaccination program to be dropped and the number of new cases to continue to rise. In 1952 there were 58,000 cases, 3,000 of which were fatal.

Amid growing demands by the public for something to be done, the National Foundation turned to Jonas Salk (1914–1995), who had begun to study polio at the University of Pittsburgh in the 1940s. In the early 1950s he developed a vaccine using formaldehyde that killed the polio virus but kept it intact enough to trigger the body's response. On July 2, 1952, Salk tried a refined vaccine on children who had already had polio and recovered. After the vaccination the childrens' antibodies increased. In January 1953 Salk reported the success of these early trials (including vaccinations carried

trials began on PAS. Finally it was announced in 1950 that giving streptomycin and PAS together over several months had cured 80 percent of patients with tuberculosis.

In the years that followed, the treatment of tuberculosis was further improved by the use of isoniazid. Isoniazid was a sulfa drug—one of a large family of drugs that had been developed since the 1930s as treatments for a variety of diseases, including pneumonia and leprosy. Developed by

Squibb and Hoffmann-La Roche in the United States, testing began on it in 1950. Like streptomycin, it was prone to resistance. However, it was found that when it was given in combination with the other two drugs for up to two years, patients were cured. The drug was relatively nontoxic and, in contrast to aminosalicylic acid, was well tolerated by almost everyone. Consequently, after 1953 the fear of tuberculosis disappeared until the late 1980s, when AIDS patients with out on himself and his family). Requiring multiple shots and a booster, the vaccine was tested on 1.8 million schoolchildren in 1954, and on April 12, 1955, the vaccine was declared safe. A nationwide vaccination program was quickly established, and the number of new polio cases each year declined, reaching around 1,000 in 1962. In that year Salk's vaccine was replaced as the vaccine of choice in the United States by the live-virus vaccine developed by the Polish-American virologist Albert Sabin (1906–1993) at the University of Cincinnati School of Medicine. Sabin's vaccine was taken orally on a sugar

lump and provided lasting immunity. By 1986 the number of new cases of polio each year in the United States was down to just three.

The discovery of cortisone

Although efforts to combat tuberculosis and polio were crucial, many of the discoveries that had an enormous influence on medicine in the 1950s did not arise out of the fight against infectious diseases. One important earlier discovery was cortisone, a naturally occurring hormone that is now used to cure or reduce the symptoms of many illnesses by stimulating the capacity of the body to heal itself. Among those responsible for its discovery was Dr. Philip Showalter Hench (1896–1965) of the Mayo Clinic in Rochester, Minnesota.

Rheumatoid arthritis occurs when the body's immune system attacks the tissues in and around joints, causing them to become inflamed and swell up. It usually begins in middle age but can also afflict children. On April 1, 1929, Hench noted that the arthritis of a 65-year-old doctor being treated at his clinic started to improve the day after he became jaundiced. The jaundice passed in four weeks, but the man's improvement lasted seven months.

Hench saw further examples of the alleviation of the symptoms of rheumatoid arthritis during jaundice and also during pregnancy, and he postulated that an innate substance, which he called "substance X," was responsible for the effect, either by correcting a chemical deficiency or oversufficiency or by exerting an antibacterial effect. By

This picture shows workers on a production line manufacturing cortisone tablets at the Upjohn Company in Kalamazoo, Michigan, in 1952.

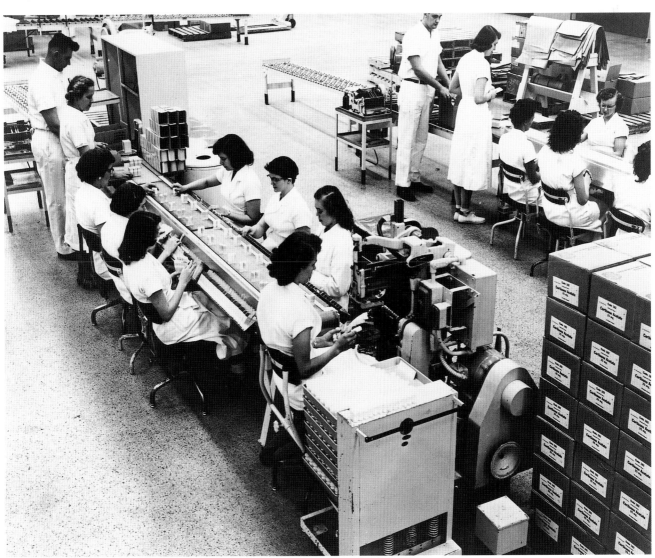

PERCY JULIAN

At a time when African Americans faced as much prejudice in the scientific world as in almost all other aspects of life, Percy Julian (1899–1975) succeeded in becoming a renowned and wealthy chemist, most notably for his work on cortisone. Born in Montgomery, Alabama, to a railway clerk and a school teacher, Julian majored in chemistry at DePauw University in Indiana and subsequently studied for a master's degree at Harvard University. Unable to obtain a teaching post at any major university because it was thought that white students would not want to be taught by an African American, he lectured at West Virginia State College for Negroes before going to the University of Vienna to study for a doctorate. Having obtained one in 1931, Julian returned to the United States and taught at Howard and DePauw universities. While at the latter he and a colleague succeeded in synthesizing the drug physostigmine, used in the treatment of glaucoma.

In 1936 Julian joined the Glidden Company in Chicago, a paint and varnish manufacturer, to direct research into soybeans. He was particularly interested in the ways in which simple compounds in natural products are altered to become chemicals essential to life, such as hormones and vitamins, and how these compounds can be created

Percy Julian developed artificial cortisone from soybeans. Cortisone was used to treat pain in sufferers from rheumatoid arthritis.

artificially. He developed a process for isolating and preparing soybean protein, and used it to produce "AeroFoam," a substance for suffocating gasoline and oil fires, which was adopted by the military. He also synthesized the male and female hormones testosterone and progesterone from soybeans. However, the achievement for which Julian was most famous was his synthesis of cortisone from soya in 1949. It was far cheaper than any synthetic form that had been produced before and made it possible for cortisone to be used widely throughout the 1950s.

In 1950 Julian was named Chicagoan of the Year, but this did not save his home, in the all-white suburb of Oak Park, from being firebombed. He refused, however, to be intimidated into moving away from the area. When he left the Glidden Company in 1953, he established a company to produce his synthetic cortisone in Oak Park. He went on to sell the company for over $2 million in 1961. Julian held more than 100 chemical patents, wrote many papers on his work, and received numerous awards and honorary degrees. He was also an active supporter of the National Association for the Advancement of Colored People (NAACP).

the end of the 1930s Hench had still not discovered the identity of "substance X." However, he had concluded that it was probably a hormone that would alleviate the symptoms of several illnesses.

Meanwhile, Hench's colleague at the Mayo Clinic, Edward C. Kendall (1886–1972), had identified a number of different chemicals in the hormones secreted by the cortex of the adrenal

glands, which he called Compounds A, B, E, and F. Both Hench and Kendall speculated whether one of these compounds might be "substance X." However, without additional funds it was impossible to attempt to synthesize enough of the compounds to investigate them further.

The situation changed when the United States became involved in World War II and began investing in

programs to improve military medicine. While working on a U.S. Air Force program, Dr. Lewis Sarett succeeded in synthesizing a few grams of Compound E, soon to be renamed cortisone. In 1948 Hench acquired a small quantity and gave it to a 29-year-old female patient who had been suffering from rheumatoid arthritis for more than five years and could barely walk. Three days later she was able to walk without pain. Hench then gave the treatment to a further 13 patients with equal success, and in 1949 he announced his findings to the world.

In 1950 both Hench and Kendall received the Nobel Prize for medicine, together with Tadeus Reichstein, a Polish-born Swiss chemist who had worked independently on the structure of the hormones of the adrenal cortex. However, Hench already knew by this time that while cortisone alleviated the symptoms of rheumatoid arthritis, it could not cure it. The drug also had an alarming number of side effects, including the accumulation of fat on the neck and face, the growth of facial hair on women, and the loss of hair elsewhere. More serious were gastro-intestinal ulcers and osteoporosis. As a result, sufferers from rheumatoid arthritis began to turn away from cortisone at the same time that it was being tried out on other conditions for which there was no known treatment, including chronic asthma and eye diseases such as conjunctivitis. Since smaller doses were used over a shorter period of time, there were not the same side effects as with arthritis.

Cortisone and its derivatives, now known as steroids, were to transform the treatment of a wide variety of illnesses whose precise causes are still not known—among them various allergies such as asthma and eczema, serious infectious diseases such as meningitis, and autoimmune disorders such as chronic active hepatitis. However, it would not have been possible to use cortisone so widely if a number of scientists had not become involved in the late 1940s in a competition to find a cheap way of producing it. The African American chemist Percy Julian (*see box opposite*) succeeded in synthesizing it from soya in 1949, ensuring that its price would drop from hundreds of dollars to a few cents for each drop.

Research into hormones

Pioneering research into hormones was also carried out by the American team of Rosalyn Yalow (*see box*) and Solomon Berson (1918–1972). They studied insulin, the hormone that is most easy to obtain in a purified form and whose function is to lower the level of sugar in the blood. Its absence results in diabetes, a condition that had been treated with injections of insulin since the 1920s. In the 1950s Yalow and Berson demonstrated that the body's immune system could recognize and respond to smaller molecules—such as those of insulin and many other hormones—than had previously been thought possible. Furthermore, they did this using a breakthrough technology called radioimmunoassay (RIA), an analytic radioisotopic technique that allows the quantification of trace amounts of biological substances within body fluids.

The development of RIA was to revolutionize medical research and enable the effective diagnosis and treatment of many diseases. Among the numerous uses to which it would be put were screening blood for the hepatitis virus, treating small children with growth hormone, testing and correcting hormone levels in infertile couples, and establishing the correct dosage levels of drugs and antibiotics.

Transplantation of organs

Knowledge of how the body's immune system works was to be of great importance in the development of another area of medicine in the 1950s—that of organ transplantation. Inevitably, it was kidneys that doctors first attempted to transplant, since they are simple to remove, and more importantly, everyone has two kidneys while only actually needing one, which meant that living donors could be used.

ROSALYN YALOW AND RIA

A research scientist who made a particularly vital contribution to the development of medicine from the 1950s onward was Rosalyn Yalow. Yalow was born in 1921 in New York City. She left school with a great enthusiasm for chemistry; but by the time she graduated from Hunter College in 1941, it had been replaced by a growing interest in physics. She eagerly accepted the offer of a job to work as a teaching assistant in physics at the University of Illinois, where she was the only woman in a department with 400 members. Having obtained a doctorate in nuclear physics in 1945, she took up a teaching post at Hunter College and became a consultant in nuclear physics at the Veterans Administration Hospital in the Bronx, where research was being carried out into the medical applications of radioactive materials.

In 1950 Yalow took up a full-time job at the hospital, where she formed a research partnership with Solomon Berson, chief of the radioisotope unit. They worked on a method for determining the rate at which the thyroid gland clears blood of iodine before turning to the study of insulin and other hormones for which they became famous. Together they developed the radioimmunoassay (RIA) technique to measure tiny quantities of various biological substances—such as hormones, vitamins, and viruses—in the blood that had previously been considered too small to detect. The ability to detect these substances paved the way for many medical advances, such as the discovery of previously unknown truths about the reaction between insulin and the immune system. Yalow and Berson both refused to patent their new technique, preferring instead to see the method used as widely as possible.

In 1977 Yalow received the Nobel Prize for medicine for her work on RIA. Berson did not share the award with her; he had died of a heart attack in 1972.

A method for treating people suffering from kidney failure was pioneered during World War II by the Dutch physician Willem J. Kolff. In 1941 he built his first dialysis machine, which did the job of the kidneys by removing waste material—in particular, urea—from a patient's blood. It was an extremely time-consuming process, and of the 15 patients whom Kolff treated before the end of the war in 1945, only one survived. However, when Kolff emigrated to the United States, the doctors at Boston's Peter Bent Brigham Hospital were sufficiently impressed by his machine to set up a renal dialysis program. The machine would prove vital to any kidney transplant operation because it would keep patients alive not only before the operation but also after it, before the transplanted kidney had begun to work.

The first attempts to transplant kidneys were made in the United States in 1951. The death rate was, however, very high. The problem was not the surgical techniques involved, since they had been developed through the pioneering work of the Frenchman Alexis Carrel (1873–1944) in the first decades of the 20th century. However, as Carrel had shown with his attempts to transplant the organs of animals, there was a biological process that resulted in the rejection of the new organ. During the 1940s the problem was investigated in Britain by the zoologist Peter Medawar (1915–1987), who concluded that the recipient of an organ—the host—will fight a transplant in the same way that it fights disease, treating the organ as an invader that must be repulsed. In 1951 Medawar proposed using cortisone because of its ability to suppress the functioning of the immune system, but this was not the ideal solution. A better drug for this purpose had yet to be found.

First successful transplants

Meanwhile, it was clear that a transplant would be more likely to succeed if there was a perfect match between the tissues of the host and donor. This was exactly the situation that presented itself to the doctors at Brigham Hospital when 24-year-old Richard Herrick was referred to them in 1954. Richard was close to death, suffering from the effects of kidney failure. He did, however, have an identical twin brother, Ronald, and in December the surgeons carried out an operation in which they gave Richard a healthy kidney from Ronald. The operation, led by Joseph Murray

Alexis Carrel was a French physician who led pioneering research into the transplantation of tissues and whole organs. He was a recipient of the Nobel Prize for medicine.

GIBBON'S PUMP

John H. Gibbon's heart-lung machine, or pump, transformed cardiac surgery. Gibbon (1903–1973) first had the idea for the pump in 1931 while working as a junior research surgeon at Massachusetts General Hospital. He spent 17 hours sitting by the bedside of a woman who, while recovering from a gallbladder operation, suffered a clot in the lungs. It prevented blood from moving into her lungs and receiving the oxygen that she needed to live. The patient was operated on, but she died.

Gibbon thought that the patient's condition would have been improved by a device—which did not yet exist—to take deoxygenated blood out of her veins, replace the carbon dioxide with oxygen, and then pump oxygenated blood back into the arteries. His idea seemed fantastical to his colleagues, who would continue to be skeptical about his work for years to come. However, throughout the 1930s Gibbon worked with his wife, a medical researcher, to develop a pump. They tested the pump on cats, and by 1939 three cats, out of a total of 39, had survived for more than a year after being operated on.

The war interrupted Gibbon's research, but in 1945, as professor of surgery at the Jefferson Medical College in Philadelphia, he started again. He worked on a refined method of cascading the blood down a thin sheet of film for oxygenation. In 1952 he used the pump while performing his first open-heart operation on a 15-month-old child. The child died, but Gibbon attempted three more operations in 1953. Of these just one was successful, with the pump maintaining the patient's circulation for nearly 30 minutes. The final operation was a harrowing experience. The diagnosis of the patient's condition was incorrect. When Gibbon opened up the child's heart, it flooded with blood, and he was unable to carry on. Gibbon decided that he could not continue with open-heart surgery, and it was left to others to take up the idea of his pump and prove that it could work.

(1919–)—who was to be awarded a Nobel Prize for this and other work in the field of transplant surgery—led to Richard's rapid recovery. However, it was to be some years before there would be a high chance of this success being repeated with anyone other than identical twins.

Murray and other surgeons attempted to transplant kidneys from other close relatives, using X-ray treatment to weaken the recipient's immune system by destroying the white cells in the blood, but such operations nearly always ended in failure. Even when the organ was not rejected, the patient invariably died because his or her immune system could no longer fight off infections. Over a period of about 10 years there were 28 transplants between identical twins, of whom 21 survived. In comparison, of 91 transplants between close relatives, only five resulted in the recipient living for a year, while those who died often did so after months of suffering.

All this was to change with the development of azathioprine in the late 1950s by George Hitchings and Gertrude Elion. Azathioprine could prevent patients from developing antibodies to a donor kidney, as Thomas Starzl of the Veterans Administration Hospital in Colorado demonstrated in 1962–1963. In less than a year he carried out transplants on 33 patients and enabled 27 of them to survive by giving them azathioprine coupled with high doses of steroids during any episodes of rejection of the new kidney. From this point the transplantation of not only kidneys but also of other organs began to flourish.

Open-heart surgery

Before the 1950s all heart surgery involved working on the heart while it continued to pump out blood. In this form of surgery, called "closed heart," surgeons could not actually see what they were doing as they used fingers and a knife to carry out the only operation they could manage in those circumstances—the dilation of narrowed valves. They had no way of dealing with defects such as holes in the heart in children and replacement of diseased valves in adults.

Today children born with holes in the heart are operated on while still babies, but in the 1950s they grew up considerably underweight and under-developed, with a blue-tinged skin, and frequently suffered from convulsive seizures caused by a lack of oxygen to the brain. A successful operation would transform the child's life, but it would require opening up the heart and using a device to take over the heart's job of pumping the blood through the lungs. One such device was a pump designed by John H. Gibbon, Jr. However, Gibbon's attempts to use the pump in open-heart surgery were only partially successful, and in 1953 he decided not to try conducting such an operation again (*see box*).

Other surgeons had also been experimenting with open-heart surgery, among them C. Walton Lillehei (1918–1999) at the University of Minnesota and John Kirklin (1917–2004) at the Mayo Clinic. Experiments with dogs showed that a donor circulatory system could function like a placenta: By connecting the patient's system to a donor's, the donor's heart and lungs were temporarily able to pump and oxygenate blood for the patient. In 1954 Lillehei began a series of 45 operations that relied on "cross-circulation." On August 13, 1954, he used the technique to link up a boy

In 1954 Joseph Murray performed the first successful kidney transplant. Ronald Herrick (standing) donated a kidney to his identical twin brother, Richard.

with a 29-year-old man. The operation to repair a hole in the heart and stretch a pulmonary valve was completed successfully, and 14 days later the boy left the hospital. He found that he could now do things that had been impossible before, such as baseball games and cycling.

Of the 45 operations in which a donor was used, in only one were there serious complications for the donor. However, it was clear that the procedure exposed the donor to unacceptable risk, and an alternative method would have to be used. Both Lillehei and Kirklin decided that a pump such as Gibbon's had to be the answer. After making various improvements to the pump, the two surgeons began the task of trying it out. Kirklin's first five patients died during or immediately after their operations, but he persisted. Five of the next ten patients survived, and within two years fewer than one in ten were dying.

By 1960 Kirklin and Lillehei had operated on what they regarded as every "operable" heart condition in children and were ready to begin to work on replacing diseased valves in adults in operations that would take several hours. Initially, these operations also had a death rate of around 90 percent, but by the mid-1960s the problems were resolved.

New challenges would present themselves to doctors and surgeons in the years that followed, as the fight against the infectious diseases that had so preoccupied medicine since the mid-19th century was replaced by mounting concern over the number of deaths caused by noninfectious illnesses such as heart attacks, strokes, and cancer.

See Also:

Birth Control • Health and Healthcare • Nobel Prizes • Polio Vaccine • Science and Technology

THE *MICKEY MOUSE CLUB*

Walt Disney's first television project aimed specifically at children, The Mickey Mouse Club *aired five days a week for nearly four years. Its popularity helped enlarge the Disney entertainment empire and left a generation of Americans with some memorable catchphrases.*

The ABC network broadcast *The Mickey Mouse Club* for the first time on October 3, 1955. Named for the Walt Disney cartoon character, the hour-long program (later shortened to 30 minutes) ran five days a week for almost four years. By the time the last show aired, 360 episodes had been made.

The program followed a variety-style format. It featured Disney cartoons with characters like Donald Duck, Pluto, and of course, Mickey Mouse; serials such as *Spin and Marty* and *The Hardy Boys*; guest performances; and short documentaries usually relating to Disney activities. The hosts, adult leader Jimmie Dodd (1910–1964) and his sidekick, former Disney animator Roy Williams (1907–1976), presented a different themed show each day: Monday was "Fun with Music Day," Tuesday "Guest Star Day," Wednesday "Anything Can Happen Day," Thursday "Circus Day," and Friday "Talent Round-Up Day."

One of the most important in-gredients of the show, however, was the Mouseketeers, a group of white pre-teens who crowded the studio wearing distinctive mouse ears attached to black beany hats. The Mouseketeers had various tasks, including taking part in games and activities and singing and dancing. At the start of cartoontime one of the Mouseketeers would chant, "Meeska Mooseka Mouseketeer, Mouse Kartoon Time Now Is Here" before revealing the cartoon of the day. At the end of the show the Mouseketeers bid the audience a heartfelt goodbye on behalf of all Mickey Mouse Club members. Some of the early Mouse-keteers later went on to have successful careers—actress Annette Funicello, for example, appeared in many beach

Wearing the distinctive Mouseketeer ears, *Mickey Mouse Club* hosts Jimmie Dodd (left) and Roy Williams clown for a publicity shot in 1957.

movies in the 1960s—while others featured regularly in Disney movies. Famous Mouseketeers from later incarnations of the show include Britney Spears and Christina Aguilera.

Disney and television

Although *The Mickey Mouse Club* was Disney's first television program aimed exclusively at children, the company had already ventured onto the small screen. It had produced two highly popular one-hour programs for NBC in 1950 and 1951, and *Disneyland*, a family show, for ABC in 1954, when it wanted to raise investment for the Disneyland park in Anaheim, Cali-fornia. The show was successful both in terms of ratings and as a vehicle for advertising Disney products and the forthcoming theme park.

The Mickey Mouse Club, however, was even more popular with audiences. Unlike most other TV shows of the time, it was filmed rather than broadcast live. The result was a much higher-quality finish to the show. *The Mickey Mouse Club* also energized the toy industry, creating a new market for advertisers and merchandisers.

The series was syndicated around the world after 1959, and generations of children grew up singing, "Who's the leader of the club that's made for you and me? M-I-C-K-E-Y M-O-U-S-E." The show reemerged in 1977 as *The New Mickey Mouse Club* but only lasted two seasons; it resurfaced yet again in 1989 as *The MMC* but was only available on the Disney Channel.

> **See Also:**
>
> **Cartoons and Animation • *Crockett, Davy* • Disney, Walt • Leisure Industry • Television**

MIDDLE EAST

The Cold War was a major influence on the events that shaped the Middle East in the 1950s. Several countries in the region claimed to pursue a policy of "positive neutrality," which meant that the balance of power between the United States and the USSR was constantly shifting.

The Middle East comprises an area of southwestern Asia and northern Africa, stretching from the Mediterranean Sea in the west to Pakistan in the east and including the Arabian Peninsula. Although the region includes countries such as Saudi Arabia and the Gulf States, the Middle Eastern nations that were most relevant in terms of an active, if sometimes covert, involvement by the United States during the 1950s were Iran, Iraq, and Israel. Events involving Egypt and Syria also gave the U.S. government cause for concern, especially toward the latter part of the decade.

The 1950s were a revolutionary decade for the Middle East, one that involved three major interconnected upheavals. The first was political and saw the removal of colonial domination from the region and the replacement of some traditional Islamic monarchs with more radical, nationalist regimes. Lebanon and Syria had recently gained independence from France, although not without a struggle, and 1952 saw the overthrow of Egypt's monarch, King Farouk, and the rise to power of the charismatic Gamal Abdel Nasser (*see box opposite*). For many Nasser was the anti-imperialist, reforming leader that the peoples of the Middle East had been waiting for.

A second major influence was the Cold War, which led the United States and the Soviet Union to become increasingly involved in the politics of the region as each jockeyed for a position of influence over the new governments. Britain had been the dominant power in the Middle East for the first part of the 20th century, but in the wake of Britain's decline as a world power following World War II (1939–1945), and particularly after the Suez Crisis of 1956, the Americans became concerned that they should not "lose" any countries to communism.

The third upheaval was a dramatic rise in oil consumption by the world's major industrial nations as the early part of the decade saw the dawn of a new era of economic growth and prosperity. This oil came mainly from large new oil fields discovered in the Persian Gulf, Arabia, and Libya.

America's vision

In the wake of World War II proponents of the so-called "modernization theory" became influential in U.S. foreign policy. These theorists and the policy-makers they advised were mainly interested in what was going to happen in the future and how that future was going to produce a region that was anticommunist and democratic, one that was in favor of free markets and free enterprise, and—crucially—one that was pro-American.

With hindsight a number of latter-day commentators now believe that the United States' approach to the Middle East during the 1950s and until the revolution that brought Ayatollah Khomeini to power in Iran in 1979 collapsed because it failed to include religion—Islam in particular. According to modernization theory, religion was irrelevant to current affairs. Instead, U.S. foreign policy in the Middle East was determined by three

Iranian Prime Minister Mohammad Mosaddeq (seen on the right with Soviet Ambassador Ivan Sadchikov) was overthrown in a coup instigated by British and U.S. intelligence agencies.

NASSER AND ARAB NATIONALISM

World Wars I and II saw the imposition of artificial state barriers throughout the Middle East. This gave rise to a general feeling among wide sections of the region's population that such barriers had to be overcome either through the reunification of individual groups or in a wider pan-Arabism—unification among all Arab peoples and nations of the Middle East. Indeed, President Gamal Abdel Nasser (1918–1970) of Egypt and the Ba'ath parties in Syria and Iraq derived much of their popular support from their stated program of unification of all Arab peoples.

It was Nasser in particular who advocated pan-Arabism along with a policy of "positive neutrality," which held that Arab nations were entitled to enjoy profitable relations with both Cold War parties. In 1956 Nasser signed a military alliance with Syria, Saudi Arabia, and Yemen that developed into a more serious attempt at unification with the establishment of the United Arab Republic (UAR), a political union with Syria, in February 1958. Nasser also had allies in a number of opposition parties in other Arab countries. By 1959—to increasing American alarm— Nasser's power had risen to the point at which he could influence the leadership struggles in other Arab nations such as Iraq and Saudi Arabia.

Nevertheless, Nasser's relationship with the Soviet Union soon began to deteriorate, and his UAR fell apart after just three years, allowing the United States to switch from unsuccessful attempts to isolate Egypt to a policy of accommodation. Ultimately, most countries of the Middle East abandoned the rhetoric of pan-Arabism in favor of individual nationalism.

Egyptian President Gamal Abdel Nasser was instrumental in promoting pan-Arabism, or the unification of Middle Eastern peoples.

main interests: the security of Israel, the security of energy (principally oil) supplies, and opposition to the Soviet Union (the Cold War). Oil had long been and remains a major factor in U.S. policy in the region, but the influence of the Cold War was a new development in the 1950s.

Jockeying for position

During the early Cold War period of the 1950s the U.S. government promoted the belief that influence in far-off countries was necessary to protect "freedom" from the threat of communism. There were limits to America's military and political power abroad at the time, so rather than direct intervention, U.S. foreign policy was often forced to employ other methods of exercising influence and control: covert operations, financial assistance, behind-the-scenes help in repressing popular uprisings, and the cultivation of local nationalist regimes. In this respect the administration of Dwight D. Eisenhower (1953–1961) mainly employed the Central Intelligence Agency (CIA), which, along with its official intelligence-gathering role, had developed certain unofficial capabilities.

In addition to opposing the spread of Soviet influence, the U.S. government was also determined to put down any left-leaning nationalist movement that appeared to be gaining sway. The fear was not just that such movements could inflict great harm on U.S. interests but that a broad socialist movement taking hold in Iran, Iraq, or elsewhere could pose a danger in terms of the rise of communism in the Middle East as a whole. In 1957, with the development of the so-called

THE BAGHDAD PACT

The Baghdad Pact, formally known as the Middle East Treaty Organization, was an alliance created in 1955 in response to the crisis in Iran in 1953. It was signed by Iran, Iraq, Pakistan, Turkey, and Britain. The members agreed to a policy of mutual cooperation and protection, along with nonintervention in each other's affairs. Although American pressure and promises of military and economic support were key in the negotiations leading up to the agreement, the United States itself did not formally join the pact, hoping that this would avoid alienating other Arab states that it still hoped to cultivate.

The United States intended that the pact members would form the basis for U.S. influence in the region and would contain the expansion of the Soviet Union by providing a belt of strong, pro-American states along its southwestern frontier. However, the pact was not a particularly successful alliance. It was renamed the Central Treaty Organization (CENTO) when Iraq backed out in 1959 and was finally dissolved in 1979.

Representatives of Baghdad Pact states and U.S. Secretary of State John Foster Dulles (far right) sign a declaration in London in 1958.

Eisenhower Doctrine, the United States pledged to provide assistance to any nation that requested help to deal with armed aggression from any nation or group of nations controlled by international communism.

The geopolitical situation of the Cold War during the 1950s thus allowed the governments of the Middle East to gain a degree of independence by employing a policy of "positive neutrality"—playing off the two superpowers against each other, appealing to one for economic or military aid, for instance, so as to ward off intervention by the other. In this way nations such as Egypt and Iraq were able to stave off American intervention (at least temporarily) by playing on their relations with the Soviet Union. The legally constituted but leftist regime in Iran, led by Prime Minister Mohammad Mosaddeq (1880–1967), was less fortunate in this respect.

Iran

During World War II the Allies kept Iran and its oil fields out of German hands. However, in the years that followed, the West saw Iran as politically vulnerable, with its weak political and social institutions and a population mired in poverty. The British had remained the chief Western presence in Iran, where they had been exploiting oil supplies since 1909. In 1950 the British made £50 million in taxes alone, while the Iranian government took only one-third of that amount in profits. Iranian protests were received with contempt by the British, fueling a rise in nationalism in the country. By the early 1950s Mohammad Mosaddeq had come to lead this movement, and he soon became prime minister.

Meanwhile, given the more equitable arrangements being forged by American oil companies in the region (notably a 50 percent deal with Saudi Arabia), the British were forced to accept that times were changing. However, an offer of 50 percent of the oil profits came too late for the Iranians, who decided to nationalize the country's oil industry in May 1951.

The last shah (monarch) of Iran, Mohammad Reza Pahlavi was forced into exile by Prime Minister Mosaddeq. However, U.S. and British intervention helped restore him to power.

In October of that year Mosaddeq ordered all British oil employees out of the country, and Iranian troops occupied the massive refinery at Abadan. This was an alarming development for the Americans, who were already worried about the possibility of a pro-Soviet coup. However, meetings with Mosaddeq—both in Iran and shortly after in America—failed to settle the dispute with the British. The situation became even more tense as the West boycotted Iranian oil, and Mosaddeq broke off diplomatic relations with the British.

The plot

For the United States the decision to topple Mosaddeq represented a move into uncharted territory—the overthrow of an apparently legitimate government. As the Eisenhower administration was preparing to take office toward the end of 1952, CIA Director

Walter Bedell Smith was pushing for a covert operation against Mosaddeq. From early February 1953 meetings between British and U.S. agents began taking place regularly on the subject.

A last-minute meeting took place on June 22, 1953, involving Secretary of State John Foster Dulles, new CIA Director Allen Dulles (brother of John Foster), Walter Bedell Smith (now undersecretary of state), and Secretary of Defense Charles Erwin Wilson. Kermit Roosevelt, a CIA operative who was to be in charge of the operation in Tehran, was also present to explain the plans for the coup. The Dulles brothers were both strong supporters of the operation and between them had easily bypassed the usual channels of government decision-making. At the same time, Smith was one of Eisenhower's most trusted and influential aides; he acted as the president's proxy at the meeting.

The coup

The plan for the coup was based on a theory that if the Iranian people were given a choice between their monarch, the shah of Iran, Mohammad Reza Pahlavi (1919–1980), and Mosaddeq, a mere politician, they were certain to prefer the former. The shah was young and immature, but Mosaddeq's support base was weak—the religious leaders (mullahs) did not trust him, the students were volatile, and the Tudeh (Iran's communist party) was widely believed to be using him. Crucially, a majority of the military was likely to remain loyal to the shah if a power struggle were to take place.

The operation, named Ajax, began on July 19, 1953, when Roosevelt drove from Beirut, Lebanon, to Baghdad, Iraq, and from there across the Iranian border. From then on it was a matter of his moving around Tehran quietly, preparing for Iranian agents to arrange demonstrations in favor of the shah, meeting with the shah, and arranging for him to be out of the country at the time of the coup.

The coup itself began badly, with messages not delivered on time and Mosaddeq getting in the first strike when he broadcast on August 16 that the shah, "encouraged by foreign elements," had tried to oust him as prime minister. He announced that he was seizing all power, and for a time Mosaddeq–Tudeh forces appeared to control the streets. However, the tide turned quickly. On August 19 pro-shah crowds took to the streets of Tehran, shouting slogans and blocking any retaliatory protest by Mosaddeq and his allies. When the pro-shah forces made their move, the army did indeed remain loyal to the shah. Mosaddeq fled, and the shah returned to Tehran from Baghdad triumphant.

Meanwhile, under a new charter the Anglo-Iranian Oil Company (later known as British Petroleum) retained 40 percent of Iranian oil, and an American syndicate got the rights to another 40 percent. The whole operation had been a huge success for the United States: A dangerous radical had been removed, the threat of a Soviet takeover quashed, and British and U.S. economic interests in Iran preserved.

Israel

After World War I (1914–1918) mandates over former German and Turkish colonies were granted to the victorious Allied powers by the newly formed League of Nations. In the Middle East Iraq and Palestine were assigned to Great Britain, while Syria and Lebanon were assigned to France. One complication was the British government's announcement in 1917 that it wanted to establish a "national home" for Jews in Palestine. The declaration reneged on promises that the British had made to Arabs about postwar independence in Palestine. In the years that followed, the Mandate for Palestine resulted in one crisis after another for the British, with riots, murders, and acts of terrorism on Jewish settlements. Zionism, the drive to establish a Jewish state in Palestine, and the arrival of many Jewish settlers meant that violence between Arabs and Jews was a constant throughout the 1930s. Then in the 1940s, as the full horror of the Holocaust in Nazi-occupied Europe became known, there was a wave of Jewish violence against the British. Having failed to impose a plan of partition through the United Nations, the British left Palestine, and Zionist leaders proclaimed the State of Israel on May 14, 1948.

Almost immediately Israel was attacked by Egypt, Iraq, Lebanon, Syria,

This map shows Israeli territory between 1949 and 1967. In 1956 Israel occupied the Egyptian-held Sinai Peninsula and the Gaza Strip but was forced to withdraw in 1957.

and Transjordan (now Jordan), which claimed to be protecting the Palestinian Arabs. Israel survived but went into the 1950s surrounded by defeated and vengeful enemies. The Arab nations of the Middle East were to disagree over much in the years that followed, yet they could present a united front on one issue—their continuing and growing hostility to Israel. The price for stepping out of line on this issue was also clear: In 1951 King Abdullah of Jordan was assassinated on a visit to Jerusalem for holding secret talks with the Israelis.

Promoting peace

In a speech on October 28, 1948, President Harry S. Truman (1945–1953) declared: "It is my responsibility to see that our policy in Israel fits in with our policy throughout the world; second, it is my desire to help build in Palestine a strong, prosperous, free, and independent democratic state. It must be large enough, free enough, and strong enough to make its people self-supporting and secure."

Truman's commitment was tested soon after Israel's victory in the First Arab–Israeli War, when the fledgling nation applied to the United States for economic aid to help it absorb an increasing number of immigrants. Truman responded by approving a $135 million loan. In 1951 Congress voted to help Israel cope with the economic burden imposed by the continuing influx of Jewish refugees from displaced-persons camps in Europe and from its increasingly hostile Arab neighbors through direct aid in the form of economic grants, loans, and surplus commodities.

In those early years of Israel's statehood aid of this kind was seen by the United States as an effective means of promoting peace in the region. The prevailing view in Congress was that if Israel was not strong economically and militarily, all-out war in the Middle

East was more likely. If such a war were to come about, the United States would face a much higher cost than that of economic aid and other forms of support for Israel.

Nevertheless, in contrast to the huge political and financial support that Israel received from successive U.S. administrations from the early 1960s, the 1950s were actually a period of frequent conflict between the United States and Israel. For example, toward the end of 1955 an offer from John Foster Dulles to sell arms to Israel was withdrawn following an Israeli raid that killed 73 Arabs. The United States also

declined to back Israel when the Israelis themselves appeared to be provoking conflict with their neighbors.

Israel and the Suez Crisis

One such instance occurred during the Suez Crisis, when Israel entered into a secret arrangement with Britain and France over military action that would force President Nasser of Egypt to reverse his decision to nationalize the Suez Canal Company, in which the British and French had held controlling interests. Israel's interest in this respect was that Israeli and Israel-bound shipping had been prevented from going through the canal since Nasser had taken charge. In October 1956 Israel invaded the Egyptian-held Sinai Peninsula. Britain and France then delivered an ultimatum, demanding that both Egypt and Israel withdraw their forces 10 miles (16km) from the canal. Shortly afterward, Britain and France invaded Egypt.

The international community widely condemned the action. In the United Nations (UN) General Assembly John Foster Dulles called the invasion "a grave error inconsistent with the principles and purposes of this Charter." Facing an imminent election and angered by British and French duplicity, Eisenhower was prevented from condemning Soviet reaction to the uprising in Hungary while his European allies took similar aggressive action in the Middle East. In the face of such pressure Britain and France withdrew.

Israel, however, did not withdraw its troops from the Sinai or the Gaza Strip, which had also been seized during the campaign. The United Nations threatened economic sanctions against Israel in February 1957. The United States announced its support for the sanctions, forcing Israel to withdraw unconditionally not only from the Sinai but also from the Gaza Strip.

Syria

In the wake of the Suez affair the United States became worried about the Soviet Union's increasingly vocal support of Arab nationalism. Its alarm increased in November 1956, when Syria's President Shukri al-Kuwatli visited Moscow; but intelligence warnings of a massive Soviet arms buildup in Syria were denied by the Syrian regime.

However, as pro-Soviet elements became stronger in the Syrian capital, Damascus, U.S. officials were accused of plotting to overthrow the government and were expelled. In turn the United States accused the Soviets of seeking to take control of Syria. It shipped arms to Turkey in case Syria was "pushed into aggressive acts" as a "victim of international communism." The Soviet Union, meanwhile, pledged support to Syria and accused the United States of deploying troops on the Turkish border.

The military and political maneuvering reached crisis point after a smuggling incident provoked an exchange of gunfire across the Syrian–Turkish border on October 8, 1957. Syria declared a state of emergency on October 16, drawing renewed charges against the Soviets by the United States and its allies. The crisis was defused by U.S. and UN diplomacy, a pullback by Turkey, and plans by President Nasser of Egypt and the Syrians to form a political union, the United Arab Republic (UAR).

Iraq

In 1958 the Iraqi monarchy was overthrown in a military coup led by Brigadier Abdul Karim Kassem (1914–1963), resulting in the death of King Feisal II. A nationalist and

Jordan's King Hussein (seated left) and Egypt's President Nasser sign a defense pact in the 1960s. The two rulers had hostility to Israel in common, but little else.

SADDAM HUSSEIN

Saddam Hussein (1937–) came from a poor Arab Sunni Muslim family and was raised by his mother and shepherd stepfather. During the 1950s he moved to Baghdad to live with his uncle, Khairallah Talfah, and soon fell under the influence of his nationalist beliefs.

Saddam joined the Ba'ath Party in 1957 and not long after was involved in the assassination of his brother-in-law, a Communist Party member. He came to prominence with the Ba'athists when he was chosen by the party leadership in 1959 to participate in an unsuccessful assassination attempt against the Iraqi

prime minister, Abdul Karim Kassem, during which Saddam was shot in the leg. He then fled to his hometown of Tikrit but soon left Iraq altogether for Syria and then Egypt. Saddam did not return to Iraq until after the Ba'ath Party conducted a successful (CIA-backed) coup against Kassem in February 1963.

However, Saddam's activities against Kassem and the left during the 1950s had been sufficient to bring him to the attention of the United States, which began to view him as an individual with whom it might be possible to do business in the future.

member of the so-called Free Officers, Kassem quickly withdrew Iraq from the Baghdad Pact (*see p. 70*) and opened up diplomatic relations with the Soviet Union. For the first year of his rule he also had close relations with the Iraqi Communist Party. Despite strong Iraqi support for the UAR, Kassem did not bring Iraq into the federation. In 1959 pan-Arab opponents of Kassem launched a rebellion in Mosul, but it was crushed. Nasser was suspected to have had a hand in the attempt.

Journalist and historian Dilip Hiro noted, "[Kassem's] non-aligned stance went down badly in Washington—as did his convening a meeting of the representatives of the oil-rich Iran, Kuwait, Saudi Arabia, and Venezuela in Baghdad in September 1960 to form the Organization of Petroleum Exporting Countries (OPEC)." OPEC was soon to become the instrument through which its oil-rich member nations could control world oil prices.

Kassem also took steps to curtail the influence of foreign companies in domestic oil extraction. The main company operating in Iraq at that time was the Iraq Petroleum Company (IPC), a joint venture between British, French, Dutch, and U.S. firms. Kassem moved to limit IPC's scope of operations and went on to set up the Iraq National Oil Company in 1961. In this way he sought to ensure that a greater portion of the profits from oil stayed within his own nation.

Throughout this maneuvering Kassem was able to use the existence of the Soviet Union as a means of extracting concessions from American and other foreign companies.

However, Kassem's moves to regulate oil exports and his friendly relations with the Soviet Union and Iraq's communists were seen as a direct threat to American interests. From the very beginning of his rule, therefore, the CIA worked to have Kassem assassinated. One failed plot reportedly involved a poisoned handkerchief.

Rise of the Ba'ath Party

The Ba'ath ("Renaissance") Party was founded in the 1940s in Syria. Its influence gradually spread to other Middle Eastern states, including Iraq, Lebanon, Jordan, and the Persian Gulf states. In Iraq the movement—which from 1953 was known as the Arab Socialist Ba'ath Party—combined pan-Arabism with rather contradictory appeals to the socialist aspirations of poorer sections of the population. As then-leader of the party, Michel Aflaq, declared: "All differences among the sons [of the nation] are incidental and false and will vanish with the awakening of the Arab consciousness."

During the 1950s the Ba'ath Party in Iraq remained underground—members had little choice, since their calls for the overthrow of the monarchy meant that they could be arrested. The Ba'athists joined in the activities that led to the

1958 revolution, but Kassem's new republican government did not favor pan-Arabism or other Ba'ath principles. Some of the younger party members, including Saddam Hussein (*see box*), became convinced that Kassem had to be removed from power.

Crucially for the Americans and British the Ba'athists in Iraq were deeply opposed to the rule of Kassem. In particular, the Ba'ath Party favored closer ties with Egypt, a more distant relationship with the Soviet Union, and attacks on the Iraqi Communist Party. Given the American aim to establish a regime that would be more sympathetic to U.S. interests and would take a harder line against the left, the Ba'ath Party was looked on with growing favor by the U.S. government. By the beginning of the 1960s the Ba'athists had become a major political force in the country. In 1963 a CIA-backed coup led by the Ba'ath Party and a section of the military succeeded in overthrowing Kassem, paving the way for the eventual rise to power of one of the Ba'athists' most ruthless and ambitious members, Saddam Hussein.

See Also:

Cold War • Dulles, Allen • Dulles, John Foster • Eisenhower Doctrine • Foreign Policy • Soviet Union • Suez Crisis • United Nations

ARTHUR MILLER 1915–2005

Arthur Miller transformed American theater with his realistic characters and provocative, socially conscious dramas. His plays explore the responsibility each person has to others and the tragedy to be found in ordinary lives.

Arthur Aster Miller was born in New York City on October 17, 1915, to Austrian Jewish parents. His father was a clothing manufacturer, his mother a schoolteacher. The family lived in Harlem until Miller was 14 but moved to Brooklyn when the Great Depression ruined his father's business. As a boy Miller enjoyed playing football and baseball and reading adventure stories. His ambition to write was sparked by reading *The Brothers Karamazov* by the 19th-century Russian novelist Fyodor Dostoyevsky, but the family could not afford to send him to college when he graduated from high school in 1932. Miller worked for two years, taking an assortment of jobs from shipping clerk in an automobile-parts warehouse to radio singer and truck driver in order to save enough money to enrol at the University of Michigan in 1934.

Miller studied economics and history before switching to an English major. He took classes in journalism and playwriting, and won an award for his comedy *The Grass Still Grows* before he graduated in 1938. When the United States joined World War II in 1941, a football injury exempted Miller from the draft. He joined the Federal Theatre Project in New York City, writing scripts for radio programs such as *Columbia Workshop* and *Cavalcade of America* while working during the day in the Brooklyn Navy Yard.

Miller's first Broadway play, *The Man Who Had All the Luck*, opened in 1944. Although it won the Theater Guild National Award, the play closed after only a few performances. *Focus*, an acclaimed novel about anti-Semitism, followed in 1945. Miller's first major success, however, came in 1947 with *All My Sons*, a family drama exploring the repercussions of a factory owner's decision to sell faulty airplane parts during World War II. The play won the New York Drama Critics Circle Award and is still regularly performed.

Death of a Salesman, which won the Pulitzer Prize, a Tony Award, and the New York Drama Critics Circle Award in 1949, established Miller's international reputation. Miller's attempt to elevate the hopes and disappointments of salesman Willy Loman to the level of Greek tragedy provoked intense debate. Many critics felt that Willy was not so worthy of pathos as the heroic characters of Greek tragedy, such as Oedipus. Miller argued that "the tragic feeling is evoked in us when we are in the presence of a character who is ready to lay down his life, if need be, to secure one thing—his sense of personal dignity."

The Crucible

Responding to the paranoia and fanaticism ignited by the Cold War—the United States' long ideological

Arthur Miller, photographed here in 1955, was one of the most important American dramatists of the 20th century. Most of his major works were written in the late 1940s and 1950s.

standoff with the Soviet Union—and the anticommunist witch hunts led by Senator Joseph McCarthy, Miller wrote *The Crucible* (1953), an allegory for the mass hysteria of the time. A fictionalized account of the Salem witch trials of 1692, the play concentrates on an individual's capacity to resist pressure to conform to society's demands. Controversial when it was first produced, the drama initially received hostile reviews, and Miller found himself shunned by many within the theater community.

In 1956 Miller himself was subpoenaed to appear before the House Un-American Activities Committee (HUAC) on suspicion of communist sympathies. Although he denied being a communist, he did admit attending a number of writers' meetings supported by the Communist Party in 1947 and a peace conference in New York, as well as signing several petitions for various causes to express his "fear of a looming victory of fascism." Miller refused to name other writers he believed had communist sympathies, arguing that he would not "use the name of another person and bring trouble on him." He was found guilty of contempt of Congress; his conviction was quashed by the United States Court of Appeals in 1958.

The later 1950s

Miller followed *The Crucible* with a tale of jealousy and betrayal, *A View from the Bridge*, which premiered in a joint production in 1955 with *A Memory of Two Mondays*. The following year Miller revised the play into two acts. He was by now acknowledged as one of America's most significant playwrights; he was awarded an honorary doctor of human letters from the University of Michigan in 1956. That same year his public profile rose dramatically when he married his second wife, movie star Marilyn Monroe (1926–1962). In 1958 he was elected to the National Institute of Arts and Letters, which awarded him the Gold Medal for drama in 1959.

Miller's next project was developing a screenplay of *The Misfits*, based on a short story he had originally published

Miller's marriage to Marilyn Monroe, pictured with the playwright soon after their wedding, was strained by Monroe's psychological decline and by Miller's dislike of celebrity.

in *Esquire* magazine in 1957. Directed by John Huston, the film starred Monroe, Clark Gable, and Montgomery Clift in an elegiac study of the death of the old West. Filming showed the toll that psychological problems and addiction were taking on Monroe. She and Miller divorced in 1961; she died the following year. Miller married photographer Inge Morath in 1962.

Miller returned to the theater in 1964 with *After the Fall*, a play widely seen as an account of his marriage to Monroe, although he always denied this. Over the next four decades Miller wrote plays, including *Incident at Vichy*, *The Price*, *The American Clock*, *Broken Glass*, and *Mr. Peter's Connections*; a children's book, *Jane's Blanket*; a novella, *Homely Girl*; short stories; and an autobiography, *Timebends*.

Miller enjoyed a renaissance in 1991 with the production of *The Ride Down Mount Morgan* and *The Last Yankee*, both of which explored his familiar

themes of success and failure. Their popularity encouraged revivals of his earlier plays.

Miller received many awards, including a Special Lifetime Achievement Tony Award and a John F. Kennedy Life Achievement Award. He held honorary doctorates from the universities of Oxford and Harvard, and in 2002 was the first American to be awarded Spain's illustrious Principe de Asturias Prize for literature. Miller died on February 10, 2005.

See Also:

Broadway • House Un-American Activities Committee • Literature • Monroe, Marilyn • Theater

MARILYN MONROE 1926–1962

One of the biggest movie stars of the 1950s and an icon of the 20th century, Marilyn Monroe paved the way for modern actors. She broke out of the Hollywood studio system and demanded creative control over her work.

Born Norma Jeane Mortensen in Los Angeles, California, on June 1, 1926, Monroe spent most of her childhood in foster care and orphanages as a result of her mother's mental illness. At age 16 she married her neighbor, James Dougherty, to avoid returning to the orphanage. During World War II (1939–1945) she worked at a local factory inspecting parachutes. A photographer took her picture for a *Yank* magazine article about women's contribution to the war effort, and she was soon in demand as a model, appearing on the cover of 33 national magazines by 1945. Her magazine work soon led to offers of screen tests from various Hollywood studios, and Norma Jeane signed with the influential Twentieth Century-Fox. At the same time, she changed her name, creating her stage name by combining Marilyn with her mother's maiden name, Monroe.

Fox dropped Monroe after two minor film roles. She was signed briefly by Columbia in 1948 and appeared with the Marx Brothers in *Love Happy* (1949) before signing a second contract with Fox, when she began to attract attention with small parts in *The Asphalt Jungle* and *All about Eve* (both 1950). Monroe's first lead role followed in 1952, when she played a psychotic babysitter in *Don't Bother to Knock*. International stardom arrived in 1953 with a string of hit films: *Niagara*, *Gentlemen Prefer Blondes*, and *How to Marry a Millionaire*. By the end of the year Monroe had been named best new actress by *Photoplay* magazine and had signed her name in the cement outside Grauman's Chinese Theatre on Hollywood Boulevard. Fifty years later her rendition of "Diamonds Are a Girl's Best Friend" from *Gentlemen Prefer Blondes* was voted number 12 on the American Film Institute's list of the top movie songs of all time.

A struggle for control

In January 1954 Monroe made headlines by marrying baseball player Joe DiMaggio (1914–1999); they became one of America's most famous and newsworthy couples. The following month her four-day tour to entertain troops stationed in Korea nearly caused a riot. Later the same

Marilyn Monroe poses on the cover of *Picture Post* in July 1956. By this time in her career she was increasingly determined to be taken seriously as an artist.

year, however, Monroe and DiMaggio divorced due to a "conflict of careers"; they maintained a close friendship for the rest of her life.

Meanwhile, Monroe fought for creative and professional control of her career. During the filming of *Niagara* she earned less money than her make-up artist because she was still under contract as a stock actor. As her popularity grew, Monroe began to ask to approve the script before agreeing to play a role, failing to show up on set when her request was refused. Fox suspended her twice for her actions, once in 1954 for *Pink Tights* and again in 1955 for *How to Be Very Popular*. Monroe fell out with her studio again when she tired of her sex siren image, which Fox was eager to promote in order to capitalize on its undoubted popularity. During the filming of a famous scene from 1955's *The Seven Year Itch* some 5,000 spectators gathered on a Manhattan corner to watch a draft from a sidewalk vent lift Monroe's skirt.

Monroe broke her contract and went to New York City to study under Lee Strasberg at the Actors Studio; in December 1955 she formed her own production company, Marilyn Monroe Productions. Both these moves were derided by Hollywood; but when studio bosses failed to find an actress with the same appeal to replace Monroe, Fox was forced to offer her a new contract with an increase in salary, a percentage of the profits, script and director approval, and the right to make one non-Fox film a year.

Monroe's company produced her next two projects. She delivered a critically acclaimed performance in *Bus Stop* (1956) and starred with Laurence Olivier in *The Prince and the Showgirl* (1957). In between the two projects Monroe married the leading playwright Arthur Miller (1915–2005).

A tragic decline

In 1959 Monroe won a Golden Globe starring with Jack Lemmon and Tony Curtis in her most successful film, *Some Like It Hot*. During production, however, Monroe became increasingly

dependent on sleeping pills, frequently arriving on the set late and unable to remember her lines. Director Billy Wilder later commented, "Anyone can remember lines, but it takes a real artist to come on the set and not know her lines and yet give the performance she did." Monroe made her final completed film in 1961, starring with Clark Gable and Montgomery Clift in John Huston's *The Misfits*, in a part written for her by Miller. The film was also to be Gable's last. Miller and Monroe divorced later the same year.

At the 1962 Golden Globes Monroe proved her popularity once more when she was presented with an award as "female world film favorite." She made her last public appearance at Madison Square Garden in May 1962, when she sang "Happy Birthday" to President John F. Kennedy, with whom she is believed to have had an affair, at his gala birthday celebration.

Monroe began filming *Something's Got to Give* but was frequently sick and missed many days of filming. Elizabeth Taylor's *Cleopatra* had previously incurred serious debts for Fox. Not prepared to lose money on another movie, the studio fired Monroe and

Marilyn Monroe poses playfully on top of a piano. Although her early career took advantage of her pin-up looks, she proved herself a comedy actress of great talent.

filed a lawsuit against her production company. The suit was later dropped, however; on August 1 Monroe was rehired to complete the film.

Four days later, on August 5, 1962, Monroe was found dead at her home in Brentwood, California. The apparent cause of death was an overdose of sleeping pills, although it has been the subject of many conspiracy theories. She was 36. Joe DiMaggio arranged her funeral and had red roses placed on her grave each week for the next 20 years.

Forty years after her death Monroe's charisma remains; more has been written about her than any other movie star, and many magazines, including *People*, voted her the sexiest woman of the century as the end of the millennium approached.

See Also:

Miller, Arthur • Movie Industry • *Playboy* Magazine • Theater

MONTGOMERY BUS BOYCOTT

The boycott of buses in Montgomery, Alabama, in 1955 was a remarkable show of the potential power of coordinated action by black Americans. The boycott marked a turning point in U.S. history: the emergence of the civil rights movement.

The roots of the boycott came on the evening of December 1, 1955. Rosa Parks (*see box opposite*), secretary of the local chapter of the National Association for the Advancement of Colored People (NAACP), the leading organization representing America's black citizens, left her job as a seamstress in a Montgomery department store and boarded a bus to take her home.

At the time buses in Alabama were segregated, like public facilities throughout the southern states. They had three sections: a rear section for African Americans, a front section for "whites only," and a middle section where blacks could sit only if there were no white passengers. Since all the seats reserved for African Americans at the back of the bus were taken, Parks joined three blacks already sitting in the middle section. Two stops later a number of white passengers boarded the bus, one of whom was left without a seat. The bus driver ordered Parks and the other black passengers to vacate their seats. The others moved, but Parks refused. The driver threatened to have her arrested. "You may do that," she replied. A policeman was found, and she was arrested. Four days later she was fined $14. Parks's courageous defiance has gone down in history as the moment that the modern civil rights movement began. "Somewhere in the universe," wrote 1960s civil rights activist Eldridge Cleaver, "a gear in the machinery had shifted."

The next evening church leaders and other prominent members of Montgomery's black community gathered in Parks's home and decided to challenge the constitutionality of Montgomery's segregated bus system. They had little money for a legal challenge, however. They had barely $500 among them, and the local chapter of the NAACP had no money, although there was a chance of receiving support from the national NAACP Legal Defense and Educational Fund. Meantime, they decided to organize a bus boycott.

On Sunday ministers in all the town's black churches spread the word that no black person should board a bus the next day. The success of Monday's boycott was remarkable. About 17,000 blacks who normally used the bus—three-fourths of the daily total—joined the boycott. Blacks walked to work, bicycled, shared cars, or took taxis. Black taxi drivers offered support by taking fares for 10 cents, the price of a bus ticket. Although police were wary, there was no violence.

An organized movement

When the leaders of the protest met to review the situation, they formed the Montgomery Improvement Association (MIA); they chose Martin Luther King, Jr. (1929–1968), a local Baptist minister, as president. That evening King addressed a crowd of 4,000 supporters at his church. "There comes a time when people get tired," he said. "We are here this evening to say to those who have mistreated us for so long that we are tired—tired of being segregated and humiliated, tired of being kicked about by the brutal feet of oppression."

Ralph Abernathy (1926–1990), a friend of King, read out the MIA's three demands: that bus drivers treat black

Rosa Parks sits toward the front of a Montgomery bus in this photograph taken in 1956; that December the U.S. Supreme Court ordered the integration of buses in the city.

ROSA PARKS

"A few days ago I met Rosa Parks," former First Lady Eleanor Roosevelt wrote in her syndicated newspaper column on May 14, 1956. "She is a very quiet, gentle person and it is difficult to imagine how she could ever take such a positive and independent stand." Rosa Parks's decision not to give up her seat on a Montgomery bus was not premeditated, but in many ways her life had been a preparation for that epochal moment.

Rosa Louise McCauley (1913–) was born of mixed Scotch–Irish and black descent in Tuskegee, Alabama, before moving to Pine Level when she was two. Tuskegee attracted black intellectuals thanks to Booker T. Washington's Tuskegee Institute, and Washington's *Up from Slavery* was one of the two books that were prominent in the family home, along with the Bible. Rosa's carpenter father and schoolteacher mother brought her up to accept Washington's doctrine of hard work and self-help, to memorize chunks of the Bible, and to sing hymns. The man who radicalized Rosa, however, was Raymond Parks, a man 10 years her senior and a charter member of the Montgomery branch of the NAACP, whom she married in 1932.

Parks involved his wife in NAACP drives to register black voters and to force hospitals to take black patients. Rosa Parks fought without success to get her own name onto the electoral register in time to vote for Franklin D. Roosevelt in 1940; she was told that she did not pass the literacy test. Her anger rose when, after the attack on Pearl Harbor, her brother was drafted into the U.S. Army to fight against fascism in defense of a democracy in which he and his family were denied the vote. In 1943 Parks joined the NAACP. Later she joined a workshop in Monteagle, Tennessee, on racial desegregation.

Another key event in Parks's life directly prefigured the 1955 bus boycott. In 1943 she was thrown off a Montgomery bus for boarding by the front door by the

A deputy sheriff takes Rosa Parks's fingerprints in 1956.

same driver, James Blake, whom she confronted 12 years later. She neither agreed to leave nor struck back when she was forcibly thrown off. It was an act of intuitive passive resistance. She never again got on a bus driven by Blake, but in December 1955 she did not notice him until he asked her to move. Her actions may have been motivated in part by her resentment of Blake.

Whatever Parks's immediate motivation, her heroism has taken its place as a key moment of individual defiance in history. The Southern Christian Leadership Conference, a leading civil rights organization, established an annual Rosa Parks Freedom Award in her honor. In 1999 she received the Congressional Gold Medal of Honor, the highest civilian award in the United States.

passengers with courtesy; that all passengers be permitted to take seats on a first-come, first-served basis, although blacks would begin from the rear of the bus; and that the Montgomery bus company hire black drivers.

When the demands were formally presented at a meeting with city and bus company officials on December 8,

however, they were rejected. "If we grant the Negroes these demands," said City Commissioner Clyde Sellers, "they would go about boasting of a victory that they had won over the white people, and this we will not stand for."

Montgomery's white establishment did everything in its power to halt the boycott as the mayor, police chief, and

city commissioner joined forces with the White Citizens' Council. Police officers constantly stopped black car drivers for questioning and arrested them for speeding. Segregationists bombarded the boycott leaders with death threats. Black workers who were employed by whites lost their jobs; they included Rosa Parks herself. Every day

MEETING HATRED WITH LOVE

On January 30, 1956, while the civil rights leader Martin Luther King, Jr., was attending a service at the First Baptist Church, a bomb exploded on his front porch. He rushed home to find the windows of his house shattered but his wife Coretta and his baby unharmed. The mayor and the city commissioner were waiting in King's living room, while outside an angry crowd of black citizens gathered, outraged by the attack on their leader. Police officers tried in vain to clear the street while more protesters arrived at the scene. A number of the crowd were armed with guns, knives, and broken bottles. King spoke to his supporters, urging them to take their weapons home if they had them. He told them that he believed that violence was no solution to their problem: "We must meet violence with nonviolence." King, who was a powerful orator throughout his career, quoted the words of Jesus from the Bible: "He who lives by the sword will perish by the sword," he told his listeners, and "Love your enemies; bless them that curse you; pray for them that despitefully use you."

King's words in Montgomery managed to calm an inflamed crowd and prevent violence. His conclusion was to set the tone for his approach to the civil rights struggle throughout the decade: "We must meet hate with love."

blacks walking to work were subjected to verbal abuse. They continued to walk, however, even through the rain and cold of the winter months. "My feet are tired," one frail, elderly woman told King after service one Sunday, "but my soul is rested."

The white backlash peaked on February 10, 1956, when more than 10,000 whites from all over Alabama and Mississippi gathered at the Montgomery Coliseum for the largest segregationist rally in the United States since the Civil War (1861–1865). The main speaker, the Republican senator from Mississippi, James O. Eastland, called on white southerners to "organize and be militant." Determined to beat the boycott, officials found in the statute books an old, disused piece of state legislation banning boycotts. They used the 1921 act to charge 89 people with breaking the law.

Leaders of the Montgomery Bus Boycott wait at a bus stop on December 26, 1956, following the end of the year-long protest.

Reverend Ralph Abernathy uses his pulpit as a platform to denounce the policy of segregating African Americans in the back of public buses in this photograph taken in November 1956.

The trials began in the Montgomery circuit court on March 19. King, the first defendant, was convicted by an all-white jury and ordered to pay a $500 fine or serve 386 days of hard labor in prison. King appealed, and the trials of the rest were deferred.

Legal maneuvers

Meanwhile, a case brought against the bus company by MIA members was proceeding in the Montgomery district court. The plaintiffs claimed that in the light of the desegregation of schools by the U.S. Supreme Court in its ruling *Brown v. Board of Education* (1954), a segregated bus service was unconstitutional. On June 5 the court decided in a 2 to 1 majority ruling of the judges that the *Brown* judgment did indeed reach beyond schools to other areas of segregation; it declared Alabama bus statutes to be violations of the due process and equal protection clauses of the Fourteenth Amendment. The judgment was, like *Brown* itself, a landmark decision. Its implications were to be felt far beyond the issue of civil rights. It became clear to many Americans that the Fourteenth Amendment—which had granted citizenship to former slaves and provided for "equal protection" under law—gave them an opportunity to use the courts as much as the political process to gain redress for grievances. The result was the so-called "rights revolution" of the 1960s.

The district court decision was, however, a long way from ending the Montgomery struggle. The city commissioners appealed the decision to the U.S. Supreme Court, while the boycott dragged on with no sign of weakening on the part of the boycotters. The bus company lost hundreds of thousands of dollars.

On November 13, 1956, the Supreme Court unanimously upheld the district court's ruling against Alabama. That night black church choirs sang, and people danced on the streets of Montgomery. When Ku Klux Klan members took to the streets, they found themselves intimidated and had to flee from black districts.

Resisting the inevitable

The Supreme Court decision did not end prejudice in Montgomery. In the ensuing months segregationists continued to attack black churches and the homes of black leaders, including Ralph Abernathy. Ku Klux Klanners continued to parade in the streets, and mobs pulled black passengers off buses; one pregnant woman was shot and wounded in both legs. In the spring of 1957 Rosa Parks and her family were forced to leave Alabama for a new home in Detroit. But the legal and political drama was over. On December 20, 1956, the curtain fell. Montgomery's buses were integrated by law, and the boycott came to an end.

See Also:

Black Americans • *Brown v. Board of Education* • **Civil Rights** • **King, Martin Luther, Jr.** • **National Association for the Advancement of Colored People** • **Segregation and Desegregation**

MOTOR RACING

During the 1950s many forms of motor racing flourished. Often starting from simple beginnings with nonprofessional drivers, they became standardized during the decade, ranging from the high-tech Indy cars to the everyday autos used in stock-car racing.

In its early years motor racing was a sport of the wealthy, car-owning elite, but by the 1950s mass automobile ownership had dramatically diversified the sport. From exotic sports cars to cheap junk racers, motor racing in one form or another became accessible to almost anyone. Many of the major forms of motor racing were officially established during the decade, making it one of the most significant in the sport's history.

The period immediately after World War II (1939–1945) was a boom time for the American auto industry.

Demand for new models was high, and the industry rose to the challenge, producing vast fleets of new cars. Along with the many premium models there was also a wide choice of affordable new cars in the showrooms. As a result, by the beginning of the 1950s most American families owned a car, and an increasingly influential automobile culture had been established. This culture was fueled by the ever-more fantastic chrome-clad creations rolling out of Detroit, Michigan, the heart of the nation's auto industry. To maintain their sales, manufacturers produced

cars that were not only utilitarian but also exciting and desirable. The 1950s saw the birth of classics such as Chevrolet's Corvette (1953) and Ford's Thunderbird (1954).

Power under the hood

As well as eye-catching style, many car buyers during the decade also wanted "big cubes"—engines with large cubic capacities. The larger the capacity, the more powerful the engine, and the more power the better. With the cost of gasoline so low at the time, at around 20 cents a gallon, the fuel costs associated with large engines were not a great issue. Consequently, even family cars were available with V8 engines and capacities over 370 cubic inches (6 liters), producing more than 300 horsepower. It was during the 1950s that legendary engines such as the V8 "small block" Chevy and Chrysler "hemi" V8 were developed to satisfy the mass demand for powerful cars. These engines, and those evolved from them, would go on to power generations of future mainstream autos and racing cars.

Much of the evolution of motor racing during the 1950s was directly related to the huge popularity that the automobile had gained in society. Motor racing had already been developing into an increasingly varied sport, involving many different types of cars, drivers, and racetracks. But it was during the 1950s that many of these motor sports experienced the first major growth in their popularity. Forms that had once been purely

A pit stop takes place during the Indianapolis 500. The track gave its name to the "Indy" class of racing, in which individually built high-performance cars raced on an oval track.

Champion racing driver Bill Vukovich is pictured in his car after he qualified for his third Indianapolis 500 in May 1955. He was tragically killed in a crash during the race.

MINIATURE RACERS

An American motor-racing innovation of the 1950s was karting, which started in California around 1956. The first regular races were run in the parking lot of a mall in Covina. Karts are miniature, open-wheeled versions of Indy cars, although not nearly as fast. They proved to be great fun and were very popular for a number of reasons: Their open bodies and closeness to the ground exaggerated the sense of speed, they exhibited sharper handling than any other type of racing car, and they were comparatively cheap to buy and run. Karting soon spread abroad and became popular in Europe, Australia, New Zealand, and Japan. International karting competition began in the 1960s, and the sport still attracts many participants. In fact, many of today's Indy and Formula One drivers started their careers in kart racing.

regional, such as hot-rod racing, which originated in the deserts of Southern California, spread out from their areas of origin and were enthusiastically taken up across the country. If they did not already have them, many motor sports created their own organizing associations to govern racing, arrange and publicize events, and allow for fair nationwide competition. By the middle of the decade each of the four major forms of the sport—Indy racing, sports-car racing, stock-car racing, and drag racing—had its own sanctioning organization.

Formula One

By the beginning of the 1950s Formula One was Europe's premier race series, but the popularity of rival Indy racing meant that the influence of Formula One in the United States had been limited. The two types of cars were broadly similar, being highly specialized, open-wheeled, one seaters. There were differences, however: Formula One cars raced on twisting, European road-type courses, while the Indy racers were designed for the oval speedway.

In 1950 Formula One racing finally reached the United States. The sport established a world drivers' championship during that year, and the

Indianapolis 500 Mile Race (Indy 500) was incorporated as one of its events. The world championship was decided by points gained from some 15 international races, including those of Belgium, Canada, France, Italy, Mexico, Monaco, South Africa, the United Kingdom, the United States, and West Germany. In 1958 a constructors' championship was also added. It awarded points to the companies that built the racing cars on a similar basis to those awarded to the drivers. The dominant constructors of the decade were Alfa-Romeo, Ferrari, Maserati, Mercedes-Benz, Vanwall, and Cooper-Climax.

Indy racing

Despite the arrival of Formula One, Indy (or Championship) racing remained America's most popular premier form of motor racing during the 1950s. The Indianapolis Motor Speedway had been closed during World War II, but its reopening in 1946 had given the sport a significant revival by the turn of the decade. Some of the drivers were wealthy amateurs or full-time drivers whose business interests supported their racing. However, even at this high level of racing competition many of the drivers had other occupations because earnings from racing usually were not enough to support a family. Perhaps the most notable driver of the decade was Bill Vukovich (1919–1955), who won the

Indy 500 in 1953 and 1954. Vukovich was killed in a crash with Rodger Ward (1921–) at the 1955 Indy. Ward was a popular driver who, despite success elsewhere, had experienced a lot of bad luck at Indianapolis. His accident with Vukovich made him consider quitting driving. However, his career began to improve in 1956, and he finally won the Indy 500 in 1959.

Most Indy drivers drove midgets and sprint cars on local dirt-track quarter-mile and half-mile ovals throughout the week. Eight to ten times each season they would gather at larger tracks to run the full-size Indy cars. This series, which included the Indy 500, was called the "Championship Trail." Indy cars were mainly custom-built "specials," as opposed to the many factory-built racers then found in Formula One. Perhaps because of this no particular cars dominated during the decade, but one of the most successful was the Offenhauser-powered Central Excavating Special, built by Floyd Trevis. It was one of a number of new, smaller designs that challenged and replaced the heavy front-wheel-drive Indy cars, such as the Blue Crown Spark Plug Specials, that had dominated since the war.

Sports-car racing

Sports-car racing was popular in the United States long before the Sports Car Club of America (SCCA) was formed in the eastern United States in

A Mercedes Benz 300 leads a Cunningham in the 1952 Le Mans 24-hour race in France. The Cunningham was the most successful American sports car of the 1950s.

1944. By the 1950s, however, the sport's popularity had spread across the country. Most postwar sports cars were European exotics such as Aston Martins, BMWs, Ferraris, Jaguars, MGs, and Porsches, but by the 1950s American sports cars such as Corvettes had joined the starting grids. The most successful was the Cunningham, which was produced by Briggs Cunningham (1907–2003) between 1950 and 1956.

Sports cars were series-produced automobiles, so they could be bought by anyone who could afford them. This made the sport accessible to many more people than the specialized Indy or Formula One race series, in which drivers needed either to be wealthy or talented enough to receive sponsorship.

Sports cars were grouped into different classes depending on their performance. There were many different types of sports-car races run throughout the United States in the 1950s, usually on road circuits such as Watkins Glen in New York. Many of these races were run for amateur drivers by local and regional organizations, but there was also a world sports car championship, which was run from 1953 to 1961.

Outstanding drivers included Dan Gurney (1931–), who began racing in West Coast sports-car races before competing in the 24-hour race at Le Mans, France, in 1958. He joined the Ferrari Formula One team and in 1962 became one of the few Americans ever to win a Grand Prix race. Carroll Shelby (1923–) was another renowned racer. He dominated SCCA events in 1955 and 1956 and was named *Sports Illustrated*'s Sports Car Driver of the Year in 1956 and 1957.

Stock cars

The National Association for Stock Car Auto Racing (NASCAR) was founded at Daytona Beach, Florida, in 1947, and the first organized racing took place on the beach in 1948. Early stock-car races were run both on beaches and on dirt ovals until, on September 4, 1950, the first paved "superspeedway" was built at Darlington, South Carolina, to host the first Southern 500. The Daytona International Speedway, home of the Daytona 500, opened in 1959.

The popularity of stock cars in the 1950s was largely attributable to the stylish, powerful automobiles available in showrooms at the time. Stock cars are based on standard ("stock") cars that the average person owned, so stock-car racing was accessible for almost any keen racer. The cars were modified and tuned to various degrees by owners and amateur mechanics to extract maximum performance. The V8 engines that were available in many standard cars provided almost endless opportunities for tuning.

JALOPIES, JUNK RACERS, AND STOCK CARS

As well as the major, organized auto-racing series popular in the 1950s, racing also took place on a local, less expensive, and less regulated scale. Automobile culture had transformed cars from being simply a method of transportation, making them exciting. So as well as visiting the drive-in restaurants and movie theaters that had appeared in many towns and cities, people would also go out driving just to show off their cars and, inevitably, to race. If a driver had a new V8 under the hood of his car, he wanted to show that it was the most powerful around. Out-of-town roads frequently became impromptu drag strips for tuned and modified cars, or for those who took things more seriously, basic stock-car racing took place at local tracks. Those drivers who did not want to risk new cars used old ones for racing. Usually bought for a few dollars, these were called jalopies or junk racers. The cars were stripped of all unnecessary weight and built with the best parts that could be obtained, or often made. Junk racing took place all over the country.

This picture shows the NASCAR International Sweepstakes auto race at Daytona Beach in 1959. It was the first running of the race that became known as the Daytona 500.

During the 1950s NASCAR began to flourish. Corporate sponsors, such as Pure Oil and Champion Sparkplugs, took an active role in the sport. Even the major automobile manufacturers, such as Ford, Chevrolet, and Chrysler, gave "factory backing" to individual drivers, and the best cars started to become the highly tuned, thoroughbred racing machines that they are today. One outstanding driver was Marshall Teague (1921–1959), AAA National Stock Car Champion in 1952 and 1954, who became in 1951 the first driver sponsored by a company (Pure Oil Company) for NASCAR racing. Lee Petty (1914–2000) was another of NASCAR's first superstars. He won 54 races in 433 starts, including the first Daytona 500 in 1959. That year he also finished 41 of 49 races and won 12 times. Herb Thomas (1923–2000) won 48 NASCAR Grand National races during his career and was the first driver to win three Southern 500s, in 1951, 1954, and 1955. His career came to an end after a crash in 1956.

Drag racing

Drag racing had begun in the 1930s and after the war became massively popular. In 1949 the first Southern California Timing Association (SCTA) "Speed Week" was held at Bonneville Salt Flats. It was here that drag racers first began running "against the clock," coaxing their vehicles to accelerate quicker rather than simply to attain high top speeds. In 1950 the first commercial drag strip, the Santa Ana Drags, opened on an airfield in Southern California and quickly gained popularity because of its revolutionary computerized speed clocks.

Drag strips were straight and a standard ¼ mile (0.4km) long. Both the elapsed time (in seconds) and the final speed (in miles per hour) of racers were recorded. As with other forms of motor racing, there were a number of classes

of drag racers. As the 1950s went on, the fastest cars became increasingly sophisticated machines.

The National Hot Rod Association (NHRA) was formed in 1951 to establish safety rules and performance standards and help legitimize the sport. It held its first official race in April 1953 on the Los Angeles County Fairgrounds parking lot in Pomona, California. In 1955 the NHRA staged its first national event, called simply "the Nationals," in Great Bend, Kansas. That year Dick Craft gained a top speed of 110 mph (177km/h) in the quarter-mile with his V8-powered Mercury. Emery Cook ran a top speed of 168.85 mph (271.68km/h) in 1957. Cook's achievement prompted the NHRA to ban nitromethane fuel. The American Hot Rod Association and the Automobile Timing Association stepped in to run nitromethane-fueled races, and the NHRA felt a loss. There were now three major drag-racing groups competing for fans and drivers.

Rallying

Road rallies became popular during the 1950s and were organized by many local car clubs. One of the most

influential clubs was the Midwest Sports Car Club of Chicago (MSCC), which had been incorporated in 1948. As well as road rallies, the MSCC also organized many other sports-car activities. Some of the early rallies were short, but others gradually became longer events. Eventually the MSCC attempted to stage a big rally. On July 30, 1955, it ran the first El Diablo rally. Drivers started on the paved streets of the Chicago suburbs and drove far out into the country across dirt tracks. El Diablo proved a great success, and the following year the event was run again, starting at midnight to add to the challenge. From then on, most rallies were run at night. After 1959 the majority become all-night-long "navigational" rallies, in which the navigation was as much of a trial as the driving. These events were both long and arduous, running between 11 and 14 hours and covering between 300 and 375 miles (480–600km).

See Also:

Automobile Culture • Automobile Industry • Leisure Industry • Sports

MOVIE INDUSTRY

The Hollywood studios dominated the movie industry in the 1950s. Threatened by the popularity of television, by McCarthyism, and by shifting public tastes, the studios fought to keep their audiences with technical innovations, sophisticated subject matter, and exciting new stars.

The 1950s marked the last phase of the classic Hollywood studio era, which began in 1930 and drew to a close in 1959. In 1950 the "Big Five" studios—Metro-Goldwyn-Mayer, Warner Brothers, RKO Radio Pictures, Paramount, and Twentieth Century-Fox—dominated the movie industry, leaving little room for the smaller studios—Universal, United Artists, and Columbia—or other independent production companies. The major studios were dependent on funding from external investors, who demanded scores of generic "audience-pleasing" movies, including musicals, mysteries, comedies, westerns, costume dramas, newspaper or prison dramas, and character-led films such as MGM's Mickey Rooney/Judy Garland "Andy Hardy" series.

The studio system resembled a factory production line, with each studio producing a movie to order each week to ensure the greatest profit. The cast and crew, from scriptwriters to directors, were under long-term contracts to the studios and obliged to make whatever films the studio requested. A studio's major stars would appear in up to 40 movies a year, and each studio worked hard to publicize and promote its significant actors or couples, even making up gossip to guarantee maximum exposure for a particular star. The studio system produced technically high-quality films, generally because it repeated successful combinations of crew and cast. Pressure exerted by investors made high profits extremely important. The studios devised two methods of capitalizing on

their product. First, they became "vertically integrated," owning all areas of the industry from production to transportation and exhibition. The studios then introduced "block booking" so that independent theaters wishing to show the big-name films were obliged to buy several "B movies"—low-budget pictures produced to accompany the main feature—at the same time. This system guaranteed huge profits for the studios; in 1946 alone the movie industry's gross income was almost $2 billion. However, these measures created a stranglehold on the industry that was so detrimental to the smaller studios and independents that in 1948 the Supreme Court stepped in and outlawed both vertical integration and block booking. This move signaled the beginning of the end of the studio system by reducing the big studios' profits and narrowing the gap between the "Big Five" and the independent producers. Studios cut salaries and fired staff in an effort to stay afloat. By this time the studios were also fighting another threat: television. The arrival of television provided serious competition because it delivered free entertainment directly to people's living rooms.

The arrival of television

A sharp fall in movie audiences coincided with a swift increase in home television sets during the 1950s; by the mid-1960s movie attendance figures were one-fourth of those recorded in 1946. Whereas an estimated 44,000

Paramount Pictures' *Sunset Boulevard* (1950) exposed the Hollywood studio system. Gloria Swanson, seen here on set, played a faded, delusional star of the silent-movie era.

homes had a TV set at the end of 1946, by 1949 there were sets in three million homes, and by 1953 half of all American homes had television. With their income fast depleting, the studios had to find ways to make money from television. Hollywood studios were converted to produce films for television, and by the mid-1950s the big studios were selling movie rights to pre-1948 films for broadcast. *The Wizard of Oz* was the first feature film to be screened on American prime-time television, on November 3, 1956.

Disney, an independent studio, devised another survival strategy when it collaborated with the ABC network in 1954 to produce *Disneyland*. A weekly show hosted by Walt Disney (1901–1966) himself, *Disneyland* became ABC's first top-10-rated series. The program simultaneously publicized Disney movies, merchandise, and its new theme park, also called Disneyland, which had been funded in part by money generated by the program.

The 1955–1956 season heralded a new age for the major Hollywood studios as, quick to follow Disney's example, they ventured into television production. The first show to appear was *Warner Brothers Presents*, broadcast on the ABC network. It was followed by *Twentieth Century-Fox Hour* on CBS and *MGM Parade*, again on ABC. *Warner Brothers Presents* set aside the last 10 minutes for "Behind the Cameras at Warner Brothers," featuring exclusive behind-the-scenes footage and interviews. This provided the studio with free publicity for its most recent motion pictures. However, the program was unpopular with both critics and audiences, and was speedily dropped. By the late 1950s Warner Brothers had begun to produce successful television drama series, including *Cheyenne*, *Maverick*, and *77 Sunset Strip*. By 1960, 40 percent of network television was produced by the major movie studios, and their output continued to grow over subsequent years.

Television did have some advantages for the movie industry. It provided a training ground for many aspiring actors, directors, and writers. Charlton

Walt Disney (center) explains the process of animation in Lucerne, Switzerland. Disney's studio made four of the top 10 highest-grossing movies of the 1950s.

Heston was the first of many TV stars to cross over to movie stardom; Clint Eastwood was another. Directors Arthur Penn, John Frankenheimer, and Robert Mulligan learned their craft on television during the fifties and went on to make some of the best Hollywood films of the following decade, including *Bonnie and Clyde*, *To Kill a Mockingbird*, and *The Manchurian Candidate*. Television also provided the screenplays for a number of important films. *Marty* (1955), which followed the fortunes of a lonely Bronx butcher, was originally written as a play for television and was directed by TV director Delbert Mann. It was the first American movie to win the Palme d'Or at the Cannes Film Festival and remains the only film to win both the Palme d'Or and the Academy Award (Oscar) for best picture. Other feature films that started as TV dramas include *Twelve Angry Men* and *The Bachelor Party* (both 1957).

A further innovation, the spin-off television series, was also developed in the fifties, when one of the decade's biggest movies, *Broken Arrow* (1950), became a TV series in 1956. A "grown-up" western exploring the relationship of an Apache chief, Cochise (played by white actor Jeff Chandler), and an Indian agent (James Stewart), *Broken Arrow* is also noteworthy as being the first film to portray Native Americans sympathetically.

Technical innovations

The pressing need for the studios was to find ways of enticing audiences away from their television sets at home and back to the movie theaters. The studios began to specialize in areas that

THE HOLLYWOOD MUSICAL

Musicals became more complex and artistic during the 1950s. Previously, a composer's music had often been arranged around his fictionalized biography in a traditional "songbook" musical—for example, the 1945 biography of George Gershwin, *Rhapsody in Blue*—and the plot was generally incidental to the musical numbers. Under the guidance of producer Alan Freed MGM transformed the genre. For *An American in Paris* (1951) director Vincente Minnelli, star and choreographer Gene Kelly, and screenwriter Alan Jay Lerner were able to use the title as a starting point for an original story interspersed with a number of Gershwin songs. Shot in Technicolor on the MGM sound stage, the movie was an "integrated" musical, with the musical numbers blending into the action; the film's characters burst into song to express their emotions or to move the plot along. Its groundbreaking finale, a 17-minute "dream ballet" costing half a million dollars to produce, is the longest continuous dance sequence in a Hollywood picture.

An American in Paris led the way for future films with bolder, more ambitious choreography, such as *Singin' in the Rain* (1952) and *The Band Wagon* (1953). *Singin' in the Rain* was codirected by its star, Gene Kelly, and also featured Donald O'Connor, Debbie Reynolds, and Cyd Charisse. The movie's dialogue is frequently replaced with song and dance, and parts of the story are told in flashback. Much of the film's interest lies in its depiction of Hollywood's expansion into sound in the twenties.
The Band Wagon, starring Fred Astaire and Cyd Charisse, demonstrated a subtle awareness of Hollywood's insecurity during the fifties by sending up the excesses of the musical genre itself. The movie explores what an audience really wants to see and celebrates the more traditional forms of entertainment. Featuring witty and sophisticated stories, innovative choreography, and extravagant set and costume designs, these films set a new standard for the future of the musical.

Gene Kelly's dynamic choreography for *Singin' in the Rain* (1952) led to the movie receiving a host of award nominations.

television could not. The first step was color. Despite the expense and the unwieldy cameras needed for the color process, the studios began to churn out as many Technicolor films as they were able, so that by the mid-1950s half of all Hollywood films were made in full color. Lavish productions such as MGM's *King Soloman's Mines* (1950),

shot on location in Africa, and Cecil B. DeMille's biblical epic *The Ten Commandments* (1956), starring Charlton Heston and Yul Brynner, were intended to tempt viewers back to the movie theaters and proved very profitable.

Color was not the only new process employed by Hollywood to attract greater audiences. The studios invested

in new technology and pioneered the most far-reaching cinematic innovations since the 1920s. A succession of developments was introduced throughout the decade that changed the shape and dimension of the picture and the screen it was projected on, as well as the way that sound was recorded and reproduced.

New screen images

The premiere of the first feature-length color 3-D film in 1952, *Bwana Devil*, caused its audience to scream at what appeared to be a lion leaping from the screen. Three-dimensional film requires filming through twin lenses; the resulting images are simultaneously projected onto the screen by two projectors. Viewers wear special glasses with polarized lenses that allow them to perceive the image in three dimensions. Over the course of the next two years the major studios released around 40 3-D movies, boasting effects that "come off the screen right at you." However, there were many people who believed that 3-D added little of artistic or dramatic value to a film, and with regular 2-D films often outperforming 3-D movies at the box office, the studios soon abandoned the gimmick.

More influential was the extensive adoption of widescreen production processes. Cinerama, a new projection

The production of 3-D movies involved a complex and laborious process. Technical developments made such films possible, but their popularity was short-lived.

system, also premiered in 1952. A wide, curving screen was used to display a tri-panel panoramic image, which, although produced by three projectors, appeared to the audience as a single image. The effect was further enhanced by stereophonic sound. The documentary film produced to show off this new technology, *This Is Cinerama*, reportedly caused the audience to rock in their seats as though on a rollercoaster ride. The introduction of Cinerama was greeted with widespread excitement: *The New York Times* for the first and probably only time placed its review of the movie on its front page.

In February 1953 Twentieth Century-Fox declared that all its future films would be shot in CinemaScope. Fox purchased the rights for the process from the French inventor Henri Chrétien, who had developed the technique in the 1920s. An aerial photography lens was used to spread an exceptionally detailed picture over a surface larger than a standard movie-theater screen. The first motion picture to be made using the process was *The Robe* (1953), advertised by Fox as "The modern miracle you see without

glasses!" referring to both its superiority over 3-D movies and its biblical subject matter. Starring Richard Burton, Victor Mature, and Jean Simmons, the film opened to lukewarm reviews, although the CinemaScope process itself was welcomed and admired. Fox followed *The Robe* with the more memorable comedy *How to Marry a Millionaire* (1953), starring Marilyn Monroe, Betty Grable, and Lauren Bacall.

Although MGM chose to employ CinemaScope under license from Fox, other studios developed their own widescreen processes. Paramount developed VistaVision, first used for the 1954 musical *White Christmas*, starring Bing Crosby and Danny Kaye. In 1956 the independently produced *Around the World in 80 Days*, which starred David Niven and Mexican comedian Cantinflas, was filmed using another widescreen system, the 70mm Todd-AO process. In spite of the competition, CinemaScope swiftly became the most common widescreen system because it required the least number of technical changes—new lenses, a new screen, and some minor modifications to existing production

equipment—yet provided a very different picture. Like Technicolor before it, the new format became associated with particular genres that were stylized rather than realistic: historical pageants like *The Robe*, musicals such as *Carmen Jones* (1954), *Seven Brides for Seven Brothers* (1954), and *Oklahoma!* (1955), and westerns such as *Broken Lance* and *Sitting Bull* (both 1954). Widescreen systems created impressive screen images and for a short time slowed the drift of audiences away from movie theaters.

There were other changes to the way that movies were made during the 1950s. Rather than building expensive studio mockups, filmmakers took to shooting their pictures on location, making their movies appear more authentic at the same time as cutting their budgets. The decade saw production teams filming *Three Coins in the Fountain* (1954) in Rome, *Love Is a Many-Splendored Thing* (1955) in Hong Kong, and *Sayonara* (1957) in Japan. Partnerships with filmmakers from Britain were also successful. John Huston's *The African Queen* (1951), an Anglo-American production starring Humphrey Bogart and Katharine Hepburn, and British director David Lean's *The Bridge on the River Kwai* (1957), starring Alec Guinness and William Holden, both won Oscars.

Content and censorship

Risqué topics that Hollywood had previously avoided became commonplace during the decade. With the content of television programs tightly controlled by commercial sponsors, a more permissive age was dawning in Hollywood, and this was used to draw audiences away from their televisions and back to the movie theaters.

In its 1952 decision *Burstyn v. Wilson* the Supreme Court ruled that movies were a form of free speech and were therefore protected under the First Amendment. The following year the Production Code Administration, which for 20 years had decreed what was appropriate to show on film, began to lose its hold over Hollywood, when director Otto Preminger refused to remove words such as "virgin," "seduce," and "mistress" from the script of his picture *The Moon Is Blue*. Released without the Production Code Administration's seal of approval, *The Moon Is Blue* was a box-office success. Other films touching on previously taboo subjects followed, including adaptations of Tennessee Williams's plays *A Streetcar Named Desire* (1951), starring Marlon Brando and Vivian Leigh, and *Cat on a Hot Tin Roof* (1958), with Paul Newman and Elizabeth Taylor, which incorporated themes of marital disharmony, homosexuality, rape, and madness.

Social change also was explored through film: *Rebel without a Cause* (1955), starring James Dean and Natalie Wood, and *Blackboard Jungle* (1955), the first movie to use rock 'n' roll in its soundtrack, both examined juvenile delinquency; Frank Sinatra fought drug addiction in *The Man with the Golden Arm* (1955); and Tony Curtis and Sidney Poitier challenged racial intolerance in *The Defiant Ones* (1958). These films generated controversy, and many people were anxious about how their content should be controlled. Movies like *Rebel without a Cause*, which depicted a teenager's rage toward his middle-class parents and society's family values, were considered too free in their portrayal of sex and religion. Public concern about their effect on young people was rife, with some groups, such as the Woman's Christian Temperance Union, claiming that young people were more at risk from movie "addiction" than from alcoholism. By 1956 the only grounds for censorship of a movie was obscenity. State and municipal censors often pressed for this judgment in order to delete scenes from a film.

Even well-established genres underwent a shift in subject matter. Westerns, a genre popularized by the studios, matured into psychological and social studies rather than action-led stories of frontier aggression. Cowboy heroes became less straightforward good guys and more ordinary, flawed, human

During the 1950s westerns began to flesh out their characters and storylines. George Stevens's *Shane* (1953) starred Alan Ladd as a mysterious drifter.

AUDREY HEPBURN

The antithesis of the blonde bombshell, gamine and stylish Audrey Hepburn (1929–1993) achieved an Academy Award for her debut performance as a disaffected princess in *Roman Holiday* (1953). Hepburn was the daughter of a prosperous British banker and a Dutch baroness, and was born in Belgium and educated in England. She spent the war years in the Nazi-occupied Netherlands, where she suffered malnutrition. After the war Hepburn worked as a dancer and model while studying acting. The French novelist Colette discovered her and insisted she be cast in the title role in the Broadway adaptation of her novel *Gigi*. Hepburn became an instant star after *Roman Holiday*, as much for her style as her acting, and continued her successful career with *Sabrina* (1954), collaborating for the first time with Hubert de Givenchy, who designed her costumes for the film. A string of popular movies followed, including *War and Peace* (1956), *Funny Face* (1957), and *The Nun's Story* (1959), for which she received an Oscar nomination. The 1960s saw Hepburn play her two most memorable roles, Holly Golightly in *Breakfast at Tiffany's* (1961) and Eliza Doolittle in *My Fair Lady* (1964), but from 1967 she became semiretired, concentrating on her family and her humanitarian work. In 1988 she became a special goodwill ambassador for the United Nations Children's Fund (UNICEF), helping children in developing countries. She continued this work until just before her death and was posthumously awarded the Jean Hersholt Humanitarian Award by the Academy of Motion Picture Arts and Sciences. Hepburn remains a style icon to this day.

Audrey Hepburn's petite frame and elfinlike looks set her apart from the typical female movie stars of the 1950s.

figures. Played by Gary Cooper, the retiring marshal Will Kane in Fred Zinnemann's *High Noon* (1952) is not afraid to show his vulnerability: He looks frightened and even cries when, forsaken by all around him, he is forced to face the bad guys alone. By focusing on the themes of honor and social responsibility, *High Noon* signaled the western's adoption of more adult themes. George Stevens's *Shane* (1953) developed the complexity of the western even further. This tale of a territorial dispute between a cattle baron and a homesteader is told from the perspective of the young son of the

homesteader. The boy is fascinated by the appearance of the enigmatic Shane (played by Alan Ladd), a drifter who comes to his family's aid. All the characters in *Shane*, from the law-abiding homesteaders to itinerant cattlemen and lawless gunfighters, are portrayed as fully rounded individuals instead of simply "good guys" or "bad guys." *The Searchers* (1956), described by its director John Ford as a "psychological epic," broadened the scope of the western even more by examining the racism inherent in the genre. Once again the characters did not fit the traditional hero or villain

mold. The lead character, Ethan, played by John Wayne, is not wholly sympathetic, does not always do the right thing, and is left out of the happy ending afforded to other characters at the end of the film.

Teenage audiences

Rebel without a Cause and *Blackboard Jungle* brought a new audience to the movies: teenagers. Until this point Hollywood had usually portrayed young adults as conventional and carefree, like the Andy Hardy character made famous by Mickey Rooney in the 1930s and 1940s. Realizing that

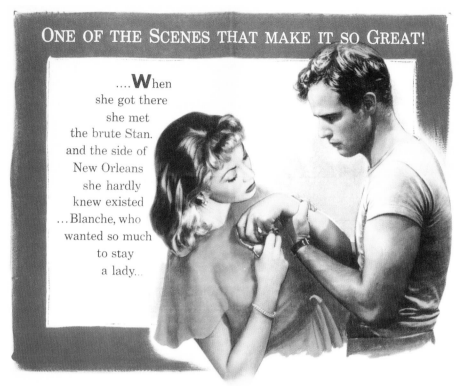

The 1950s saw gritty performances by method actors such as Marlon Brando, who played Stanley Kowalski in Elia Kazan's *A Streetcar Named Desire* (1951).

disturbed teenager is transformed into a werewolf by an wicked doctor, and Ed Wood's debut *Glen or Glenda* (1953), about a man who, in the words of the tagline, "loved women so much, he dared to dress like one!" Wood, often dubbed the "world's worst director," persuaded veteran horror actor Bela Lugosi to appear as a mad doctor in the transvetism-themed movie.

Another genre that targeted teenagers—the rock-'n'-roll movie—appeared for the first time in 1956. *Rock around the Clock*, starring Bill Hayley and His Comets, was a worldwide hit. The film was banned in a number of cities across the United States because it generated such excitement that young people jived in the aisles and ripped up seats. Quick to capitalize on its success, the same production team produced the equally successful *Don't Knock the Rock* (1956). Frank Tashlin's *The Girl Can't Help It* (1956), starring Jayne Mansfield, also made use of rock 'n' roll, featuring performances by Little Richard, Fats Domino, and the Platters, among others. Elvis Presley was another idolized singing star who signed a film deal during the decade. His movies were not a hit with the critics, but young audiences loved them. His most successful film was *Jailhouse Rock* (1957). By 1959 the youth market was worth approximately $10 billion a year.

1950s antiheroes

The studios nurtured young stars to appeal to the new self-expressive and rebellious generation, and a series of antiheroes was introduced to the big screen. In 1954 Marlon Brando (1924–2004), wearing a white T-shirt and leather jacket, became a symbol of antiauthoritarian rebellion when he played the arrogant yet sensitive leader of a motorcycle gang in *The Wild One* (1953). The film presented a disturbing picture of modern youth, and its subject matter was considered

disaffected teenagers with a disposable income could provide a lucrative market, Hollywood was soon devising films and grooming stars to attract them. A new genre of movies was created especially for the drive-ins frequented by teenagers. Short, low-budget, science fiction horror films became popular, such as those directed by Roger Corman. They had sensational titles like *Not of This Earth* (1957), *Attack of the Crab Monsters* (1957), and *A Bucket of Blood* (1959), and boasted such taglines as "From the depths of the sea ... a tidal wave of terror!" Other examples of this new genre included Gene Fowler's *I Was a Teenage Werewolf* (1957), in which a extremely controversial. Brando, along with other new stars including James Dean, Paul Newman, and Marilyn Monroe, trained at Lee Strasberg's Actors Studio, which advocated method acting, a realistic and intense style of performance that reinterpreted the acting technique devised by the Russian Konstantin Stanislavsky. Actors who employed this technique delivered edgy and emotional performances.

Another antihero, James Dean (1931–1955), became a screen legend at the age of 24 when he died in a car crash shortly after completing work on *Giant*, his third major film. Only one of his movies, *East of Eden* (1955), was released during his lifetime. Nevertheless, Dean had already become a cult figure for the alienated teenagers of the 1950s, a status that could only grow following his untimely death and the posthumous release of *Rebel without a Cause* (1955) and *Giant* (1956).

After a shaky start in *The Silver Chalice* (1954)—a picture he was so embarrassed about that he placed a full-page ad in *Variety* magazine to apologize to movie audiences—Paul Newman (1925–) followed the antihero trend by specializing in outsider roles, including *Somebody up There Likes Me* (1956), a film for which he garnered glowing reviews, and his Oscar-nominated performance in *Cat on a Hot Tin Roof* (1958).

Ava Gardener (1922–1990), "the world's most beautiful animal" as one 1950s movie poster proclaimed her, was an antiheroine who demonstrated her "bad girl" qualities in films such as *Pandora and the Flying Dutchman* (1951) and *Mogambo* (1953). In 1951 she married Frank Sinatra (1915–1998), who himself had an extremely successful movie career during the decade after his singing career was almost ended by a vocal-cord hemorrhage in 1952. After winning an Academy Award for best supporting actor for *From Here to Eternity* (1953), Sinatra delivered impressive performances in a string of films, including *Suddenly* (1954) and *The Man with the Golden Arm* (1955). He returned to his musical roots with *Guys and Dolls* in 1955, *High Society* in 1956, and *Pal Joey* in 1957.

The big stars of the 1950s

A more wholesome heroine, Doris Day (1924–) had both critical and commercial success with a series of musicals, including *Calamity Jane* (1953) and *The Man Who Knew Too Much* (1956), while also enjoying a solo singing career. In *Pillow Talk* (1959) she was paired for the first time with another big star of the fifties, Rock Hudson (1925–1985). Hudson began the decade playing bit parts before scoring a huge hit as an alcoholic playboy-turned-surgeon in *Magnificent Obsession* (1954). He starred in a number of big-budget movies and received an Oscar nomination for his role in *Giant* (1956).

Scottish-born Deborah Kerr (1921–) decided to shrug off her "good girl" image by frolicking on the beach as an adulteress with Burt Lancaster in *From Here to Eternity* (1953), a role for which she was Oscar-nominated. Kerr made some of her most famous films in the late 1950s, including *The King and I* (1956) and the romantic movies *Heaven Knows, Mr. Allison* and *An Affair to Remember* (both 1957).

The handsome and talented Montgomery Clift (1920–1966) emerged as the biggest male star of the early 1950s after Oscar-nominated turns in *A Place in the Sun* (1951) and *From Here to Eternity* (1953). Following a terrible car crash during the production of *Raintree County* (1957), his face had to be rebuilt, and his self-confidence was irreparably damaged. He continued to work, however, starring opposite Brando in *The Young Lions* (1958) and Elizabeth Taylor in *Suddenly, Last Summer* (1959). Also good-looking and talented, Sidney Poitier (1927–) delivered a number of remarkable performances during the decade in movies such as *No Way Out* (1950) and *Blackboard Jungle* (1955). Turning down roles he found degrading, Poitier became Hollywood's first African American leading man and won an Oscar nomination for best actor for his depiction of an escaped convict in *The Defiant Ones* (1958). His costar, Tony Curtis (1925–), had spent the fifties

James Dean became the role model for disaffected youth. In the posthumously released Rebel without a Cause *(1955), in which he starred with Natalie Wood, he epitomized the 1950s angst-ridden teenager.*

WILLIAM HOLDEN

Between 1954 and 1958 one of the biggest Hollywood box-office draws was William Holden (1918–1981). Signed to both Paramount and Columbia in 1937, he became an instant star following his first lead role as a young boxer in *Golden Boy* (1939). Considering him too inexperienced in film acting, Columbia almost replaced Holden in the role until his costar Barbara Stanwyck guided him through the process. A casualty of the studio system, Holden found himself poorly paid and cast in unsuitable roles before his career-defining performance as an unsuccessful screenwriter turned gigolo opposite Gloria Swanson in Billy Wilder's *Sunset Boulevard* (1950), for which he was Oscar-nominated. Despite being pushed by his studio contract to make films undeserving of his talent and star-power, Holden produced his most significant work during the 1950s. He won an Oscar for *Stalag 17* (1953) and consolidated his popularity in a series of successful movies, including *Born Yesterday* (1950), *Sabrina* (1954), and *Love Is a Many-Splendored Thing* (1955). Before agreeing to star in David Lean's *The Bridge on the River Kwai* (1957), Holden negotiated a landmark deal with Columbia, making him part-owner of the film and guaranteeing him an income for years to come. He continued to make movies in the sixties and seventies but devoted most of his time and money to wildlife conservation in Africa.

William Holden won an Academy Award for his performance as Sgt. J.J. Sefton in *Stalag 17* (1953).

slowly transforming his image from pin-up boy to critically acclaimed actor via such films as *Sweet Smell of Success* (1957), playing a despicable press agent, and *Some Like It Hot* (1959), starring as a cross-dressing musician on the run from the Mob. His partner in drag for the movie, Jack Lemmon (1925–2001), launched his film career in 1954 in *It Should Happen to You* and won his first Oscar for his role in the comedy *Mister Roberts* (1955). A gifted comedian, Lemmon was Oscar-nominated for a second time for his role in *Some Like It Hot*.

Curtis and Lemmon starred with arguably the biggest screen idol of the decade in *Some Like It Hot*: Marilyn Monroe (1926–1962). Monroe achieved international superstardom through a series of colorful comedies, including *Gentlemen Prefer Blondes* (1953) and *The Seven Year Itch* (1955). However, she was uncomfortable with her sex symbol image and sought to develop her range and reputation with grittier pictures like the critically acclaimed *Bus Stop* (1956). Monroe's 1953 movie *How to Marry a Millionaire* also starred Betty Grable (1916–1973) and Lauren Bacall (1924–), two stars who had made their names in the 1940s. Grable's career had slowed down after World War II, and she made her last film in 1955. Bacall, who took Hollywood by storm and married Humphrey Bogart in the mid-1940s, also had success during the 1950s with *Young Man with a Horn* (1950) and *Designing Woman* (1957).

Many of the stars of the thirties and forties continued to be among the top-drawing names of the fifties. A popular leading man, Gregory Peck (1916–2003) had already secured his position as a celebrated actor and continued to develop his impressive repertoire, playing a cynical killer in *The Gunfighter* (1950), a love-struck journalist in *Roman Holiday* (1953), and the tortured Captain Ahab in *Moby Dick* (1956). Katharine Hepburn (1907–2003), who established her star-power in the thirties and forties, garnered her fifth Oscar nomination for *The African Queen* (1951) and further nominations for her roles in *Summertime* (1955), *The Rainmaker* (1956), and *Suddenly, Last Summer* (1959), in which she played Elizabeth

Taylor's menacing aunt. Taylor (1932–) had enjoyed a successful career since 1942 and earned critical acclaim and Oscar nominations for her roles in *Raintree County* (1957) and *Cat on a Hot Tin Roof* (1958).

John Wayne (1907–1979) continued to be a big box-office draw throughout the fifties, frequently collaborating with director John Ford to make, among others, *Rio Grande* (1950), *The Quiet Man* (1952), and *The Searchers* (1956). Clark Gable (1901–1960) starred in *Mogambo* (1953), a remake of *Red Dust*, a film in which he had starred 21 years earlier. Judy Garland (1922–1969) began the fifties collapsing on the set of *Annie Get Your Gun* and being dropped by MGM, only to make a spectacular comeback with *A Star Is Born* in 1954. Ingrid Bergman (1915–1982), who had been exiled from Hollywood amid scandal over her affair with Italian director Roberto Rossellini in 1949, marked her return by winning a second Oscar for her starring role in *Anastasia* in 1956. Both Bette Davis (1908–1989) and Joan Crawford (1904–1977) continued to make films throughout the fifties, although after Oscar-nominated roles in the early 1950s—for *All about Eve* (1950) and *The Star* (1952) for Davis, and *Sudden Fear* (1952) for Crawford—both their careers gradually went into decline.

Several established European stars rose to international prominence during the decade. French actress Brigitte Bardot (1934–) became very popular in the United States. She made her American debut in *Un acte d'amour* with Kirk Douglas in 1953, but remains most famous for kick-starting the sexual revolution in the 1956 French movie *Et Dieu … créa la femme* ("… And God Created Woman"). Italian stars Sophia Loren (1934–) and Gina Lollobrigida (1927–) also both made several Hollywood movies, acting with some of the leading male stars of the time: Loren with Cary Grant and Frank Sinatra; Lollobrigida with Burt Lancaster and Rock Hudson.

ALFRED HITCHCOCK: "MASTER OF SUSPENSE"

Purveyor of taut, stylish thrillers, English-born Alfred Hitchcock (1899–1980) had already established his name as a director of technically innovative psychological movies by 1950. He saw it his mission as a filmmaker to "scare the hell out of people" by focusing on the shadowy side of human nature. His reputation grew over the course of the fifties as he produced a variety of big-budget, often witty tales of mistaken identity, espionage, and murder, starring some of the biggest names of the period. James Stewart epitomized the ideal everyman for Hitchcock, although each of the characters he played in *Rear Window* (1954), *The Man Who Knew Too Much* (1956), and *Vertigo* (1958) had a darker, obsessive side. Cary Grant, too, was cast in roles that undermined his debonair image: a reformed cat burglar in *To Catch a Thief* (1955) and an advertising executive mistaken for a spy in *North by Northwest* (1959). Both Stewart and Grant costarred with the quintessential Hitchcock "cool blonde," Grace Kelly. Kelly had made her film debut in 1952's *High Noon*, but it was not until she teamed up with Hitchcock for *Dial M for Murder* (1954), *Rear Window*, and *To Catch a Thief* that she gained real recognition. Hitchcock's other "cool blondes" of the 1950s included Doris Day (*The Man Who Knew Too Much*), Kim Novak (*Vertigo*), and Eva Marie Saint (*North by Northwest*). A tense thriller, polished comedy, and sophisticated romance, *North by Northwest* is viewed by some experts as the highpoint of Hitchcock's career, and it features some of the most famous scenes ever filmed, including the inventive crop dusting and Mount Rushmore chase sequences. Hitchcock remains one of the most widely imitated directors in movie history.

Alfred Hitchcock, seen here in St. Moritz, Switzerland, was notorious for appearing as an extra in his own movies.

The independent star

The end of the Hollywood studio system was most effectively indicated by the rise of independent stars—actors who retained creative control of their work by handpicking their roles. Gregory Peck had maintained his power and sparked a bidding war by refusing to sign with an individual studio, while long-time MGM star Clark Gable went freelance and became the highest-paid independent actor in Hollywood. Some actors remained within the studio system but renegotiated their contracts to suit their needs and ambitions. James Stewart at Universal and William Holden at Columbia both managed to get contracts that gave them a share of the profits of the films they were making. Other stars, including Marilyn Monroe, set up their own production companies and produced their own pictures. The most successful and adventurous of them were Burt Lancaster (1913–1994) and Kirk Douglas (1916–), who acted, produced, and often directed their own movies. Lancaster's company, Hecht-Hill-Lancaster, produced *Marty* (1955) as well as vehicles for Lancaster himself, including *Apache* (1954) and *Sweet Smell of Success* (1957). Douglas's Byrna Productions' first movie, an adventure called *The Vikings* (1958), was followed by *The Devil's Disciple* (1959), made in collaboration with Lancaster's company. Gradually, independent production became standard practice, with the studios increasingly acting only as distributors. By 1958, 65 percent of Hollywood films were produced by independent companies, and by 1960 the studios employed staff for individual projects rather than keeping production teams on long-term contracts.

EUROPEAN FILM

Filmmaking in Europe was evolving in other directions than the Hollywood studios. The *Nouvelle Vague*, or New Wave, movement originated in France when critic and film historian François Truffaut inspired a generation of directors with an article for the journal *Cahiers du cinéma* in 1954 that established the *auteur* theory. The theory held that a director is the central creative power behind a motion picture. From the late 1950s onward a group of unconventional directors—Louis Malle, Claude Chabrol, and Jean-Luc Goddard, in addition to Truffaut himself—pioneered a new kind of topically and technically radical filmmaking. Written and directed by Chabrol, *Le Beau Serge* (1958) was an influential New Wave film about a man returning to his home town to find his friend has become an alcoholic. Directors Tony Richardson, Lindsay Anderson, and Jack Clayton took the movement to Britain with films such as *Room at the Top* (1959), which was part of a wider movement known as the "angry-young-man school" or "kitchen-sink drama." Such movies focused on the working class and displayed a dissatisfaction with the oppressive British class structure in stark, frank language and cinematography. Another important film in this genre was Richardson's *Look Back in Anger* (1958), adapted from the play by John Osborne. Italian neorealism—a nationalistic movement that developed in the 1940s to depict the turmoil of a country recovering from the effects of World War II—gradually gave way to modernism under the guidance of directors like Federico Fellini and Michelangelo Antonioni in movies such as *Le notti di Cabiria* (1957) and *Le amiche* (1955), and was very influential on European New Wave cinema.

French actress Brigitte Bardot achieved success in America in movies such as *Un acte d'amour* (1953) and *Et Dieu ... créa la femme* (1956) but remained very much an icon of European cinema.

THE AMERICAN FILM INSTITUTE'S TOP 10 BOX-OFFICE LEADERS OF THE 1950s

Lady and the Tramp (1955)

Peter Pan (1953)

Cinderella (1950)

The Ten Commandments (1956)

Ben-Hur (1959)

Sleeping Beauty (1959)

Around the World in 80 Days (1956)

This Is Cinerama (1952)

South Pacific (1958)

The Robe (1953)

The movie version of the Rodgers and Hammerstein musical *South Pacific* starred Rossano Brazzi and Mitzi Gaynor as lovers.

Communism in Hollywood

The House Un-American Activities Committee (HUAC) first descended on Hollywood in 1947 to investigate communist influence in the entertainment industry. HUAC interrogated witnesses about their political beliefs and affiliations. The hearings culminated in a group of directors and screenwriters—the so-called Hollywood Ten—being held in contempt of Congress and imprisoned for up to one year. The studios quickly succumbed to the mass anticommunist hysteria sweeping the country and issued a declaration, vowing that they would not intentionally employ anyone with suspected subversive connections. This decision initiated an unofficial blacklist: Anyone implicated in any way by the HUAC hearings was considered guilty by association and therefore unemployable. HUAC's return to Hollywood in 1951 resulted in

hundreds of people being blacklisted in three years, damaging their careers or destroying them altogether. Scriptwriter Carl Foreman was blacklisted shortly after the production of *High Noon* ended because his tale of a man standing firm in his beliefs against the rest of society was considered to be a criticism of the activities of HUAC. Some members of the movie industry cooperated with the committee by naming names. Among such "friendly" witnesses were director Elia Kazan and scriptwriter Budd Schulberg. Their 1954 film *On the Waterfront* portrayed a man's difficult decision to turn informer and is often interpreted as an allegorical justification for the roles they chose to play before HUAC.

There were other repercussions from the HUAC investigations: Hollywood distanced itself from political concerns, scripts were scrutinized for subversive content, the Academy Awards refused

to reward the work of "unfriendly" witnesses, and information was collated on movie stars. Katharine Hepburn, for example, caught the attention of agents for wearing red to a political rally as well as for her affair with Spencer Tracy. However, HUAC never uncovered any evidence of overt communist propaganda generated by Hollywood.

See Also:
Blacklist • Brando, Marlon • Cartoons and Animation • Dean, James • Disney, Walt • Garland, Judy • *High Noon* • House Un-American Activities Committee • Legion of Decency • Monroe, Marilyn • Musical Theater • *On the Waterfront* • Oscars • Poitier, Sidney • Presley, Elvis • Sinatra, Frank • Teenage Culture • Television • Wayne, John • Western Movies • Williams, Tennessee

ED MURROW 1908–1965

Ed Murrow set the standard of excellence in news reporting as television developed in the 1950s. Honest, independent, and always controversial, he remains one of the most influential TV reporters of all time.

Edward R. Murrow was born Egbert Roscoe Murrow on April 25, 1908, near Greensboro, North Carolina. His family moved to Washington, where Murrow attended Washington State College. He majored in speech and changed his name to Edward. In 1929 he became president of the National Student Federation, then worked for the Institute of International Education.

Witness and reporter

Murrow began his broadcasting career in 1935 as director of talks and education at CBS. From 1937 he headed the network's European Bureau. When Germany occupied Austria in 1938, Murrow found himself obliged to report on the events, making the first of more than 5,000 broadcasts. World War II (1939–1945) sealed Murrow's reputation. His eyewitness reports from London, prefaced by the words "This is London," made Americans feel as though they were there in person. Murrow's unique style of presentation was simple but vivid, with the emphasis on telling things as they were.

After the war Murrow returned to the United States as vice president of CBS news operations but soon went back to radio broadcasting. His show *Hear It Now* ran successfully between 1950 and 1951. Initially resistant to the growing popularity of television, Murrow was eventually persuaded to adapt his program to a television format. He hosted *See It Now* between 1951 and 1958. "This is an old team trying to learn a new trade," announced Murrow as the show premiered on

Ed Murrow, seen here in the CBS studios in 1954, was an influential broadcast journalist throughout his career. His challenging style made him popular with American audiences.

November 18, 1951. By April 20, 1952, *See It Now* had moved to prime time, where it stayed until July 1955. Over the next few years the show pioneered many features, such as the news magazine format, the in-depth feature, and the investigative report. During the 1952 Christmas season, for example, the program featured a one-hour report on the everyday difficulties that American soldiers faced during the Korean War (1950–1953). For the duration of the show Murrow used a signature sign-off line: "Good night and good luck."

Murrow, along with his managing editor Fred W. Friendly, wanted to use his show to inform Americans. With this in mind they broadcast a stinging critique of Senator Joseph McCarthy (1908–1957) on March 9, 1954. Murrow urged the audience to speak out against the fear that McCarthy had engendered, and the studio received 100,000 letters in support. CBS, however, was less pleased. The network wanted to preserve its advertisers.

As well as *See It Now*, Murrow hosted the very popular Friday prime-time show *Person to Person* between 1953 and 1959. Each week he chatted from the studio with a celebrity at home; his interviewees included Lauren Bacall, Marilyn Monroe, Marlon Brando, and the newlywed John F. and Jackie Kennedy.

Murrow received four Emmys for *See It Now* and numerous awards for *Person to Person*, but his relationship with CBS deteriorated. At a media convention in 1958 he criticized television for "being used to detract, delude, amuse and insulate us."

From 1958 to 1959 Murrow moderated and produced *Small World*, a television series featuring discussions among world figures. In 1959 he took a year's leave of absence, and although he hosted the occasional show, he had effectively retired from broadcasting. In 1961 President Kennedy appointed him director of the U.S. Information Agency. A heavy smoker, Murrow died of lung cancer on April 27, 1965.

> **See Also:**
> Communications • McCarthy Hearings • News and Current Affairs • Radio • Television

MUSICAL THEATER

The 1950s saw the stage and screen debuts of many of the finest and most well-loved musicals in the history of the form, yet it also saw a gradual decline in the mass popularity of the musical as it faced stiff competition from television and rock 'n' roll.

The 1950s were an important and exciting decade in the history of the American musical theater, which was based, as before and after, around the theaters on Broadway in New York City. Although not a prolific period—the 1955–1956 season, for instance, offered only five new musicals—most of the musicals presented in the decade were innovative and groundbreaking, and many ran for more than 1,000 performances. The decade featured the continuing development of the integrated musical, the rise of director/choreographers such as Jerome Robbins and Bob Fosse, and creative partnerships such as Rodgers and Hammerstein, and Lerner and Loewe; it was the decade of *Guys and Dolls*, *The Pajama Game*, *West Side Story*, and *My Fair Lady*.

Overview

In a period of postwar optimism, prosperity, and risk-taking each season in the decade offered at least one big musical hit. Broadway musicals of the time were elaborate and had high production values; they were rich in variety and replete with social meaning as well as entertainment value. The cost of producing high-quality, large-cast shows was the reason for the small number of new musicals presented each season, especially compared with the number of straight plays, which were much less costly to produce. In addition, Broadway audiences were shrinking, due in part to rising ticket prices and to the arrival of new forms of entertainment, especially television.

With the growing popularity and accessibility of television in the fifties people were trading in outside entertainment for evenings at home, especially with new programs such as *Studio One* and *Play of the Week* bringing televised versions of Broadway plays into people's living rooms free of charge. The onset of rock-'n'-roll music changed audiences' musical tastes, and the styles of music associated with musical theater and with popular music, which shared a resemblance before the war, began to diverge more sharply. In the decade that also saw the emergence of teenagers as a distinct cultural group for the first time, these differences in musical style also began to be associated with the differing tastes of teenagers and their parents' generation. Many teenagers grew up in the fifties without exposure to musical theater and therefore had no understanding or appreciation of it. However, despite growing production costs, rising ticket prices, and shrinking audiences, musical theater remained viable both financially and artistically, and the decade offered some of the genre's greatest achievements.

Rodgers and Hammerstein

The end of the 1950s saw the termination of one of the most prolific, successful, and popular composer/lyricist teams in musical theater history. Composer Richard Rodgers (1902–1979) and lyricist Oscar Hammerstein

The 1959 hit *The Sound of Music* was created by Richard Rodgers, Oscar Hammerstein, Mary Martin, Russel Crouse, and Howard Lindsay, pictured here from left to right.

WINNERS OF THE TONY AWARD FOR BEST MUSICAL

1950	*South Pacific*
1951	*Guys and Dolls*
1952	*The King and I*
1953	*Wonderful Town*
1954	*Kismet*
1955	*The Pajama Game*
1956	*Damn Yankees*
1957	*My Fair Lady*
1958	*The Music Man*
1959	*Redhead*

II (1895–1960) saw no end to their popularity in the 1940s, boasting three simultaneous shows on Broadway in 1947, and rounding out the decade with *South Pacific* in 1949. They started the fifties with a bang, receiving the Tony Award and a Pulitzer Prize (only the second ever for a musical) for *South Pacific*, and their reign continued with *The King and I* in 1951, *Flower Drum Song* in 1958, and *The Sound of Music* in 1959. They also offered two minor hits with *Me and Juliet* (1953) and *Pipe Dream* (1955).

Set in Bangkok in the 1860s, *The King and I* is based on the novel *Anna and the King of Siam*. It tells the story of Welsh teacher Anna Leonowens, who is hired to educate the children of the king of Siam. Like *South Pacific*, *The King and I* drew attention to issues of prejudice and tolerance, and examined the differences and lack of understanding between Western and Eastern cultures. The show offered a strong female lead for comeback star Gertrude Lawrence and made a star of the then-unknown Yul Brynner. It was choreographed by Jerome Robbins (1918–1988) and included his famous ballet "Small House of Uncle Thomas," based on the story *Uncle Tom's Cabin*. The show played 1,246 performances, despite Lawrence's death in 1952.

Flower Drum Song, based on the novel of the same name, shows the need for tolerance and understanding between generations. It tells the story of Asian American adults trying to maintain traditional values while their largely modernized children have assimilated to their surroundings. Featuring a largely Asian American cast, the show was the only Broadway musical directed by film star, dancer, and choreographer Gene Kelly.

One of the more popular musicals still produced today (and recently revived on Broadway) is *The Sound of Music*. Set in Austria in 1938, it is based on the autobiography *The Trapp Family Singers* and tells the story of Maria, a woman hired to care for the children of a wealthy captain, Georg von Trapp. Maria wins the favor of the children and eventually the captain, whom she marries. However, their happiness is interrupted by the Nazi annexation of Austria. The second longest running musical of the 1950s, the show played for 1,443 performances and proved to be its creators' last production: Hammerstein died nine months after its opening.

Lerner and Loewe

The longest-running Broadway musical of the 1950s (and, before 1975, in history) was written by the other reigning composer/lyricist team of the

Julie Andrews and Rex Harrison star in the classic 1956 Lerner and Loewe musical *My Fair Lady*, which won the Tony Award for best musical in 1957.

GWEN VERDON

Gwen Verdon (1925–2000), an extraordinarily talented dancer, singer, and actor, set the precedent for the "triple threat"—performers who could dance, sing, and act with equal proficiency. Verdon made her Broadway debut in 1950 in the revue *Alive and Kicking*, but she gained attention in 1953's *Can-Can*, set in Paris in 1893 and based on true stories of attempts to shut down dance halls for showing the high-kicking cancan. Although its star was French actress Lilo as the proprietress of the Bal du Paradis, she was inadvertently upstaged by Verdon as the lead cancan dancer. Verdon powerfully and expertly carried out the strong, energetic movements of choreographer Michael Kidd (1919–), bringing the house down night after night with her sexy "apache" dance.

Verdon created the role of Lola, the seductress working for the devil in the Adler and Ross musical *Damn Yankees* (1955). Her perfect execution of choreographer (and later husband) Bob Fosse's exquisitely sensual movements catapulted her to stardom. She and Fosse worked together on two other musicals in the 1950s. The first was *New Girl in Town* (1957), based on the Eugene O'Neill play *Anna Christie* and featuring music and lyrics by Bob Merrill. Two years later Fosse's initial effort as director as well as choreographer was the musical whodunit *Redhead*, also starring Richard Kiley. Both shows were intended to be vehicles for Verdon; *Redhead* won a Tony in 1959.

Gwen Verdon jokes at a recording session for *Damn Yankees* in 1955, with composer Jerry Ross to her right and lyricist Dick Adler to her left.

Verdon continued her collaboration with Fosse after their separation in the 1970s and helped continue his legacy after he died in 1987. She was artistic adviser for the stage show commemorating his work, *Fosse*, in 1999.

The Music Man by Meredith Willson opened on Broadway in 1957. It tells the story of a con man who sells musical instruments.

era, lyricist Alan Jay Lerner (1918–1986) and composer Frederick Loewe (1901–1988). *My Fair Lady* (1956), adapted from George Bernard Shaw's 1914 play *Pygmalion* and set in London, epitomized the height of the golden era of Broadway musicals. Its star Julie Andrews, fresh from her debut in the 1920s pastiche *The Boyfriend* (1954), and her costar Rex Harrison are forever identified with their roles: Eliza Doolittle, a lower-class cockney flower seller, and Henry Higgins, a pompous English professor who decides to make Eliza into a proper lady. The show was immensely popular, with music offering glimpses of the English music hall ("Get Me to the Church on Time") and Viennese operetta ("I Could Have

GEORGE ABBOTT

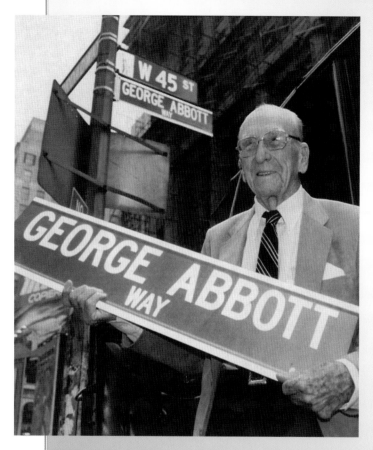

A director, producer, writer, and actor, George Abbott (1887–1995) led an extraordinarily long life and had a prolific career. In the 1950s alone he contributed to eight musicals, including the smash hits *Damn Yankees* and *The Pajama Game*, the Pulitzer Prize-winning *Fiorello!*, *New Girl in Town*, *Me and Juliet*, and *Once upon a Mattress*.

Significant to the success of many musicals, Abbott collaborated with talents such as Jerome Robbins, Bob Fosse, Leonard Bernstein, and Harold Prince (who debuted with *The Pajama Game* in 1954). Abbott directed while Robbins choreographed Irving Berlin's penultimate musical, *Call Me Madam* (1950), which starred Ethel Merman and offered hits similar to Berlin's earlier *Annie Get Your Gun* (1946). Abbott worked with Fosse on his choreographic debut, *The Pajama Game* (1954), and they collaborated again on *Damn Yankees* (1955) and *New Girl in Town* (1957). *Wonderful Town* (1953) featured Abbott's direction of Bernstein's score.

Abbott directed two very different and charming musicals in 1959: *Once upon a Mattress*, the only show composed by Richard Rodgers's daughter Mary, was based on the fairy tale "The Princess and the Pea" and starred Carol Burnett in her Broadway debut; and *Fiorello!*, based on the life of New York Mayor Fiorello LaGuardia, featured music by Jerry Bock and lyrics by Sheldon Harnick, the team who later wrote *Fiddler on the Roof* (1964).

Abbott's long career in the theater came to an end with his involvement with the 1994 revival of *Damn Yankees* at the age of 107; its original lyricist Jerry Ross had died at the age of only 29 during its initial run.

Musical theater veteran George Abbott collaborated on many of the great musicals of the 1950s. A street off Broadway was named for him.

Danced All Night") traditions. Part of its huge success was due to the advances made in sound-recording technology during the 1950s, the first full decade of the long-playing record (LP), and to the wide audiences—well beyond the ranks of New York City theater-goers—that the LP brought to the show. *My Fair Lady*'s original mono cast recording became the biggest-selling show album in history, had radio airplay, and was rerecorded in stereo. From that time on, LPs of new musicals became an integral part of the marketing and financing of new theatrical productions.

Competing directly with *The King and I*, Lerner and Loewe offered *Paint Your Wagon* in 1951, about the California Gold Rush. Although its run was comparatively short (289 performances), the show remains popular, with hit songs such as "They Call the Wind Maria."

Giants of the integrated musical

The musicals of the 1940s had set a new precedent for musical theater by having a well-constructed "book," or libretto (spoken dialogue) and lyrics (sung text), often by different writers, that were no longer just frameworks for catchy musical numbers but fully fleshed-out plots, as important as the songs. In addition, songs and dances seamlessly furthered the plot and illuminated the characters. As musicals developed in the 1950s, therefore, they

were expected to be fully integrated, smoothly combining not only drama, music, and choreography, but sets, costumes, lighting, and props, all aspects of the production working together to establish the narrative, mood, and meaning of the show. As a result, musicals took on more complex, socially significant, and interesting stories. Many musicals of the decade, including those already mentioned, helped further these concepts.

Integrated musicals demanded more not only from their creators but also from their actors. The early days of musicals with a group of singers and a separate group of dancers were gone. Performers were now expected to be able to sing, dance, and act—those who could do so were described as a "triple threat" because of the challenge they posed to performers with only one or two of the skills. The precedent was established by a young, up-and-coming entertainer, Gwen Verdon, who took Broadway by storm (*see box on p. 103*).

Striving for a more integrated musical often resulted in working toward the creative vision of one person who controlled the production, direction, and choreography. Brilliant minds such as Jerome Robbins, Bob Fosse, Michael Kidd, Joshua Logan, and David Merrick controlled many aspects of the shows in which they were involved.

Jerome Robbins

A great example of creative vision is *West Side Story* (1957), an honest, socially significant work, with the first tragic ending in the history of musicals. Conceptualized, directed, and choreographed by Robbins, the story is Shakespeare's *Romeo and Juliet* set in 1950s Manhattan. Leonard Bernstein (music), Stephen Sondheim (lyrics), and Arthur Laurents (book) headed a brilliant creative team that worked toward realizing Robbins's vision. The simultaneously beautiful and cutting score and intense lyrics worked with Robbins's new vocabulary of movement to capture the perfect balance of power, relentless energy, vulnerability, and panic felt by the gang members. Everything came together to paint a clear picture of the story and its players.

Robbins was also behind 1959's *Gypsy*, working again with Sondheim (1930–) and Laurents (1918–), with music by Jule Styne (1905–1994). This remarkable show is based on the memoirs of stripper Gypsy Rose Lee, but the action focuses on her stage-mother Rose, a role written for Ethel Merman. Sondheim and Styne gave Rose a powerhouse score of forceful songs expressing her pure drive and desire for a better life, with her children caught in the crossfire. Robbins's

staging for the strippers' "You Gotta Get a Gimmick" famously captures the advice of the young women. *Gypsy* has been revived on Broadway three times, with Angela Lansbury, Tyne Daly, and Bernadette Peters respectively in the role of Rose.

Robbins choreographed and directed a version of the popular children's tale *Peter Pan* (1954), starring

Mary Martin. Initially only a marginal box-office success, it has since been revived several times. Robbins shared directing duties with one of Broadway's most creative minds, George Abbott (*see box opposite*) on *Wonderful Town* (1953, revived on Broadway in 2003) and *The Pajama Game* (1954). The latter featured the debut of choreographer Bob Fosse (1927–1987),

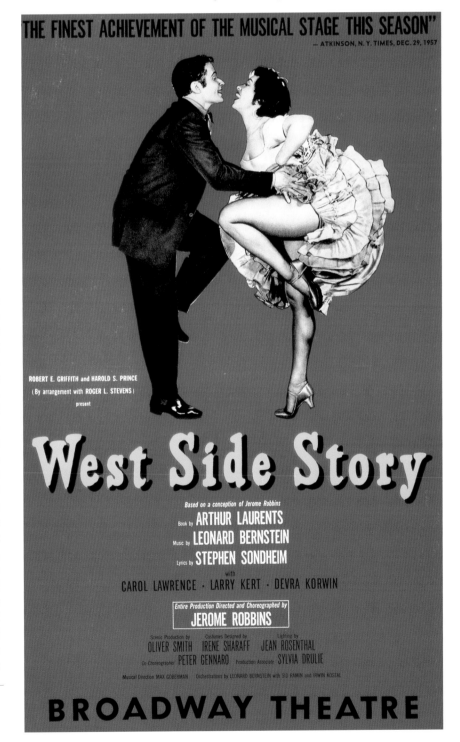

The striking design of this 1958 promotional poster for *West Side Story* reflects Jerome Robbins's overall vision for his musical.

FRANK LOESSER

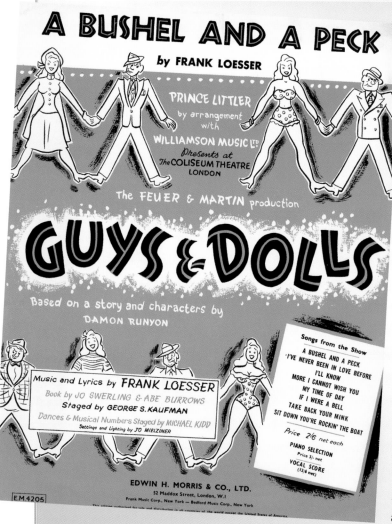

Frank Loesser (1910–1969) started his career writing lyrics for film songs, eventually adding his own tunes. His Broadway debut as composer/lyricist was *Where's Charley?* (1948), which featured the song "Once in Love with Amy." Loesser struck Broadway gold with the innovative and nearly perfect "musical fable of Broadway" *Guys and Dolls* (1950). Based on Damon Runyon's short story "The Idyll of Miss Sarah Brown," the action follows gambler Sky Masterson's pursuit of "mission doll" Sarah Brown, while Nathan Detroit, the organizer of the "oldest established permanent floating crap game in New York," tries to put off marrying Miss Adelaide, his fiancee of 14 years. Loesser's brilliant lyrics use vernacular speech to define the characters, while the songs advance the mood and action of the play; Michael Kidd's exhilarating choreography presents the dancers as real people. The dazzlingly funny and touching show is a cornerstone of American musical theater. It played 1,200 performances and toured for an additional two years; it was also adapted for film and has been revived several times.

Loesser wrote songs for Hollywood's *Hans Christian Andersen* (1952), a biography of the Danish fairy-tale writer, starring Danny Kaye, and then wrote music, lyrics, and libretto for his next Broadway work, *The Most Happy Fella*, in a rich, fluid, operatic vein. Its seamless integration was apparent in the lush score, which combined arias and choral pieces with classic musical numbers. The show opened in 1956 and was the first musical to be recorded in its entirety on LP.

The music and lyrics of favorite songs from popular musicals, such as "A Bushel and a Peck" from *Guys and Dolls*, were widely published.

with whom Robbins worked on *Bells Are Ringing* (1956), starring Judy Holliday as a phone service operator.

Bob Fosse

Fosse's debut made an indelible mark on Broadway. The *Pajama Game* number "Steam Heat," featuring dancer Carol Haney, established Fosse's trademark erotic style, combining stillness and meticulous attention to detail, complete with bowler hats and gloves. With influences from ballet and modern dance Fosse brought his own idiosyncrasies to the mix, combining everyday movements with dance. Fosse and the rest of *The Pajama Game*'s creative team followed it up with *Damn Yankees* (1955), a baseball story starring Gwen Verdon. Both shows were written by the young composer/lyricist team of Jerry Ross (1926–1955) and Richard Adler (1923–), whose collaboration was cut short by Ross's early death. Both shows were also hits, each playing for more than 1,000 performances.

Following *Damn Yankees* and *Bells Are Ringing*, Fosse choreographed *New Girl in Town* (1957), a musical based on the Eugene O'Neill play *Anna Christie*, starring Gwen Verdon and with music and lyrics by Bob Merrill and libretto by George Abbott, who also directed. Fosse's debut in the dual role of director/choreographer was with the show *Redhead* (1959), also starring Verdon, a musical whodunit set in a wax museum in early-1900s London.

Other important musicals

Despite the growing popularity of the integrated musical, the decade began with one of the last popular examples of the revue—a collection of songs and sketches without narrative connection to each other. *New Faces of 1952* featured performers who were new to Broadway. Since the first *New Faces* in 1934 the series had been updated seven times, and the 1952 show was the most popular as well as the last. Featuring the debuts of Alice Ghostley, Eartha Kitt, and Mel Brooks, the revue offered, among other things, such unlikely numbers as a hoedown about the trial of murderer Lizzie Borden.

Many Broadway shows, such as *Damn Yankees, Guys and Dolls,* and *Fiorello!* (1959), used very American themes in their story and setting. The epitome of Americana, however, was *The Music Man* (1957), by Meredith Willson (1902–1984). Encouraged by Frank Loesser, Willson based his musical on memories of his home town in Iowa, supplying music, lyrics, and libretto for the show. Starring Robert Preston and Barbara Cook, the musical featured a variety of musical styles, including barbershop and ragtime, and won the 1958 Tony Award. Cook came to *The Music Man* fresh from her work on 1956's *Candide*, a commercial failure (73 performances) that has since become a classic. Featuring a beautiful and challenging operatic score by Leonard Bernstein (1918–1990) and based on the writing of Voltaire, the musical has been reworked several times and is a staple of opera and concert repertoire.

A long-running musical that seems to have been forgotten is *Little Mary Sunshine* (1959), featuring music, lyrics, and book by Rick Besoyan

(1925–1970). The show ran for 1,143 performances and helped establish the contrast between lush Broadway and less expensive but high-quality Off-Broadway musicals (those staged away from the main theater district in New York City).

After *Wish You Were Here* (1952; *see box*) Harold Rome (1908–1993) and Joshua Logan collaborated on *Fanny* (1954), starring Ezio Pinza and Florence Henderson, the first musical show produced by entrepreneur David Merrick. At the same time, Merrick began work on a musical in the classic western tradition, *Destry Rides Again*, once more with a score by Rome. Michael Kidd (1919–) contributed his exciting choreography, complete with cracking whips. The show, starring Andy Griffith, opened in 1959.

German-born composer Kurt Weill (1900–1950) made his mark on the 1950s musical despite his death at the beginning of the decade. In 1954 Broadway produced the first English-language version of his *Threepenny Opera*, originally *Die Dreigroschenoper*, a collaboration with the playwright Bertolt Brecht that was first produced in Berlin in 1928. Starring Weill's wife Lotte Lenya, the play had to close after only 12 weeks due to a prior booking; however, public demand brought the production back a year later. It played for 2,611 performances. Weill's daring 1949 production *Lost in the Stars*, based on Alan Paton's novel *Cry, the Beloved Country*, became part of New York City Opera's repertoire in 1958.

Composer Harold Arlen (1905–1986), known for his score for the movie *The Wizard of Oz* (1939), wrote two complementary shows with a Caribbean locale in the 1950s. In 1954 he collaborated with Truman Capote on an adaptation of Capote's short story "House of Flowers." The primarily black cast featured Pearl Bailey and Diahann Carroll, as well as modern and ballet dancing stars Arthur Mitchell, Carmen De Lavallade, and Alvin Ailey. In 1957 Arlen again worked with *Oz* lyricist E.Y. "Yip" Harburg (1896–1981) on *Jamaica*, which became a success largely thanks to its star, Lena Horne.

Hollywood musicals

The success of the integrated Broadway musical, with its sense of realism and high-quality construction, led to a change in Hollywood musicals as movie producers and directors yearned for the same integration in their creations.

Since the 1930s Metro-Goldwyn-Mayer had been the most accomplished studio producing musicals, creating an enormous number of wonderful movie versions. Its wide range of productions attracted many Broadway artists to work in Hollywood, including choreographers such as Gene Kelly, Robert Alton, and Michael Kidd, and composers and lyricists such as Ira Gershwin, Betty Comden, Adolph Green, and Cole Porter. The involvement of such professionals helped the movies achieve the sought-after integration necessary to appeal to a

JOSHUA LOGAN AND *WISH YOU WERE HERE*

The unique *Wish You Were Here* (1952) featured a lovely score by Harold Rome and was produced, directed, and choreographed (with uncredited help from Jerome Robbins) by Joshua Logan (1908–1988). With this show Logan demonstrated the growing importance of directors to musical theater in the 1950s. Its light plot—a group of middle-class New Yorkers are on summer vacation at Camp Karefree in the Catskill Mountains—led Logan to insist on building a huge swimming pool into the stage of the Imperial Theatre. Because of the pool it was impossible for the show to have its customary out-of-town tryout, and early feedback was negative. However, Logan refused to give in and continued to work on the show, making changes even after its opening, causing influential director and critic Harold Clurman to call it "the only truly experimental theater in New York." *Wish You Were Here* sold out after three weeks and ran for 598 performances.

Gene Kelly and Leslie Caron starred in MGM's classic _An American in Paris_. Kelly's daring choreography helped earn the musical an Academy Award for best picture in 1951.

was made by adapting earlier stage shows for the screen, including movie versions of _Oklahoma!_ (1955), _The King and I_ (1956), _South Pacific_ (1958), _Guys and Dolls_ (1955), _Damn Yankees_ (1958), and _The Pajama Game_ (1957).

Four great originals

Arthur Freed's unit at MGM also managed to produce four successful original musicals during the decade. _An American in Paris_ (1951) starred Gene Kelly fighting for the attention of leading lady Leslie Caron. Replete with songs by George and Ira Gershwin, the movie daringly ended with a 17-minute ballet to George Gershwin's orchestral tone poem of the same title. Vincente Minnelli's direction and Kelly's choreography integrated narrative and dance, with the final ballet the movie's highlight. It was only the third musical to win an Oscar for best picture.

Shortly afterward MGM released _Singin' in the Rain_ (1952), starring Kelly with Debbie Reynolds; they played Hollywood actors trying to survive the transition from silent films to "talkies" in the late 1920s. The movie contains some of the greatest dance sequences ever filmed, including Donald O'Connor's duet with a dressmaker's dummy, "Make 'Em Laugh," and the title track performed by Kelly.

In 1954 Stanley Donen directed and Michael Kidd choreographed _Seven Brides for Seven Brothers_, with music by Gene de Paul. The brothers were given athletic dancing in true Kidd style, particularly in the barn-raising scene.

One of the last original musicals of the decade was also one of its finest: _Gigi_ (1958), starring Leslie Caron, Louis Jourdan, and Maurice Chevalier, featured music and lyrics by Lerner and Loewe. Despite setbacks, including reshooting part of the film, it was a smashing success, winning nine Oscars.

sophisticated audience. MGM's corps of creative talents mostly worked under contract, allowing the studio to make several musicals a year economically. They worked together to give the movies cohesive development and unity. Songs and dances developed characters and story line, and stories were more

serious and socially significant, although to a lesser degree than on Broadway. As the contract system declined, however, musical movies became more expensive to produce. Fewer were made, and good original ideas and stories were harder to come by. This was partly due to the waning overall popularity of the musical as younger tastes began to shift toward rock 'n' roll. An attempt to meet this challenge can be seen in Elvis Presley's appearance in _Jailhouse Rock_ (1957). Another effort to recapture audiences

See Also:

Bernstein, Leonard • Broadway • Dance • Horne, Lena • Movie Industry • Oscars • Porter, Cole • Recording Industry • Rodgers and Hammerstein • Theater

NATIONAL AERONAUTICS AND SPACE ADMINISTRATION

During the 1950s American space research was conducted by the Army, Air Force, Navy, and civilian agencies, which all competed for funds. The creation of NASA in 1958 brought all these efforts together and gave them the focus necessary for the great achievements of the 1960s.

Since scholars first theorized about the origins of the universe, people have dreamed of flying into space. On October 4, 1957, those dreams started on the road to reality with the launch of the world's first artificial satellite, *Sputnik 1*. This Soviet success marked the beginning of the space race—the struggle for technological superiority in space between the Soviet Union and the United States. The National Aeronautics and Space Administration (NASA) was born out of this bitter rivalry.

While American officials were quick to congratulate their counterparts in Moscow, in reality the success of *Sputnik 1* only heightened tensions between the superpowers. The space race was seen by both sides as a new front in the Cold War, part of an all-encompassing contest for political, ideological, and economic supremacy. The *Sputnik* launch prompted anxious calls to increase U.S. funding for aeronautics and space research. They were quickly answered by the National Aeronautics and Space Act of 1958, which, according to its preamble, would "provide for research into problems of flight within and outside the Earth's atmosphere, and for other purposes."

The birth of NASA

The 1958 "Space Act" made possible the creation of a new organization, the National Aeronautics and Space Administration, to assume overall control of the national space program.

T. Keith Glennan served as the administrator of NASA from 1958 to 1961. He headed a staff of scientists, engineers, and technicians all engaged in research in space matters.

NASA began operations on October 1, 1958, and President Dwight D. Eisenhower (1953–1961) appointed T. Keith Glennan (1905–1995), president of Case Institute of Technology in Cleveland, Ohio, to be the organization's first administrator.

Before the foundation of NASA many different government agencies, as well as the military, were responsible for aeronautics and space research in one way or another. Gradually these organizations were brought under the NASA umbrella, although the Department of Defense retained control over space activities related to

matters of national security, such as the development of rockets for launching missiles. First to be absorbed was the National Advisory Committee for Aeronautics (NACA), which had been created in 1915 as the civilian government agency responsible for aviation research. With 8,000 employees and an annual budget of $100 million NACA formed the core of the new organization. NASA took control of NACA's three major research laboratories—Langley Aeronautical Laboratory (in Virginia), Ames Aeronautical Laboratory (California), and Lewis Flight Propulsion Laboratory (Ohio)—plus two small test facilities, the Wallops rocket test range in Virginia and the Muroc aircraft test range in California.

Next came the transfer of the Naval Research Laboratory (NRL). The NRL was responsible for Project Vanguard—the U.S. effort to put into Earth orbit a scientific satellite as part of the International Geophysical Year (IGY, 1957–1958). Project Vanguard was conceived in 1955, but the project faltered through lack of funds and was eventually canceled following the success of *Sputnik 1* (also launched as part of the IGY). NASA then assumed control of the Army Ballistic Missile Agency (ABMA) in Huntsville, Alabama, including German-born rocket engineer Wernher Von Braun (1912–1977) and his team, who were based there, and who were beginning development of the Saturn rockets.

Work is completed on the second Project Mercury capsule in a hanger near Cleveland, Ohio, in 1959. The project was NASA's first manned spaceflight program.

Finally, the Jet Propulsion Laboratory (JPL), managed by the California Institute of Technology for the U.S. Army, was integrated into the fledgling space agency. One of the JPL's notable successes was the launch of *Explorer 1*, which took over from the failing Project Vanguard as the United States' IGY entry. On January 31, 1958, *Explorer 1* became the first American satellite to enter Earth orbit. *Explorer 1* also provided evidence for the existence of bands of charged particles trapped in space by Earth's magnetic field, which were named the Van Allen radiation belt for Dr. James Van Allen (1914–), the lead researcher on *Explorer 1*.

NASA began to operate space missions almost as soon as it was created. The agency organized its first "man-in-space" program on October 7, 1958, formally naming it Project Mercury on November 26, 1958. Following a series of test missions with the spacecraft *Pioneers 1* through *4*, NASA selected seven astronauts for the Mercury program in April 1959.

Further Soviet successes

By this time, however, the Soviet Union was enjoying considerable success with its Luna space program. *Luna 1* had already performed the first lunar flyby on January 2, 1959. Soviet officials scored yet another victory with the *Luna 2* spacecraft, which succeeded in hitting the moon on September 14, 1959. This further success helped push moon exploration closer to the center of American space policy.

NASA took delivery of its first Mercury capsule on April 1, 1960. In July that year NASA started work on the next phase of the national space program, the Apollo spacecraft.

AMERICA'S FIRST

On May 5, 1961, Alan B. Shepard, Jr. (1923–1998), became the first American to travel into space. Shepard, a U.S. Navy fighter pilot, was one of the "Mercury 7"—the original seven astronauts selected by NASA in 1959 to train for space flight. Shepard was launched into space aboard the Mercury spacecraft named *Freedom 7*. During his 15-minute flight Shepard ascended to an altitude of 116 miles (187km) and landed safely in the Atlantic Ocean some 302 miles (486km) east of his launch point.

Kennedy takes center stage

President John F. Kennedy took office in January 1961. Most people credit Kennedy with revolutionizing the national space program. When Yuri Gagarin made the first manned spaceflight for the Soviet Union on April 12, 1961, Kennedy waited until the completion of the first American manned flight, by astronaut Alan Shepard on May 5 (*see box*), before responding. On May 25 that year Kennedy made his famous declaration that a lunar exploration effort would place an American on the moon before the end of the decade. This deadline was key to maintaining the momentum needed for such a huge project. Kennedy's dream would eventually come true when *Apollo 11* landed on the moon in July 1969, but it would not have been realized without the earlier efforts of the Eisenhower administration, which established NASA on firm foundations.

See Also:

Astronomy • Cold War • National Defense Education Act of 1958 • Rocketry • Science and Technology • Space Exploration • Von Braun, Wernher

NATIONAL ASSOCIATION FOR THE ADVANCEMENT OF COLORED PEOPLE

As the leading civil rights organization in the 1950s, the National Association for the Advancement of Colored People was instrumental in landmark advances for black Americans. However, its focus on legal reform was attacked by critics who wanted more direct action.

The National Association for the Advancement of Colored People (NAACP) has spearheaded the civil rights movement in the United States for over 90 years. In the 1950s it played an important part in the ending of segregation and the birth of the civil rights movement, although its tactics of concentrating on legal challenges, public education, and political lobbying were criticized by black leaders who advocated more direct action.

Formation and early campaigns

The NAACP was created on February 12, 1909, as a body to represent African Americans and coordinate their campaign for civil rights. Its original board of eight distinguished Americans included only one black American, W.E.B. DuBois (1868–1963), who edited the NAACP journal *The Crisis* from 1910 to 1934.

From the start the NAACP focused on educating whites about the need for change. In its early campaign against lynching, or unlawful killing, for example, it placed large ads in major newspapers to provide key information about lynching and its victims.

The association expanded rapidly and by 1915 was beginning to exert political influence. It won a Supreme Court ruling against the "grandfather clause" (the stipulation that a person was eligible to vote only if his grandfather had also had the privilege), which many southern states used to prevent African Americans from voting.

The NAACP's first black executive secretary, writer and diplomat James Weldon Johnson (1871–1938), was appointed in 1917. By the 1920s the NAACP had become the leading civil rights organization in America, fighting legal battles against segregation and racial discrimination in employment, housing, education, transportation, and voting rights. In 1929 Johnson was succeeded by Walter Francis White (1893–1955), a writer whose articles on civil rights reached a wide readership through magazines such as *The Nation* and *The New Republic*, as well as *The New York Herald Tribune* and *The Chicago Defender*. In 1955 White was replaced by Roy Wilkins (*see box on p. 113*). Under Wilkins the NAACP initially continued its efforts to use the courts to end racial discrimination.

Legal defense

In 1935 the African American lawyer Charles Hamilton Houston (*see box on p. 112*) joined the NAACP as special

---

IN THE FIELD FOR THE NAACP

Black Americans working for the NAACP in the South often faced great personal risk. White employers often fired blacks who joined the NAACP, while white banks foreclosed on their loans and took their homes. In some cases, however, NAACP activists paid with their lives. On Christmas Day 1951, for example, Harry T. Moore, the first executive director of the Florida NAACP, was blown up and killed with his wife by a bomb planted beneath their home. A Klansman suspected of the murder committed suicide after being questioned by the FBI.

Later in the decade the Baptist preacher of Belzoni, Mississippi, the Reverend George Lee, worked with local NAACP president and grocer Gus Courts to register African Americans to vote. The pair had registered some 90 voters before Lee was murdered by gunfire from a passing car as he drove along a Belzoni street on May 7, 1955. The local sheriff declared the death to be a road traffic accident; no one was ever tried for the murder. Only six months later Gus Courts was shot in the arm and abdomen; he later moved to Chicago. Meanwhile, the local White Citizens' Council threatened economic sanctions against those blacks who had registered to vote. To protect their jobs and their businesses, most subsequently removed their names from the register.

CHARLES HAMILTON HOUSTON

The NAACP emphasis on tackling the legal basis of segregation, which had been established in 1896 by *Plessy v. Ferguson*, the Supreme Court ruling that laid down the principle of "separate but equal" provision of opportunity to black and white citizens, depended on the creation of talented lawyers who could argue the civil rights case in the courts. A key figure in that process was Charles Hamilton Houston (1895–1950). Houston saw the courts as a way to shape society; he argued that a lawyer was "either a social engineer or he's a parasite on society." In 1930 Houston became dean of the Howard University School of Law, where he trained numerous black lawyers, including his later assistant Thurgood Marshall. In 1935 Houston was appointed the first special counsel of the NAACP and developed a strategy for fighting racial segregation through the courts. Although Houston did not live to see *Plessy* overturned by the NAACP victory in *Brown v. Board of Education*, his one-time student Marshall, who won the case, acknowledged Houston's role by saying, "We were just carrying his bags, that's all."

Charles Hamilton Houston was the first special counsel of the NAACP.

counsel. To assist him he recruited Thurgood Marshall (1908–1993), who in 1967 would become the first black justice of the Supreme Court. Houston and Marshall set out on a series of legal battles to contest racist laws concerning transportation, housing, and education. The NAACP Legal Defense and Educational Fund was founded under Marshall's leadership in 1940, and he went on to win 29 of the 32 cases he argued before the Supreme Court, including lawsuits brought in 1944 against excluding black voters from primary elections, restrictive housing regulations in 1948, and unequal provision of facilities for state university students in 1950.

Led by Marshall, the NAACP launched a legal campaign to end segregation in public education. Established by the 1896 Supreme Court decision *Plessy v. Ferguson*, the "separate but equal" principle sanctioned separate schools for blacks and whites. School segregation was practiced by numerous southern and border states, including Texas, Oklahoma, Arkansas, Missouri, Louisiana, Mississippi, Georgia, Alabama, Florida, North and South Carolina, Virginia, and Kentucky. The NAACP case relied on presenting evidence such as a 1937 finding that for every $37.87 spent on the education of white children in the South, only $13.08 was spent on black children.

This photograph shows posters supporting a membership drive in NAACP offices in Detroit, Michigan, during the 1940s, when the NAACP was the leading advocate of black rights.

Roy Wilkins (left) and Thurgood Marshall (right) talk to Autherine Lucy, a student forced out of the University of Alabama by white intimidation in March 1956. Lucy's case helped inspire the 1960 novel *To Kill a Mockingbird* by Harper Lee.

After local district courts upheld school segregation, the NAACP appealed a combination of five lawsuits to the U.S. Supreme Court. The case is usually known for a student in one of the cases, Linda Brown of Topeka, Kansas, as *Brown v. Board of Education.*

The court heard the appeals in December 1952 but adjourned a decision until a second hearing the next year. Chief Justice Earl Warren insisted that the ruling be unanimous in order to put pressure on southern states to comply. The court reached agreement only after a major compromise: Desegregation would be gradual rather than immediate, as the NAACP wanted.

The landmark *Brown* decision was announced on May 17, 1954. The court unanimously ruled separate educational provision for black and white students "inherently unequal." A second ruling in 1955 decreed that public schools had to desegregate with "all deliberate speed," a wording that some states seized on as an excuse to delay integration. Hostile states launched intensive attacks on local branches of the NAACP; their tactics ranged from legal methods—Alabama began an eight-year legal campaign to ban the NAACP—to racial and physical abuse. The attacks resulted in a huge fall in NAACP membership in the South, which was previously home to 50 percent of the association's members. By 1957 southern membership accounted for just 28 percent.

ROY WILKINS

Roy Wilkins (1901–1981) was born in St. Louis, Missouri, and graduated from the University of Minnesota, Minneapolis, in 1923. He became a reporter and later managing editor of the *Kansas City Call*, a weekly African American newspaper. In his editorials for the paper he urged blacks to fight racism by using their right to vote. Wilkins joined the staff of the NAACP in 1931 and edited its official publication, *The Crisis*, between 1934 and 1949. At the same time, he was responsible for directing the NAACP's antidiscrimination program across the United States.

In March 1955, during the early stages of the civil rights movement, Wilkins was appointed executive director of the NAACP, a position he held until 1977. He oversaw the organization at a time when it still focused on seeking equal rights through the courts: He had played a crucial role in winning the historic Supreme Court decision to outlaw segregated public schools in *Brown v. Board of Education* in 1954. In the early 1960s Wilkins worked on President John F. Kennedy's civil rights bill and in August 1963 helped organize the civil rights March on Washington. He received the NAACP's Spingarn Medal in 1964 for his achievements.

Wilkins was opposed to violence and rejected racism in all its forms, including black separatism. Under his leadership, however, the NAACP came under increasing pressure from black activist groups to diversify its activities to include nonviolent direct action and to extend legal aid to other, more militant groups. By the early 1970s voices within the NAACP were calling for Wilkins's resignation. He refused to step down until poor health forced his retirement in 1977.

people who were standing. If any African Americans defied these rules, they would be arrested and fined.

On December 1, 1955, Rosa Parks, secretary of the Montgomery, Alabama, branch of the NAACP, refused to give up her seat to a white man, ignoring the orders of the bus driver. Parks was arrested, convicted of violating segregation laws, and fined $14. Local NAACP leaders used Parks as the cue for a boycott of the city's buses. The boycott lasted over a year before the Montgomery bus company was obliged—partly by a ruling of the Supreme Court and partly by the loss of earnings—to accept integration.

Civil rights acts

The gradual methods of the NAACP earned criticism from other civil rights campaigners such as the Congress of Racial Equality (CORE), which advocated more direct action. CORE had been founded in 1942 to use tactics of nonviolent civil disobedience to support civil rights. It had undertaken actions such as the "Journey of Reconciliation" in 1947: a trip by eight white and eight black men through the South to test desegregation of interstate travel. Although Walter White was against such action, he offered NAACP legal advice. That brought him into

Some states in the Deep South rejected the Supreme Court ruling. Orval Faubus, governor of Arkansas, used the National Guard to prevent nine black students from enrolling at Little Rock Central High School in September 1957, and President Dwight D. Eisenhower (1953–1961) sent Army troops to enforce desegregation. By 1960, however, only one-sixth of 1 percent of black students in the South attended a desegregated school. That proportion had risen to 16 percent by 1967.

Race and transportation

Another focus of NAACP activity was public transportation. Although the Supreme Court had banned racial segregation in interstate transportation in 1946, states in the Deep South persisted in segregating public transportation. Whites sat in the front of a bus and blacks sat at the back, provided that there were no white people standing. If the bus became crowded, any African Americans sitting down would give up their seats to any white

THE SPINGARN MEDAL

Named for Joel Elias Spingarn, chairman of the board of the NAACP that created it, the Spingarn Medal is conferred for outstanding achievement by a black American. The gold medal has been presented annually since 1915, with the exception of 1938. Winners of the award during the 1950s were as follows:

1950   Charles H. Houston (NAACP Legal Defense and Educational Fund)

1951   Mabel K. Staupers (leader of the National Association of Colored Graduate Nurses)

1952   Harry T. Moore (NAACP leader in Florida, murdered in 1951)

1953   Paul R. Williams (architect)

1954   Theodore K. Lawless (physician, educator, philanthropist)

1955   Carl J. Murphy (editor, publisher, civic leader)

1956   Jackie Robinson (baseball player)

1957   Martin Luther King, Jr. (Baptist preacher)

1958   Daisy Bates and the Little Rock Nine

1959   Edward "Duke" Ellington (jazz composer, orchestra leader)

THE MAKING OF AN NAACP MARTYR

Medgar Evers (1925–1963) had served in the U.S. Army in World War II and graduated from college before taking a job selling insurance to poor black farmers. Outraged by the conditions in which his customers lived, he began to organize local affiliates of the NAACP in Philadelphia, Mississippi, with his brother Charles. In 1954 Medgar Evers became the NAACP's first field secretary in the state. He moved to Jackson, from where he toured the state by car to recruit black voters and to investigate racial incidents. In 1955 he observed the trial of the two white men accused of murdering the black schoolboy Emmett Till and helped the chief prosecution witness Mose Wright escape after he was threatened for testifying in the case.

In the face of intimidation Charles Evers moved to Chicago. His brother, meanwhile, became more active in challenging segregation. In 1958 he took a "whites only" seat in the front of a bus and was beaten up. He was beaten again when he visited a courthouse to support black students arrested for reading in a "whites only" library. As Evers coordinated a local campaign of sit-ins and boycotts with the Student Nonviolent Coordinating Committee (SNCC) and the Council for Racial Equality (CORE), his profile rose to the extent that he appeared on television to talk about race relations in Jackson.

On June 12, 1963, only hours after President John F. Kennedy had appeared on television to commit himself to the cause of civil rights, Evers was shot and killed as he arrived home carrying a pile of NAACP T-shirts. His killer, Byron De La Beckwith, openly boasted about the murder but was found not guilty by two hung juries before he was finally sentenced to life imprisonment in 1994.

conflict with Thurgood Marshall; the lawyer argued that a "disobedience movement on the part of Negroes and their white allies, if employed in the South, would result in wholesale slaughter with no good achieved."

Despite such tensions, the NAACP joined with other organizations in a campaign that resulted in the Civil Rights Act of 1957, intended to secure the right of all African Americans to vote. The act required the establishment of a new division of the federal Justice Department to scrutinize civil rights abuses and necessitated representatives of both Democrats and Republicans to produce a joint report on race relations.

Not all black Americans were impressed by the legislation. Some regarded it as a sham that did little to improve, for example, access to voting rights. Others shared the NAACP view that as the first civil rights bill since Reconstruction, the legislation's short-term effects were less important than laying the foundations for later, more far-reaching changes in the law.

NAACP in the 1960s

John F. Kennedy argued for a new civil rights cct during his victorious 1960 presidential campaign; however, despite benefiting from 70 percent of the African American vote, he was slow to introduce new legislation to Congress. Eventually a new civil rights bill was brought before the legislature in 1963 to ban segregation in public places, create an Equal Employment Commission, and ensure that companies seeking federal business had a civil rights charter.

March on Washington

To support the bill, the NAACP and other civil rights groups organized the March on Washington on August 28, 1963. Demanding equal justice for all, about 250,000 people gathered at the Lincoln Memorial, where they heard Martin Luther King, Jr., make his "I have a dream" speech. The Civil Rights Act was passed in 1964, followed by the Voting Acts of 1965 and the Fair Housing Act of 1968.

Like the campaign for the Civil Rights Act of 1957, the cooperation among civil rights organizations for the March on Washington remained atypical. During the 1960s the NAACP increasingly lost members to other groups that advocated straightforward mass protest rather than a legal approach. The rivalry between the various associations caused tensions that ultimately harmed the progress of civil rights. A relatively constant charge leveled against the NAACP was that its approach was too passive and too gradualist: It worked through the very system that had enforced segregation and disenfranchisement. The accusation came from CORE and from the Student Nonviolent Coordinating Committee (SNCC), founded in 1960 to organize lunch-counter sit-ins; later it was repeated by the more radical Black Panthers and the Nation of Islam. In its turn the NAACP disapproved of the tactics of such groups.

With the establishment of a legal framework of civil rights in the United States in the late 1970s the NAACP used its Legal Defense Fund to expand its operations to support civil rights overseas. It also began to campaign on other contentious issues, such as promoting tighter gun-control laws.

See Also:

Black Americans • *Brown v. Board of Education* • Civil Rights • King, Martin Luther, Jr. • Little Rock School Crisis • Marshall, Thurgood • Montgomery Bus Boycott • Segregation and Desegregation

NATIONAL DEFENSE EDUCATION ACT OF 1958

The National Defense Education Act of 1958 had a considerable effect on the American education system for years to come. It was introduced during the Cold War primarily in order to improve education in science, mathematics, and foreign languages.

The National Defense Education Act (NDEA) was passed in 1958 as a direct result of the United States' concern that it was losing the space race with the Soviet Union. On October 4, 1957, the Soviets launched the world's first artificial satellite, *Sputnik 1*. The launch suggested to critics that political and technological supremacy were related. They blamed schools for the apparent inability of Americans to compete with the Soviets, and so education became a matter of national defense. The NDEA was created primarily to support the teaching of science, mathematics, and foreign languages. It aimed to produce a generation of students who could develop weapons and space technologies, and understand the language and culture of potential enemies and allies.

Establishing the NDEA

Other factors fostered the demand and delivery of a new education bill aside from the *Sputnik* launch. They included the "baby boom" that threatened to overcrowd existing schools, higher educational expectations brought about by postwar affluence, and fear of losing the Cold War. There was serious concern in the 1950s about the quality of education in American schools, especially about progressive, "child-centered" education and the shortage of graduates in science and technology. In fact, a "crisis in schools" had been identified as early as 1950 and had brought about a response from philanthropic foundations such as the Carnegie Corporation and the Ford Foundation and the establishment of the National Science Foundation (NSF) by Congress. The NSF, which was intended to support the teaching of science and mathematics at all levels, set the precedent for the NDEA.

The debate on how to improve education was fought between those who advocated federal aid to help the states raise standards and those who opposed it. Opponents believed that federal aid would imply federal control over education; there were also complications about funding schools that espoused a religion, because of the separation of church and state. The *Sputnik* crisis led the opposing sides of the debate to agree that improving the quality of American education was now

A teenager works on a science experiment. The NDEA was created to support the teaching of science, mathematics, and languages at elementary and secondary levels.

Students at Temple University, Philadelphia, take a test in 1951. The NDEA encouraged thousands of students to attend college through fellowships and loans.

a matter of urgency; proponents of federal aid succeeded in legitimizing their cause by linking national security with education and showing that the problem was too important to be left in the hands of the individual states.

Scope of the act

The National Defense Education Act was signed into law by President Dwight D. Eisenhower (1953–1961) on September 2, 1958. It encompassed three main provisions: first, support to individual students at universities and colleges through loans and fellowships; second, assistance to state education at elementary and secondary levels through programs to improve the teaching of science, mathematics, and foreign languages; and third, assistance to researchers for developing new means of teaching using new media (television, radio, motion pictures, and related media).

The act was administered by the Department of Health, Education, and Welfare (HEW) and gave the federal government great responsibility in policing education. Some of the act's titles required states to submit plans to qualify for funds, while others required matching funds from the states. Critics claimed that the act was too piecemeal and required too much administration. The bureaucracy of HEW expanded to suit demand, and the expenditures of the Office of Education increased 130 percent between 1954 and the end of Eisenhower's presidency in 1961. Nevertheless, the NDEA showed a good record of activity in its first year, with student loans to 1,201 colleges, 1,000 fellowships to graduate students in 23 universities, and the foundation of foreign-language centers in 19 universities, with a total expenditure of $33.7 million.

The NDEA remained the main source of federal aid to education for many years. Approved initially for four years, the act was extended without

alteration for a further two years to 1964. In 1963 President Lyndon Baines Johnson (1963–1969) extended the NDEA to 1965, with amendments to the titles concerning college loans and fellowships. The act was subsequently approved for a further three years and was extended to accommodate the antidiscrimination provisions of the Civil Rights Act of 1964. Although the word "Defense" remained in its name, the act was no longer shaped by the requirements of the Cold War. Several of the titles of the NDEA were assimilated into the Elementary and Secondary Education Act of 1965 and the Higher Education Act of 1965. The provisions of the NDEA were integrated into other legislation during the 1970s, but the act itself survived two decades to a time when the reason for having the word "Defense" in its title was no longer understood.

Commentators argue that the NDEA was more important as a precursor to the legislation that followed than as a response to the *Sputnik* crisis.

By the summer of 1958 anxiety about *Sputnik* had subsided, and the National Aeronautics and Space Act of that year established a new organization, the National Aeronautics and Space Administration (NASA), to control the space program. Moreover, an education act was a long-term strategy that could not address the immediate threat posed by *Sputnik*. The NDEA set a precedent for federal aid to education that has continued ever since. In the years after the introduction of the NDEA, however, the focus of domestic policies shifted. Policies were introduced to deal with poverty and race relations, and policy makers came to regard education as a means of helping the disadvantaged rather than of pursuing excellence.

See Also:

Civil Rights • Cold War • Rocketry • Schools and Universities • Science and Technology • Soviet Union • Space Exploration

NATIONAL SECURITY COUNCIL

During the 1950s the newly formed National Security Council provided a forum in which government leaders could discuss questions affecting the security of the nation. Presidents Truman and Eisenhower came to rely on the council to bring clarity to complex problems.

In the years immediately after World War II (1939–1945) it became apparent that the U.S. government needed to improve the coordination of foreign and defense policy between its various departments and agencies. Consequently, in 1947 Congress passed the National Security Act to establish the National Security Council (NSC). The composition of the NSC changed over the years, but initially it had seven permanent members: the president, who was chairman; the secretaries of state, defense, the Army, Navy, and Air Force; and the chairman of the National Security Resources Board. The director of the Central Intelligence Agency (CIA) attended meetings as an adviser. The president might also ask various other officials to attend particular meetings. The NSC's stated aims were to provide advice to the president on domestic, foreign, and military policies related to national security and to aid cooperation between the government departments involved.

Truman and the NSC

During the NSC's first years President Harry S. Truman (1945–1953) attended fewer than a quarter of its meetings, preferring to rely on his personal advisers in the White House. Eventually, however, events persuaded him to make greater use of the council. Concern about the spread of communism and the growing power of the Soviet Union was already mounting when in 1949 the Soviets successfully tested their first atomic warhead, and the Communists came to power in mainland China. There was an urgent need for an analysis of how the United States might respond to the challenge posed by these events, and this led to the presentation in April 1950 of an NSC report called NSC-68 (*see box opposite*). Sometimes described as the blueprint for the Cold War, NSC-68 provided a justification for the immediate buildup of the U.S. nuclear arsenal. Some two months later Communist North Korea invaded South Korea, and Truman began to attend most of the NSC's weekly meetings.

Relations with Eisenhower

President Dwight D. Eisenhower (1953–1961) was a firm believer in detailed discussion leading to effective planning, and on becoming president he did much to boost the role of the NSC in making and implementing policy. The council now consisted of five members: the president, the vice president, the secretaries of state and defense, and the director of the Office of Defense Mobilization. Among the numerous other advisers who regularly attended was the director of Central Intelligence, who provided briefings on worldwide developments affecting security. The council discussed papers sent up to it by the Planning Board and handed down all decisions for implementation to the Operations Coordinating Board, to which were attached over 40 interagency working groups. A special assistant oversaw the

President Truman (second on right) meets with the National Security Council for a briefing on the defense situation in 1951. Secretary of State Dean Acheson sits at Truman's right.

A REPORT TO PRESIDENT TRUMAN: NSC-68

In April 1950 the NSC presented a secret report to President Truman that was to lead to a massive escalation in the number of nuclear weapons built by the United States as part of the Cold War with the Soviet Union. The report asserted that the Soviet Union was attempting to dominate Europe and Asia and "to impose its absolute authority over the rest of the world." Soviet values, it argued, were incompatible with American values; the Soviet Union was "implacable in its purpose" to destroy the American system. In the face of this threat the United States was the only power capable of defending freedom from communism throughout the world.

The report argued that the United States should lead the free world in a sustained buildup of political, economic, and military strength that would send a message to the Kremlin about the resistance it would face. NSC-68 also argued that Americans had to face up to the fact that the Cold War was a real war "in which the survival of the free world is at stake."

The response, the report argued, was the launch of an aggressive program of psychological attacks designed to increase mass dissatisfaction both inside the Soviet Union itself and in its satellite countries. At home a new security and civil defense program would be developed to prepare the American people for the prospect of nuclear war. The United States also had to build up its military—nuclear—strength "in order that it may not have to be used." The Cold War arms race had begun.

President Eisenhower (left) talks with Vice President Richard M. Nixon (center) and Secretary of State John Foster Dulles before an NSC meeting about the situation in Formosa.

functioning of this system but, unlike the national security advisers who were to be appointed in the future, had no role in formulating policy.

Covert operations

Among the policies that Eisenhower supported was the organization of covert operations abroad. NSC involvement in such operations had begun as early as 1947, when it had authorized covert action in the Italian elections. During Eisenhower's first years as president the CIA overthrew two government leaders who had nationalized the assets of some U.S. companies: In 1953 Mohammad Mosaddeq was ousted from power in Iran, and in 1954 the same fate befell President Jacobo Arbenz of Guatemala. Consequently, in 1954 the NSC set up what was called the 5412 Committee, made up of representatives of the president and secretaries of state and defense, to review and recommend further covert operations.

Although Eisenhower was very committed to the NSC system and chaired 329 out of a total 366 meetings during his years as president, there were many occasions on which he stepped outside it to manage foreign-policy problems. This was particularly the case with crises, such as the Suez Crisis of 1956, when he needed to discuss the situation constantly with a small group of advisers. The NSC and its supporting machinery of sub-committees was far too large and bureaucratic to be used on a day-to-day basis, but under Eisenhower it played a very important role in determining the overall direction of policy.

See Also:

Armed Forces • Cold War • Foreign Policy • Guatemala • Middle East • Politics and Government • Soviet Union

NATIVE AMERICANS

The 1950s saw the introduction of relocation and so-called "termination" policies to assimilate Native Americans into mainstream society. However, such programs failed to yield the desired result and encouraged the development of a politically active generation of American Indians.

In the 1950s the U.S. government adopted new policies toward Native Americans: It implemented relocation programs to encourage Native Americans to move out of their reservations and into the cities, and it also instituted a so-called "termination" policy, under which federal responsibility for and jurisdiction over Native American nations was turned over to state governments. It is estimated that some 20,000 Native Americans joined the urban relocation program in the 1950s. Although incentives such as relocation assistance and job placements were offered to those who were willing to move to the cities, many found the adjustment to an urban environment traumatic, and the promised economic benefits of relocation did not materialize.

Reservation life

Reservations were areas of land that had been set aside by the federal government as a permanent home for Native American nations. Although the Northwest Ordinance of 1787 promised that land and property would never be taken away from Native Americans without their consent, their land was not always protected, and in certain periods (for example, between the 1880s and 1930s) it was opened up for sale. Today Native Americans hold about 56 million acres (23 million ha) in reservations and trust land. The U.S. government holds the title to the land for the nations, with the Department of the Interior acting as trustee. The 1960 Census recorded a Native American population of 523,591; approximately 360,000 Native Americans still lived on reservations at that time.

In the first few decades of the 20th century conditions on many of the reservations caused some concern. The death rate for Native Americans exceeded that of the U.S. population as a whole by as much as one-third. Pneumonia, dysentery, diabetes, hepatitis, and tuberculosis were common causes of death. Birthrates were high—up to two and a half times the overall U.S. rate. Average life expectancy for both men and women was barely 44 years, and alcoholism and suicide were major problems. Living conditions were primitive, and many families lived in dilapidated shanties. Before World War II (1939–1945) it was estimated that 60 percent of the reservations' dwellings had no electricity and 80 percent had no running water or sewers. Educational standards were low. Native American children typically completed no more than five years of school, and only one in six adults graduated from high school. In some areas unemployment was between 50 and 80 percent of the population.

The effect of World War II

The lives of many Native Americans were profoundly affected by World War II. Tens of thousands left the reservations to serve in the military and

Children learn arthimetic at a school in the Navajo Indian Reservation in about 1954. Education was one of the means by which the U.S. government promoted assimilation.

FLOODING THE RESERVATIONS

In the 20th century the development of hydroelectric projects as a source of power had a disastrous effect on Indian land. Native Americans were forced to resist the construction of dams that threatened to flood reservation lands and destroy fishing sites and livelihoods. In 1958 the New York State Power Authority planned to create a reservoir that would flood more than one-fifth of the Tuscarora Reservation lands. The Tuscarora protested, using both legal channels and open protest, and the Federal Power Commission ordered the project stopped. Only two years later, however, the decision was reversed by the Supreme Court, and the reservoir was built.

In the 1940s and 1950s the Pick-Sloan Program called for the damming of the Missouri River. Despite Native American protests, the Missouri River Hydroelectric Project was completed to power the cities of the Midwest. Most of the dam construction took place in locations occupied by North and South Dakota Indian reservations along the river. As a consequence, Native American nations lost 350,000 acres (142,000ha) of riverfront land for hydroelectric-power production. For these communities, already living in economically depressed areas, the loss of fertile river-valley land caused insurmountable problems.

work in ancillary wartime industries. In 1943, for example, more than 46,000 took jobs off reservations in shipyards, lumbering, canneries, mines, and farms. More than 24,000—one-third of all Native American men between ages 18 and 50—served in the armed forces. Unlike African Americans, they were not placed in segregated units. Navajo radio operators were responsible for creating an unbreakable code, employed in the Pacific theater of operations, which used the Navajo language for radio transmissions.

The experience of World War II exposed many Native Americans to urban culture and to the industrial world outside their reservations. They acquired job skills and experience, which gave them an impetus to leave their communities. At the same time, wartime experiences and achievements intensified a sense of Native American identity and self-consciousness. The GI Bill of 1944 provided a large number of Native Americans with their first opportunity to attend college, and many college graduates remained in the cities to find employment.

Against this background of growing self-consciousness Native American nationalism flourished. In 1944 leaders

from 50 nations formed the National Congress of American Indians (NCAI), the first major intertribal organization. The NCAI became an active lobby group in Washington, D.C., campaigning for protection of Indian lands, mineral rights, and timber resources, as well as fighting for better education and healthcare on the reservations.

In 1946 Congress established the Indian Claims Commission (ICC), the purpose of which was to compensate Native Americans for unfair treatment by the federal government. The commission remained in existence until 1978, heard a total of 852 claims, and awarded damages amounting to about $818 million.

During World War II the Navajo men enlisted in the armed forces used their tribal language for radio transmissions, ensuring the confidentiality of military information.

Two Navajo women weave a rug on a traditional loom in Arizona. The Navajo are renowned for their weaving skills, which are passed on from generation to generation.

Los Angeles. The architect of the relocation program was BIA Commissioner Dillon S. Myer, who had been in charge of the program that had moved thousands of Japanese Americans into internment camps during World War II. Myer's goal was to assimilate Indians into mainstream American life.

In August 1953 Congress introduced a fundamental change in its Native American policy. House Concurrent Resolution 108 declared it to be the policy of the United States to abolish federal supervision of the Native American nations as soon as possible and subject them to the same laws, privileges, and responsibilities as other U.S. citizens. As a result of the resolution the U.S. government began the process of "termination." At this time several states with substantial Native American populations were in

New policies

From 1952 the federal government established special programs to encourage Native Americans to move to the cities. The Bureau of Indian Affairs (BIA) provided transportation, vocational training, job placements, and counseling to those who wanted to leave the reservations. The first relocation offices were established in Chicago and Los Angeles, and by 1958 a total of 12 centers were operating between Cleveland, Ohio, and the West Coast. Recruits for the relocation program were moved long distances from their former homes in an attempt to discourage them from moving back to the reservations. Alaskans, for example, were usually relocated to Chicago, while Minnesota Ojibwa were moved to Oakland, California, and the Sioux of South Dakota were moved to

President Truman is presented with a pipe after signing the Indian Claims Commission Act in 1946. The ICC was created as a tribunal for the hearing of claims against the United States.

URBAN SKYWALKERS

Not all Native Americans came to the cities as a result of government relocation. Mohawks from the St. Regis Reservation in northern New York State and the Caughnawaga Reservation south of Montreal began to arrive in New York City early in the 20th century. They brought with them a reputation for their skill in bridge-building, which ensured that they were in great demand for skyscraper construction. Mohawks soon became famous for their fearlessness, especially at great heights. As early as 1714 English traveler John Lawson had noted their abilities when he witnessed Caughnawaga Mohawks crossing rushing streams "on the smallest of poles" and running "along the ridge of barn or house." In the later 19th century iron and steel bridges were built across the St. Lawrence River. In 1886, when a new railway bridge was being erected above the rapids between Caughnawaga and Lachine, Mohawk children were seen scrambling over it, while youths and men were paid to shift and bolt the great steel beams high in the air.

In New York City Mohawks sought well-paid jobs as high-steel specialists, often settling into cheap apartments in Brooklyn within easy reach of the construction boom in Manhattan. They operated in small, tribal crews, spoke fluent English, were prepared to live in urban conditions, and commuted to work by subway. When their years in the construction industry came to an end, most would then return to the reservation and a peaceful retirement. Mohawk steelworkers worked on many of the most famous New York City buildings of the 20th century, among them the Woolworth Building, the Empire State Building, the Waldorf Astoria Hotel, the RCA Tower in Rockefeller Plaza, and, in the 1950s, the United Nations Building. Working in tightly bonded units, precariously perched on wind-buffeted beams more than 50 stories up, each individual depended on the others in his team for safety. In these conditions the strength and value of age-old tribal ties were truly tested.

Mohawk construction workers in Manhattan display the fearless feats of balance that earned them the name of "skywalkers."

major conflict with the nations over taxation, water rights, and hunting and fishing jurisdictions. They petitioned Congress to transfer federal responsibilities for the nations to the state governments. Congress enacted Public Law 280, which transferred certain criminal and civil jurisdiction over Indian lands to, initially, state governments in California, Minnesota, Nebraska, Oregon, Wisconsin, and—on its statehood—Alaska. This transfer of jurisdiction was effected without the nations' negotiation or consent. In effect, the new law allowed the states to abolish agreements—for example, concerning water rights—that had previously been protected by federal legislation. Native American campaigners saw Public Law 280 as a disastrous step toward their enforced assimilation, a true "termination" of Native American culture.

The NCAI led opposition to government policies, campaigning under the slogan "Self-determination rather than termination." Earl Old Person, a Blackfoot leader, commented: "It is important to note that in our Indian language the only translation for termination is to 'wipe out' or 'kill off.'... How can we plan our future when the Indian Bureau threatens to wipe us out as a race?"

Indian Health Service

For decades the U.S. government had neglected to carry out its obligations to protect the health of Native Americans.

A lack of adequate funding, as well as problems recruiting and retaining physicians and other health professionals to serve on reservations, plagued the BIA. In 1954 Congress passed a law providing for the transfer of all functions relating to Native American health from the BIA to the Surgeon General of the Public Health Service, or PHS. As a result, 2,500 health workers of the BIA, together with the bureau's 48 hospitals and 13 school infirmaries, came under the jurisdiction of the PHS's newly created Indian Health Service (IHS). Shortly after the transfer the IHS found that "Indians of the United States today have health problems resembling in many respects those of the general population a generation ago." This was attributed to inadequate health services, substandard and overcrowded housing, and a lack of sanitary facilities. Approximately 25 percent of deaths within the Native American populations (as opposed to just 8 percent among non-Indians) were attributed to communicable diseases such as tuberculosis, influenza, pneumonia, and gastrointestinal diseases. During the next 30 years the IHS implemented infectious-disease control practices on the reservations, instituted a program of health education, and improved sanitation.

The urban experience

Many of the Native Americans who relocated to the city found the experience traumatic. In the words of Wilma Mankiller, the former chief of the Cherokee Nation of Oklahoma who moved with her family to California in the 1950s, "No one pointed a gun at me or at members of my family. No show of force was used. It was not necessary. Nevertheless, the United States government, through the Bureau of Indian Affairs, was again trying to settle the 'Indian problem' by removal. I learned through this ordeal about the fear and anguish that occur when you give up your home, your community, and everything you have ever known to move far away to a strange place."

Dislocated and disoriented, many Native Americans found that they were exchanging one form of poverty for another. Arriving in the city, newcomers were met by a relocation officer. They were issued with a small amount of money, and accompanied by the relocation officer, they were made to spend the money on clothes, cookware, groceries, bedding, and toiletries—even an alarm clock to ensure that they were on time for work. Some limited training was offered, but most Native Americans could find only casual—and frequently seasonal—work in agriculture, construction, and on the railroads. A significant number could not afford decent food or housing and soon found themselves on public aid once their relocation support ran out. Many Native Americans felt that they had been victims of an empty promise: Assured by the BIA that they were

Mohawk Chief Poking Fire stands before his tepee in front of the State House, Montpelier, Vermont, in 1953. He founded the Kahnawake Indian village in Quebec in the 1930s.

BOB BURNETTE: AN INDIAN CAMPAIGNER

Robert Phillip Burnette (1926–1984) was born on the Rosebud Reservation in South Dakota to a family of Sioux ranchers and farmers. He was educated at the Rosebud Boarding School and in 1943 enlisted in the Marine Corps, serving in the Pacific theater. The war years were Burnette's first experience of life outside the reservation, and he was able to observe firsthand the better standards of living enjoyed by non-Indians in cities such as Los Angeles and San Francisco. On his return to the Rosebud Reservation, however, he found that little had changed. The Sioux were still subjected to prejudice and discrimination, and the land allotment policies promulgated by the Bureau of Indian Affairs (BIA) were driving many Sioux away from their traditional livelihood as cattle ranchers. Under pressure from white settlers who were interested in acquiring Sioux land, the BIA began to raise Indian ranchers' rents, hoping it would be able to put pressure on the Sioux to sell or lease their allotted lands to the whites.

Burnette blamed corrupt tribal leaders, who were colluding with the BIA. In 1952, after a hard-fought battle, he won election to the Rosebud Tribal Council. Two years later he became tribal president and served for eight years. During this period Burnette gained a reputation as an assertive tribal leader who not only promoted intertribal cooperation but also gained support for his cause from non-Indians such as John F. Kennedy and Martin Luther King, Jr. In 1961 Burnette became executive director of the National Congress of American Indians, but he returned to his reservation in 1964, where he continued to fight for self-determination and sovereignty on both a local and national basis. His last years were marred by bitter political infighting at the Rosebud Reservation as he sought to undermine the power of corrupt tribal leaders. Burnette has been credited with playing a crucial role in the crusade to persuade the federal government away from the 1950s policy of termination.

going to a better life, they were effectively abandoned once they arrived in the city. Native Americans clustered together in the ghettos of uptown Chicago, Bell Gardens in Los Angeles, and elsewhere. Indian children encountered racism and dropped out of school. Their parents were unable to obtain adequate healthcare, paid high rents for substandard housing, and many suffered from alcoholism.

For many disillusioned Native Americans the only solution was to pull together as a community. In Chicago, for example, members of the various nations formed two support organizations in 1954—the All-Tribes American Indian Center and St. Augustine's Center for American Indians, both of which survive today. In fact, the arrival of many representatives of different nations in the cities created a new era of intertribal unity. In 1961 the first big intertribal conference brought together around 400 representatives of more than 60 Native American nations in Chicago. Pantribal organizations were able to mobilize support for issues that superseded the interests of individual nations.

The protest movement

Following World War II, and against the background of the government's relocation and termination programs, Native Americans became increasingly active politically, demanding equal voting rights and an end to discrimination. In Arizona and New Mexico, for example, Native Americans who paid no U.S. taxes were denied the right to vote in spite of the 1924 Indian Citizenship Act that had granted Native Americans full U.S. citizenship. In 1948, following effective campaigns by Native Americans, both states ended this denial of voting rights.

However, it was protests against the termination of federal control that were most vocal. Between 1954 and 1960 support to some 60 nations and other Indian groups was brought to an end by the withdrawal of federal services or trust supervision. Some groups lost acres of land to private exploitation.

The year 1961 was important in the history of Native American civil rights. A militant new organization, the National Indian Youth Council (NIYC), was founded in New Mexico and began to use the phrase "Red Power." It sponsored marches and demonstrations to protest against efforts by individual states to abolish fishing rights that had hitherto been protected by federal treaties. In the same year Philleo Nash was sworn in as commissioner of Indian Affairs, the first anthropologist ever to hold that position. It was an indication that the U.S. government was finally beginning to pay attention to Native American concerns. Also in 1961, at the Native American conference in Chicago, representatives from many nations drafted the Declaration of Indian Purpose, which stressed the determination of Native Americans to choose their own way of life. The declaration requested an end to the termination program and called for policies to create economic opportunities for Native Americans on the reservations.

See Also:

Architecture • Asian Americans • Black Americans • Civil Rights • Health and Healthcare • Poverty • Segregation and Desegregation

NEWS AND CURRENT AFFAIRS

Television news began the 1950s with a format like that of the movie newsreel but ended the decade looking recognizably like the TV news of today. Newspapers responded to this challenge with a new sense of their mission—to broaden and deepen public understanding.

America's burgeoning love affair with the television in the 1950s was to have a profound effect on the dissemination of news, which had previously been in the hands of radio broadcasters and the print media. Television's immediacy and its ability to capture events as they actually happened enabled it to challenge the former dominance of these rivals. In an era of Cold War paranoia and secrecy the workings of Washington were becoming increasingly oblique, and the traditional freedom of the press came under attack from those who felt it compromised national security.

The evolution of television news

Television news in the United States evolved from the radio networks. Both NBC and CBS (which began radio broadcasts in, respectively, 1926 and 1927) put out regular news bulletins focusing on current affairs, reports from abroad, political conventions, and presidential elections. The main network radio stations were dependent on wire services, such as Associated Press. These agencies specialized in supplying news stories to both the press and broadcasters, drawing on a huge pool of freelance journalists ("stringers") both at home and abroad.

Although both NBC and CBS licensed commercial TV stations as early as 1941, the television networks were not actually formed until after World War II (1939–1945), in 1947. In 1948 NBC launched its network news service with a 10-minute weekday broadcast, the *Camel Newsreel Theater*. It was presented by John Cameron Swayze (1906–1995), who seldom appeared on screen but simply read copy over newsreel film images. The newsreel companies, such as Movietone News, had news cameramen all over the world who specialized in breaking news stories, producing footage that was shown in movie theaters before the main feature. They used the same large cameras that had been developed for the slower, more static style of Hollywood filming. Developing the film and transporting it to New York City, where the television networks were based, meant that it was often out of date by the time it was broadcast. All this changed during the 1950s, when television news organizations switched to 16mm film and the smaller cameras needed to use it. Freed from the more cumbersome Hollywood equipment, television cameramen became much more mobile, able to produce footage that suited the smaller medium. In 1958 "reversal" film, which came out of the processor as a positive print, was introduced. This drastically reduced editing time, giving television images a new immediacy. The remaining stumbling block in the process—transporting the film to New York—had been removed in 1951, when a

President Harry S. Truman speaks to the nation during a TV address. Television became crucial to presidents in the 1950s as a means of appealing directly to the people.

coaxial cable link connecting the East and West coasts was completed, enabling images to be transmitted electronically rather than physically.

Network news

As technology improved, the television networks started to transmit the regular news programs that defined the era. In 1951 Fred Friendly and Edward R. Murrow (1908–1965) began producing *See It Now*, which Murrow also anchored, for CBS. The program broke new ground, introducing many features of news broadcasts that are still in evidence today. It was the first news broadcast to use its own footage rather than newsreel film. Field producers were used to put together reports from all over the country. The program was broadcast live, coast to coast (it opened with split-screen shots of Brooklyn Bridge and the Golden Gate Bridge, and truly spanned the continent). Murrow had served his journalistic apprenticeship in the late 1930s, when he set up a network of correspondents for CBS to report on the descent into war in Europe. His fearless reporting, including coverage of Allied bombing missions and Nazi death camps, had made him a household name at home. When Murrow moved to television, then in its infancy, he drew on his journalistic experience to seek out stories of ordinary Americans, which he presented as powerful commentaries on political issues. On March 9, 1954, *See It Now* broadcast a program on Senator Joseph McCarthy (1908–1957). Composed almost entirely of McCarthy's own words, it was a damning portrait of a fanatical anticommunist. McCarthy's intemperate response helped seal his fate, but the whole fiasco had caused a rift between Murrow and CBS, which by 1958 had decided to discontinue *See It Now*.

NBC had pioneered network news broadcasts with the *Camel Newsreel Theater* (later renamed the *Camel News*

Caravan), but the format soon began to look static and out of date. All this changed in 1956 when two anchors, Chet Huntley and David Brinkley, were paired to present a nightly 15-minute news program, *The Huntley–Brinkley Report*. Producer Reuven Frank is credited with the development of the show and the idea of having two anchors—Huntley in New York City and Brinkley in Washington, D.C. Frank was also responsible for the broadcast's famous closing line: "Good night, Chet." "Good night, David. And good night for NBC News." Brinkley's dry, witty style of reporting set the program apart from the more sober output of CBS (*see box on p. 128*).

The Huntley–Brinkley Report's chief competitor, also transmitted in the evening, was the *CBS Evening News*, anchored by Douglas Edwards and directed by Don Hewitt. Edwards actually did two live broadcasts—first for the East Coast, then again three hours later for the West Coast

(videotape was not yet available to record a program for later reuse, so everything that was not filmed had to be broadcast live).

NBC was also responsible for devising a new kind of news broadcast, a morning show that was structured to be watched in a semifragmentary way as viewers got ready for school and work. In the words of Reuven Frank, *Today* was considered a "brash experiment" when it premiered in 1952. But it was soon obvious that it was going to last. Much of its success was due to the ironic, amiable personality of its first host, David Garroway. In his trademark horn-rimmed glasses and bow tie he was an excellent communicator, able to look directly into the camera and engage the audience. His famous signoff was "Peace." Nevertheless, initial insecurity about the success of the show led to the addition of a chimpanzee sidekick, given the name J. Fred Muggs, who became a popular star in his own right.

During the 1956 Democratic National Convention Walter Cronkite of CBS (center) speaks with W. Averell Harriman (left), a candidate for the Democratic nomination.

DAVID BRINKLEY: A NEWS PIONEER

David Brinkley (1920–2003) was not just a news reporter. Famous for his wit and fluent writing style, he also helped change the face of television news. *The Huntley–Brinkley Report* first appeared on NBC in October 1956. Brinkley had initially teamed up with Chet Huntley (1911–1974) a few months earlier, when they had anchored the network's television coverage of the Democratic and Republican conventions.

Brinkley was born in North Carolina and first went to work for NBC Radio in 1943, where he gained experience as a newscaster. He went on to become the Washington reporter for the *Camel News Caravan*, but it was the 1956 political conventions that brought him to the public eye. Television news before Huntley and Brinkley was a combination of dull film reports in the style of movie newsreels and a flat, radio-style voice-over. But Huntley and Brinkley galvanized the news, stamping it with their own personal style and authority. While Huntley

David Brinkley helped transform the faceless, formal style of television news, making it witty and personal.

retired in 1970, Brinkley went on in the 1980s to present *This Week with David Brinkley* for ABC, which exploited his many years as the ultimate Washington insider. Brinkley was one of the first journalists to be absolutely comfortable with television. His economic writing style, with its short, declarative sentences, was ideally pitched for TV news. He was also acutely aware that the news on television was a combination of pictures and sounds; he was able to judge when to stop talking and let the news footage tell its own story. As his NBC boss Reuven Frank said, "Brinkley writes silence better than anyone else I know." Asked at the end of his career about his legacy to American television news, Brinkley replied: "We more or less set the form for broadcasting news on television which is still used. No one has been able to think of a better way to do it."

Making the news

It soon became apparent that television was not only pioneering new ways of presenting the news, it was also making the news by providing on-the-spot coverage of special events. Audiences easily became transfixed by live coverage of news stories. When a toddler named Kathy Fiscus fell down a well in California in 1949, the Los Angeles television station KTLA reported live from the scene during the two-day rescue effort and transmitted the story to TV stations along the West Coast. The story was later picked up by stations nationwide and drew an enormous audience response; people even telephoned the television station to inquire about the child's fate (she did not survive). It was a sign of things to come.

In 1951 two national news stories drew large audiences. The hearings of Senator Estes Kefauver's Special Committee to Investigate Organized Crime in Interstate Commerce were watched by millions in bars and restaurants (this was before most people had their own TV sets). The eight days of hearings held in New York City in March 1951, in particular, gripped the nation as mobsters such as Frank Costello appeared before the committee. Stores were so empty during the broadcasts that some resorted to offering major discounts in order to attract customers. It was an early indication of the potential power of television in political affairs. In the same year, when General Douglas MacArthur embarked on a short, televised national tour following his return

from Korea, including an address to Congress, the broadcasts drew an audience of 44 million. In 1952 the televised Republican National Convention attracted an audience of 60 million. By the 1956 elections the conventions were watched by audiences of 100 million.

Perhaps the most celebrated case in which television played an important role in political events was its influence on public perceptions of Senator Joseph McCarthy. The Army–McCarthy hearings were convened in 1954 to investigate charges leveled by the Republican senator against the U.S. Army and vice versa. They were broadcast live across the nation by the ABC and DuMont networks. The hearings lasted 36 days; and despite the enormous commitment of time (and

Douglas Edwards of CBS interviews Senator
John F. Kennedy at the 1956 Democratic
Convention. Kennedy ran unsuccessfully
for the vice-presidential nomination.

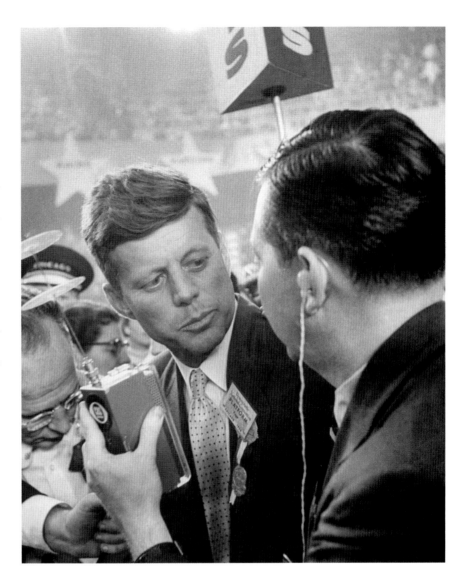

loss of advertising revenue), ABC's president, Robert E. Kintner, resolved to broadcast the entire event live.

On television the contrast between the rude and often boorish behavior of the senator and the cool demeanor of Joseph N. Welch (1890–1960), the Army's special counsel, was the stuff of daytime soap opera. The senator's repeated interjection, "Point of order," became a national catchphrase. An audience of some 20 million watched the testimony. The hearings reached a climax on June 9, when McCarthy accused one of Welch's colleagues of communist sympathies. Welch's response—"Have you no sense of decency, sir, at long last?"—drew a round of applause from the audience, and McCarthy's stunned disbelief was broadcast to the nation.

Television played its part in McCarthy's subsequent downfall. In the words of Stuart Symington, a Democratic senator: "The American people have had a look at you for six weeks. You are not fooling anyone." The hearings were a media milestone, revealing that television itself was crucial to how political events unfolded.

President Dwight D. Eisenhower (1953–1961) was acutely aware of the power of the new medium. In 1953 he suggested that television cameras should be allowed into his presidential press conferences. The idea was strongly resisted by the White House press corps, who saw presidential briefings as their own territory; but their objections were overridden, and filming was allowed from January 19, 1955. Print journalists argued that their broadcasting colleagues were ill prepared and far too aware of the entertainment value of television. Broadcasters were able to elicit news

Joseph Nye Welch was chief counsel for the
U.S. Army during the 1954 Senate hearings on
communist infiltration. His calm style was an
effective foil to Joseph McCarthy's bluster.

from press conferences and then "scoop" the print media, putting out stories before the newspapers went to press. It was not long before the entire structure of the president's working day was altered to reflect the realities of television scheduling. If, for example, the president wanted an announcement to top the evening news, it had to be made before 2:00 P.M., Eastern Standard Time. In the words of Frank Stanton, president of CBS: "Television, with its penetration, its wide geographic distribution and impact, provides a new, direct and sensitive link between Washington and the people."

Interpreting the news

Despite its increasing dominance, television was not the only important medium for news. The national daily circulation of newspapers in the United States in 1960 was just below 59 million. Newspapers had been challenged by the new medium throughout the 1950s, but they had found ways of retaining their readers.

During World War II (1939–1945) newspapers had willingly acceded to self-censorship when issues of national security were at stake, but in the immediate aftermath of the war a new mood of paranoia and secrecy developed that began to challenge freedom of speech. Secrecy was not only evident around questions of national security; it was also apparent on a more local level, even at school board meetings. Some newspapers responded with litigation, taking the government or officials to court to force them to reveal withheld information. Relationships between journalists and the government became less direct as news was fed to newspapers through the intermediaries of press officers, public relations officials, and off-the-record briefings. Many journalists felt that a barrier had been placed between them and their sources, impeding their ability to gather and report the news. Government–press relations reached a low point in 1951, when President Harry S. Truman (1945–1953) signed an executive order introducing a new system of classification of government documents (*see box*). Although Eisenhower later modified Truman's order,

many journalists felt that the government had nevertheless set a precedent on the withholding of information.

Media manipulation

The rise and fall of Senator McCarthy, so vividly documented on television, posed new problems for the newspapers. Many newspaper journalists felt that McCarthy's rapid ascent in the early 1950s was directly attributable to the fact that the newspapers gave him endless free publicity by reporting his activities. In the words of the editorial writer of *The Washington Post*, Alan Barth, the newspapers' unquestioning coverage served "Senator McCarthy's partisan political purposes much more than it [served] the purposes of the press, the interest of truth." McCarthy was a consummate manipulator of the media. He was friendly, cooperative, and helpful to journalists, always willing to provide information for a story, well aware of press deadlines, and eager to time his press releases accordingly. His status as a senator lent him a cloak of respectability, and many journalists, schooled to report news objectively but also with due deference to authority, relayed his allegations without qualification.

Alarmed by these manipulations, the editors of the important metropolitan dailies—in particular, *The New York Times*, *The Washington Post*, and *Los Angeles Times*—began to formulate a

response. They started to supplement their straightforward reportage of McCarthy with interpretive writing that attempted to analyze and explain increasingly complex news stories. This in-depth reporting was separated from the news articles and became more and more important as newspapers began to redefine their role as being to bring out the full meaning, as well as reporting the simple facts, of the news. Television news coverage accelerated this trend. Many readers, having seen a story reported on television, relied on newspapers to flesh out and explain what they had seen.

Against this background individual columnists and editorial writers took on a new prominence, bringing a dissident and inquiring voice to the news. I.F. Stone (*see box opposite*) was one of the most notable of the dissenting voices. However, writing was not the only way of challenging widely accepted orthodoxies. The cartoonist Herbert Block (1909–2001) provided an alternative way of doing so. Block started as a staff cartoonist with the *Chicago Daily News* in 1929. He became increasingly disenchanted with the right-wing views of the newspaper, and his cartoons began to focus on the rise of Nazism in Germany, winning him a Pulitzer Prize in 1942. Although his cartoons were very popular with the public, he found himself in conflict with his employer (by then *The*

EXECUTIVE ORDER 10290

In the secretive atmosphere of postwar Washington, as government devoted more and more attention to fears of communist infiltration, journalists found it increasingly difficult to penetrate official channels in their quest for news stories. But government–press relations reached an all-time low in 1951 when President Truman introduced Executive Order 10290. Under this new order 45 government agencies were required to classify all information that was necessary to "the security of the nation" into the following categories: Top Secret, Secret, Confidential, and Restricted. These categories were already used by the military, but Truman insisted that civilian departments should be given the same powers

since they too were required to handle sensitive information. He referred to a CIA report that asserted that "90 percent of all our top-secret information had been published in either the daily newspapers or in the slick magazines." Without the protection of his order, he argued, the news media would betray information that could be useful to communist enemies. The newspaper industry was horrified. *Editor & Publisher*, a trade publication, stated that it was "the most drastic peacetime censorship ever attempted in this country." Despite a series of appeals against the order, it stayed in force until 1953, when Eisenhower's administration limited classification power to 17 of the original 45 agencies.

I.F. STONE'S WEEKLY

Maverick journalist I.F. Stone (born Isidor Feinstein; 1907–1989) took on the Washington establishment and asserted his right to tell the truth at all times. Born in Philadelphia, he was editor of *The Nation* from 1940 to 1946. In 1953, at the height of McCarthyism, his name was on a list prepared for the Senate Internal Security Subcommittee of the 82 "most active and typical sponsors of Communist-front organizations." Unemployed and unemployable, Stone decided to take his fate into his own hands and, with the help of a $3,000 loan from a friend, started a political paper, *I.F. Stone's Weekly*. Totally independent, Stone could tell the unvarnished truth, denouncing war atrocities and exposing the intrigues of U.S. administrations, whether Republican or Democratic. He never attended presidential press conferences or off-the-record briefings and did not cultivate highly placed inside sources—the usual journalistic tools. Instead, he doggedly scoured public documents, burying himself in the records of obscure congressional hearings, debates, and reports. He repeatedly found contradictions of the official line, lies, and infringements of civil rights and liberties. His documentation, because of his careful research, was irrefutable. In his words: "Government lies, but it doesn't like to lie literally. Because a literal, flat and obvious lie tends to be caught up. So, what they do is, they become the masters of the disingenuous statement, of phrasing something in such a way that the honest, normal and unwary reader gets one impression—that he is supposed to get." In the course of its 18-year history (it became a biweekly in 1967 and closed due to Stone's ill-health in 1971) the weekly's circulation rose from a few thousand to 70,000. By this time Stone had inspired a new generation of journalists to test the truth behind the government line. His life showed that an idealistic individual is not helpless in the face of the powerful. In his words, "I have so much fun I ought to be arrested."

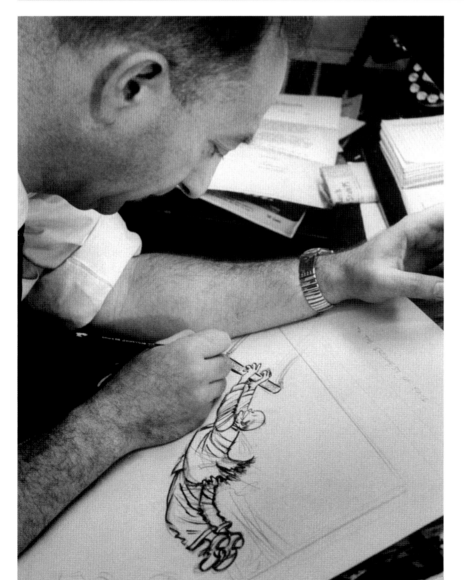

Newspaper cartoonist Herbert L. Block works at the drawing board in 1956. In a career that spanned six decades he influenced public opinion with his take on major events.

Washington Post) during the 1952 presidential campaign, when his cartoons were critical of Dwight D. Eisenhower, the Republican candidate. This led the paper's owners to refuse to publish them in the final days of the campaign. Block was also extremely critical of Joseph McCarthy; he is credited with coining the term "McCarthyism," which he portrayed in one cartoon as a hysterical attempt to douse the torch of the Statue of Liberty. McCarthy responded by calling *The Washington Post* "the Washington edition of [the U.S. communist newspaper] the *Daily Worker*." Block, however, had a wide following and won his second Pulitzer Prize in 1954.

See Also:

Cartoons and Animation • Cold War • Communications • Law and Order • McCarthy Hearings • Murrow, Ed • Newspapers • Radio • Television

NEWSPAPERS

In the 1950s newspapers faced stiff competition from a new medium—television. In addition, rapid social change, the Cold War, and the secrecy it brought about in government also made their work unexpectedly difficult, as papers struggled to retain their relevance to the reader.

At the end of World War II (1939–1945) America's newspaper industry was booming. Daily newspaper circulation stood at an all-time high at the close of 1945 and increased steadily throughout the late 1940s, proving that those people who believed that newspapers would struggle to attract readers when there were no wartime headlines had been wrong. National and local advertising revenues also increased. Healthy finances and the end of wartime shortages encouraged many newspapers to expand their offices and modernize their presses. *The New York Times* estimated that in 1948 alone $50 million worth of expansion was underway in newspapers across the nation.

This boom time did not last, however. During the 1950s America's daily and weekly newspapers faced a number of tough challenges. Foremost among them was competition from television. While the small television industry seemed to pose little danger to daily newspapers during the earliest postwar years, television came of age in the fifties, particularly in terms of the newsgathering capabilities of its reporters. As more and more households owned a television, and as television news reporting became increasingly sophisticated, newspapers witnessed a stagnation or gradual decline in their circulation. In addition, while newspapers' national advertising revenues remained relatively healthy throughout the decade, television attracted a large share of advertising revenues that had formerly been spent on newspapers.

Rising costs

At the same time, the costs of newspaper production were escalating. The printing technology used by the daily newspapers had changed little between the late 19th century and the 1940s; it entailed a labor-intensive process of setting copy into metal type on typecasting machines. These machines could be operated only by skilled typesetters. By the end of the forties cheaper alternatives to the hot-metal process—offset printing, photoengraving, and teletypesetting—were being introduced, and newspaper owners were devoting more resources to developing quicker and more economical printing methods. By the end of the fifties, however, real progress had yet to be made, and labor rates and newsprint prices had increased. To solve the newsprint cost problem, many newspapers trimmed the size of their pages by an inch or more; others introduced more columns of print. Newspapers also ran more advertising than editorial matter to maintain profits as costs rose.

Metropolitan vs. suburban

Aside from technological change, another challenge facing newspapers in the 1950s was the shift in America's population from urban areas to the suburbs. This trend profoundly affected newspapers. Metropolitan daily news-

The Daily Tribune leads with a headline about perjury in the Domestic Relations Court in 1955. Newspapers often tried to boost sales with supplements such as this.

THE NEW YORK TIMES

Also known as "The Gray Lady" or simply *The Times*, *The New York Times* was founded in 1851 by Henry J. Raymond and George Jones as *The New-York Daily Times*. It was intended to provide a serious alternative to the more partisan, sensationalist newspapers—the so-called yellow press—that were common in 19th-century America. By contrast to its rival papers, which sought to shock, anger, and excite readers, *The New York Times* set out to provide a historical record of current events. By the turn of the century, under the proprietorship of Adolph Ochs, *The Times* had achieved an international reputation and was widely distributed nationally and abroad. Arthur Hays Sulzberger (1891–1968), who married Ochs's daughter, was the paper's publisher throughout the 1950s.

The New York Times of that era was believed to be "mildly liberal" by most newspapermen and women, yet

Arthur Hays Sulzberger expanded the *New York Times*'s interpretive reporting. His son and grandson have since succeeded him.

it spent much of the decade defending itself against charges of communist sympathizing and employing procommunist staff. The paper's music critic, Olin Downes, and the dance critic, John Martin, were both on the FBI's list of people considered a potential threat to national security, and in 1956 Senator James O. Eastland led a committee investigating assertions that the *Times* staff included "100 Communist Party members."

Nevertheless, having been at the forefront of "interpretive" journalism during the McCarthy years, and as one of the few newspapers that reported the civil rights movement with anything like depth and informed analysis, *The Times* emerged from the decade with its integrity more intact than that of many newspapers.

papers lost readers, while suburban, community weeklies and dailies had new readerships. In 1950 in the United States there were about 1,800 newspapers published each weekday (with an average circulation of about 30,000 copies) and between 550 and 600 Sunday papers (with an average circulation of about 85,000 copies). Fewer than 40 daily newspapers had a circulation over 250,000 copies, although this figure increased by the end of the decade. However, the number of newspapers that had a circulation between 100,000 and 250,000 (between 80 and 90 titles) decreased slightly over the course of the decade.

There were few truly national newspapers in the 1950s. The main exception was *The Wall Street Journal*, although large metropolitan newspapers with expanded distribution networks, such as *The New York Times* and *The Washington Post*, also filled the role of national newspapers to a degree. Nevertheless, even these large city

newspapers had a mainly regional readership during the decade.

As today, in the 1950s the New York City-based *Wall Street Journal* (first published in 1889) mainly reported on American and international business and financial news and issues. It had the widest circulation of any newspaper in the United States during this time and had a reputation for being a reliable—if staunchly conservative—source of news. The more liberal *New York Times* (*see box*) tended to focus more on foreign affairs, while *The Washington Post* (first published in 1877) had a reputation for covering national politics.

New approaches to journalism

The immediate postwar years and the decade that followed were generally characterized by more serious and thoughtful journalism than in previous decades. Sensational stories of scandal and violent crime still formed the basis of attention-grabbing headlines, but in

the same editions readers could usually find clear, concise reports on education issues and politics. For the majority of small daily and weekly newspapers the emphasis was on local news. For example, a June 1956 edition of the *Los Angeles Evening Herald Express* carried about seven columns of national and international news but also devoted a couple of columns to Hollywood gossip and more than 30 columns to sports.

The "wire services"—full-time news reporting services such as Associated Press and United Press—sold stories to newspapers unable to afford a large staff of reporters. They were crucial in enabling smaller papers to cover national and international events.

Freedom of information

Journalism in the 1950s was also transformed by deteriorating relations between the press and the government. There were a number of reasons for this breakdown. Chief among them were, first, the increasing secrecy in

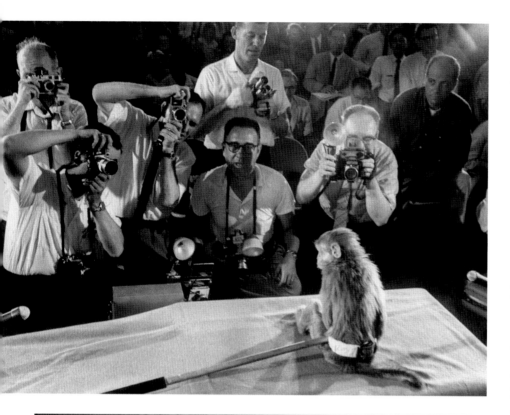

Members of the press photograph a monkey named Able, who was carried aboard a Jupiter rocket in May 1959 in preparation for eventual human space flight.

government that resulted from the national security concerns of the Cold War and, second, the rise of Senator Joseph McCarthy and the anti-communist "witch hunts" that took place in the early part of the decade.

Throughout World War II the relationship between the U.S. government and the nation's press had been fairly harmonious, resulting from a strong sense of common purpose. Journalists were proud to comply voluntarily with government requests to withhold information. As Raymond Daniell of *The New York Times* once said, "There isn't any story in the world that is good enough to justify risking the life of a single American soldier." Nevertheless, in exchange for responsible censorship journalists came to expect access to news and the people who made that news. Such access became more and more limited as the United States emerged from the war.

Initially, obstacles to free reporting existed mainly in the international arena. Despite the efforts of trade associations such as the American Society of Newspaper Editors (ASNE), the Associated Press Managing Editors (APME), and Sigma Delta Chi (now the Society of Professional Journalists) to lobby the newly established United Nations (UN) on freedom of information, such efforts were frustrated from the start. The Soviet Union, in particular, opposed UN attempts to build treaties that would protect the worldwide flow of news.

Military secrecy

As Cold War tensions grew, however, barriers to the press began to rise on the domestic front as well. Most freedom-of-information issues of the late 1940s concerned military secrecy surrounding

A man looks at the newspapers for sale at a newsstand in New York City in 1952. Foreign-language papers can be seen as well as those in English.

SYDNEY GRUSON AND THE GUATEMALA COUP

As the 1950s went on, the agenda of serious journalism and that of an increasingly secretive government appeared to move further apart—a fact that became clear in the days leading up to the CIA-backed plan to overthrow President Jacobo Arbenz of Guatemala in June 1954. Crucial to the success of the plan was the cooperation of the American press in convincing the public that the coup had originated as a result of indigenous Guatemalans rising up against a procommunist regime. One of the CIA's main responsibilities during the coup, therefore, was to ensure that journalists were kept out of the area to prevent them discovering just how ill-prepared and weak the ostensible "liberator," Carlos Castillo Armas, and his army really were.

Chief among the reporters the CIA wanted to bar from the region was one of *The New York Times*'s most talented foreign correspondents, Sydney Gruson (1916–1998). Although Gruson was not notably radical, he had a reporter's inquisitiveness in abundance. Allen Dulles, head of the CIA, had become concerned by Gruson's reporting in the preceding months and was particularly bothered by a number of stories suggesting that Arbenz's government enjoyed considerable support in the region and was not particularly procommunist.

Dulles went to his contact at *The Times*, General Julius Ochs Adler, who was a cousin of the publisher, Arthur Hays Sulzberger. He explained that some delicate events were about to take place in Guatemala, and that the CIA would prefer Gruson not to cover the story because his "political reliability" might be in question. Adler passed the information on to Sulzberger who, worried by the charges, insisted that Gruson be kept out of Guatemala. After the coup Sulzberger pressed Dulles on the question of whether or not Gruson was a subversive. It soon became clear that the newspaper had been duped into keeping one of its best reporters away from an entirely legitimate story.

the development of new weapons and technologies. Journalists began to worry about the military's attempts to suppress certain news stories, even when the information they contained was already available to the public or even known to the Soviet Union. For example, Federal Bureau of Investigation (FBI) agents questioned the publishers of *Aviation Week* about an article on the development of a supersonic aircraft despite the fact that the plane was based on a Soviet prototype. Most journalists took the view that national security should be protected by press–government cooperation and responsible journalism, as had been the case during the war, rather than by censorship. Paradoxically, the events of the Korean War (1950–1953) resulted in few concerns over the freedom of the press, since censorship followed a voluntary model similar to that used during World War II.

Secrecy in nonmilitary domestic matters also began to increase in the postwar years. During the early 1950s journalists discovered that the State Department was withholding a large volume of material from reporters, and

there were numerous instances of state governors and other local government officials and even school boards closing meetings to the public and refusing to release records and reports. At the same time, journalists increasingly found themselves having to deal with government intermediaries such as press agents and public relations people, which made the likelihood of their being manipulated into publishing government propaganda all the greater.

The early part of the decade also saw the imposition in 1951 of Executive Order 10290 by President Harry S. Truman (1945–1953). The order provided for a classification system of government information into the same categories already used by the military: Top Secret, Secret, Confidential, and Restricted. Truman defended the order on the basis that nonmilitary information could also be sensitive, and that such documents had to be protected from publication lest they provided assistance to communist enemies. The order met with instant criticism from the newspaper industry; the trade journal *Editor & Publisher* labeled it "the most drastic peacetime censorship" ever introduced in the United States.

Despite numerous protests, the order remained unchanged until President Dwight D. Eisenhower (1953–1961) took office. His revisions involved limiting the power to classify documents to 17 (rather than the original 45) government agencies, the elimination of the "restricted" category, and authority to classify information being vested only in the chief administrative officers of each of the 17 agencies. Nevertheless, some editors, such as *The Indianapolis Star*'s Jameson G. Campaigne, complained that the order remained, "a millstone around the necks of the editors of the nation."

The press and McCarthy

Another major cause of strained relations between American newspapers and the government during the 1950s was one of the biggest news stories of that decade: the rise to prominence of the junior U.S. senator from Wisconsin, Joseph McCarthy (1908–1957), who claimed that the federal government had been infiltrated by communists. McCarthy was a skilled manipulator of the news media. Partly as a result of his cooperative attitude toward the press, reputedly telephoning

As the deadline to go to press approaches, this printer completes the "imposing" of the front page in 1955. This was known as working "on the stone."

government officials while reporters listened in and providing tips to those in need of a story, he managed to dominate the nation's headlines from the moment he made his speech in Wheeling, West Virginia, in February 1950 to his eventual censure by fellow senators in late 1954. According to two of McCarthy's critics, Jack Anderson and Ronald W. May, who published a book on the senator in 1952, if McCarthy was a political monster, then the press acted as his Dr. Frankenstein.

At the start of the senator's climb to fame journalists—often starved for information by other branches of government—were happy to cooperate for the simple reason that he was news. Journalist Willard Edwards, who covered the story for the *Chicago Tribune*, remembered: "McCarthy was a dream story. I wasn't off page one for four years." The senator was also skilled at timing his press conferences in order to achieve the best exposure: He would level a charge against an individual but not allow enough time for reporters to

check the allegation before they were obliged to either print it or risk being scooped by their rivals. As a result, McCarthy's version usually appeared in print largely unchallenged; and even when a charge was later disproved, the fact was soon buried by a torrent of fresh allegations.

As time went on, newspapers and their journalists began to feel trapped by the convention that required them to report every (even the most outrageous) charge made by McCarthy. Bob Baskin, a journalist for *The Dallas Morning News*, complained, "I had to report—and quote—McCarthy. That's all I could do. How do you say in the middle of your story 'This is a lie'?"

Senator Joseph McCarthy holds up a copy of the Washington *Evening Star* as he makes a statement in 1954 while the Senate Censure Committee considers charges against him.

THE TABLOID PRESS

In 1903 the British publisher Alfred Harmsworth created the first newspaper in a tabloid format, London's *Daily Mirror*. The paper, originally aimed at women readers, became a hit with commuters because its compact size made it easy to read on crowded buses and subways. It was also popular with readers in general because it specialized in condensing hard-hitting crime stories in fewer than 250 words. In the United States the tabloid was a natural progression of the "yellow journalism" founded by Joseph Pulitzer and William Randolph Hearst in the last quarter of the 19th century. Hearst, in particular, demanded that stories in his papers be written with excitement and energy, that the editorials have a strong point of view, and that dramatic illustrations and large photos be used to break up the small print.

On June 26, 1919, the first tabloid appeared in the United States—the New York City-based *Illustrated Daily News*. The paper instantly scandalized the city's more principled journalists and residents. New York publicist Aben Kandel complained that such tabloids "reduce the highest ideals of the newspaper to the process of fastening a camera lens to every boudoir keyhole." Nevertheless, the *Daily News* went on to develop a national reputation for its crime coverage, and by the 1950s most large cities in the United States had at least one tabloid.

America's tabloid press soon developed a style known as "jazz journalism." While the tabloids maintained extensive coverage of crime and trials, they started to branch out into writing on fashion, lifestyles, and increasingly celebrity gossip, sex, and scandals. During the 1950s favorite subjects covered in the tabloid press included spies, racial issues, and even UFOs.

Notorious among tabloid papers of the era was *The National Enquirer*. The scandal sheet began in 1952, when Italian publisher Generoso Pope, Jr., bought a New York racing tip sheet and transformed it into a

newspaper version of popular scandal magazines such as *Confidential*. Before long the newspaper was infamous for inventing incredible stories, attracting readers with headlines such as "I Cut out Her Heart and Stomped on It!" Circulation rose to a million copies a week during the decade, partly as a result of the *Enquirer*'s revolutionary distribution system, which placed it in neighborhood grocery stores all over the United States.

A man offers the *Daily News* for sale. In the 1950s street vendors selling papers straight from a shoulder bag were still common.

However, *The Washington Post*'s editorial writer Alan Barth believed that reporting of the McCarthy story showed poor journalism: "[Newspapers] may have to report the statements of a demagogue, but ... [it] is part of their job to put [those statements] in perspective. Their aim must be to present not only the truth but the whole truth."

Many newspaper publishers, even the most liberal ones, worried that strong criticism of McCarthy and his methods would be playing into the hands of the enemy: the communists. A few publishers and editors decided not to cover any stories about accusations of communism. For example, one New Hampshire newspaper, *The Claremont Daily Eagle*, refused to print any news of McCarthy for more than eight months in 1950, and in 1951 it announced that it would not be publishing a list of people with alleged communist sympathies that had been released by the House Un-American Activities Committee (HUAC). Some other newspapers simply avoided using McCarthy's name in their headlines and rarely reported stories about him on the front page.

Interpretive writing
Some of America's largest and most influential metropolitan dailies solved the problem of how to report on McCarthy by turning increasingly toward interpretive writing—that is, toward opinion or comment pieces that

not only reported the facts but also explained, explored, and analyzed the meaning of an event for readers. Commentators point out that while the move toward greater analysis was already underway during the immediate postwar period, McCarthy provided greater impetus for the trend because the story was so complex. Foremost among those newspapers that advocated the use of interpretive analyses and applied this approach to investigating McCarthy's charges were *The Washington Post*, *The New York Times*, *The Baltimore Sun*, and *The Milwaukee Journal*. Such newspapers tended to have their own Washington correspondents, who had easier access to more in-depth information. By contrast, most smaller newspapers had to rely on the wire services for their news about McCarthy.

African Americans and the press

Another major challenge that newspapers faced during the 1950s was covering the rise of the civil rights movement, desegregation, and the social upheavals that they led to, particularly in the South.

Prior to the momentous Supreme Court rulings of the 1950s that provided the catalyst for desegregation, African Americans featured rarely in the nation's newspapers. The occasional mentions they did merit were usually the result of their having committed a crime or died a violent death. In a 1947 book, *Your Newspaper*, journalists in the prestigious Nieman Fellowship Program at Harvard University reported: "As pictured in many newspapers, the Negro is either an entertaining fool, a dangerous animal, or (on the comparatively few occasions when a Negro's achievements are applauded) a prodigy of astonishing attainments, considering his race."

The 1950s were to witness a gradual transformation in such reporting. In 1946 *The New York Times* announced that it would in future omit racial designations from its reports after black leaders complained that racial identification of African Americans in newspaper articles, especially crime reports, created a false impression of the entire black population. The late 1940s and early 1950s also saw newspapers, even those in the Deep South, beginning to use courtesy titles for African Americans or running regular pages or columns of their news.

Nevertheless, until the mid-1950s, even in the most liberal newspapers black news was seldom seen as being worthy of publication. Positive stories that featured African Americans appeared infrequently, while some newspapers had a policy not to publish pictures of ethnic minorities. The employment of black reporters was also rare. A study by Lincoln University in Missouri found just 21 black journalists working on white-owned daily newspapers across the country in 1955. Although they were few in number, black reporters such as Ted Poston of *The New York Post* began to attract notice nationwide with their writing on desegregation.

Newspapers were obliged to begin featuring more news about African Americans when the Supreme Court issued its landmark decision *Brown v. Board of Education* in 1954, which ruled that segregated public schooling was unconstitutional. The undisputed leader among the nation's newspapers in terms of the breadth and depth of its coverage of desegregation and civil rights was *The New York Times*. In 1955 Turner Catledge, the paper's executive editor, sent a team of reporters to survey desegregation efforts in the Deep South and border states over a period of five weeks. The paper also supported integration in its editorials. Chief among the *Times*'s reporters in the South, and a leading authority on the issues and actors involved, was John N. Popham (*see box*).

JOHN N. POPHAM

Prior to the horrific murder of 14-year-old Emmett Till in Mississippi in 1955 and the media frenzy that surrounded the following trial, *The New York Times*'s John N. Popham (1910–1999) was the only full-time national newspaper journalist working in the South. Popham had originally been sent to cover the southern states in 1947 by Managing Editor Turner Catledge, himself from Mississippi and by that time well aware of the profound changes that were about to unfold in the region.

Popham was from a long-established Virginia family. He based himself at the Hotel Patten in Chattanooga, Tennessee, near the offices of *The Chattanooga Times*, which, like *The New York Times*, was owned by the Sulzberger family. He bought a car and began traveling extensively across the South. Popham's term as The

Times's correspondent in the region lasted until 1958, by which time he had acquired a reputation for being a diplomatic and scrupulously fair reporter. His reporting won him both praise and awards. In 1953 he was named the South's most outstanding journalist by Sigma Delta Chi (now the Society of Professional Journalists).

Popham established himself as the pioneer journalist covering the South and interpreting it for the rest of the nation. He became the first point of contact for newly arrived reporters and was famed for his charming character and vast network of connections. It was Popham and later his successor at *The Times*, Claude Sitton, who set the tone for reporting civil rights during the 1950s and into the following decade. Popham became managing editor of *The Chattanooga Times* in 1958 and retired in 1978.

Roy Bryant (left) and J.W. Milam are pictured at their trial for the murder of Emmett Till in 1955. The trial was covered by an unprecedented number of reporters.

Press coverage of desegregation generally fell far below the standards set by *The New York Times*. Newspapers in both the southern and northern states mirrored the attitudes and biases of the communities they served; regardless of their personal feelings on the issue, most editors were concerned for their own survival and so tried not to offend local sensibilities. Although it came out in opposition to race-related violence, the southern press offered little in the way of support for desegregation. What little coverage the issue did receive in the South was frequently distorted and unbalanced, provided little in the way of context, and tended to emphasize conflict rather than progress.

Nor did the few moderate and liberal southern newspapers necessarily favor integration; they were simply more likely to urge compliance with the law and equal treatment of blacks. Nevertheless, these comparatively outspoken editors, who included, for example, leading moderate Ralph McGill of *The Atlanta Constitution*, were often vilified in their towns and communities. Many were later awarded Pulitzer Prizes in editorial writing.

Reporters on the scene

In the wake of the Supreme Court's 1955 ruling that ordered school desegregation to proceed "with all deliberate speed," some larger southern newspapers gradually became more balanced in their reporting of racial issues. However, they continued to rely on the wire services as their source of information rather than send reporters to cover and interpret stories as they happened. This was in contrast to the northern dailies, which began to send their reporters to the South in force. An unprecedented 75 (mainly northern) reporters were on hand in Sumner, Mississippi, in 1955 to cover the trial of Roy Bryant and J.W. Milam, accused of the murder of 14-year-old Emmett Till. (They were acquitted by the all-white

jury, then sold their story to the press, boasting of how they had carried out the murder.) In 1957 Little Rock, Arkansas, was transformed into what one NBC reporter called "a giant press room," when more than 200 out-of-town reporters descended on the city to cover the unfolding integration crisis as nine black students tried to attend classes at the previously all-white Central High School.

Little Rock, in particular, led to antagonism between northern and southern reporters, some of whom openly took sides (notably *The New York Times*'s education editor, Benjamin Fine) and were accused of inciting violence among the already volatile mob that surrounded the school.

Little Rock was also the first running story of national importance that

television fully covered and is believed by many commentators to be the scene where television news reporting got the upper hand over the more conventional reporting style of the nation's newspapers for the first time. The extensive TV coverage, live broadcasts, and dramatic pictures occasionally had newspaper reporters rushing to file new copy after watching an evening broadcast on television.

See Also:

Brown v. Board of Education • Cartoons and Animation • Civil Rights • Cold War • Communications • Guatemala • • Little Rock School Crisis • McCarthy, Joseph • Magazines • News and Current Affairs • Pulitzer Prize

RICHARD M. NIXON 1913–1994

Richard M. Nixon was a prominent member of the House Un-American Activities Committee in the late 1940s, two-term vice president, and later president of the United States. He was forced to resign in disgrace midway through his second term in the Watergate scandal.

Richard Milhous Nixon was born in California on January 9, 1913. He graduated from Duke University, North Carolina, in 1937 and began practicing law. After serving in the Navy in World War II (1939–1945), Nixon began an almost meteoric rise in politics. In 1946 he won election from Southern California to the U.S. Congress as a Republican, upsetting the well-known New Deal Democrat Jerry Voorhis. Nixon ran as a virulent anti-communist, and he immediately won appointment to the House Un-American Activities Committee (HUAC), which was engaged in an investigation of communist influence in American politics and entertainment.

When allegations were made by writer and ex-Communist Whittaker Chambers that Alger Hiss, a high-ranking State Department official under President Franklin D. Roosevelt (1933–1945), had spied for the Soviets, Nixon led the investigation. Hiss vehemently denied the charges and was eventually found guilty of perjury.

Senator and statesman

On the strength of his new fame as a champion of anticommunist right-wingers Nixon ran for the seat from California in the U.S. Senate in 1950 and won another surprise victory. After only two years in the Senate Nixon made another major career move. When war hero Dwight D. Eisenhower (1890–1969) received the Republican nomination for president in 1952, he chose Nixon as his running mate. It was believed

Richard Nixon's political career was marked in turn by success and controversy. He was eventually elected president in 1968, only to fall from grace during the Watergate scandal.

that Nixon would bring relative youth and a passionate following among hard-core conservatives.

Nixon's vice-presidential campaign was quickly threatened by allegations that he controlled a secret "slush fund," money given by wealthy donors. Nixon went on national television on September 23, 1952, to try to save his career. He defended his use of the secret money to pay for his legitimate political expenses and claimed that his own lifestyle was modest. He admitted that he had received one improper gift: a

cocker spaniel puppy, named Checkers. The favorable reaction to the "Checkers" speech moved Eisenhower to keep Nixon on the ticket, and they won convincingly in November.

As vice president Nixon found that his new job carried little power, and Eisenhower did not give him any significant role in his administration's decision-making. Eisenhower considered dropping Nixon from the ticket in 1956 but relented. In his second term as vice president Nixon was sent on several major foreign trips. During a 1958 state visit to Latin America he was spat on in Lima, Peru, and pelted with rocks in Caracas, Venezuela. While on a state visit to the Soviet Union in 1959 Nixon engaged in a surprisingly heated televised argument with Premier Nikita Khrushchev (1894–1971) over the relative merits of the American and Soviet ways of life.

In 1960 Nixon won the Republican presidential nomination, but his boss did not deliver a ringing endorsement. When asked to list some of Nixon's major accomplishments, Eisenhower replied, "Give me a week, and I might be able to think of one." Nixon lost to John F. Kennedy (1961–1963) in one of the closest presidential elections in American history.

See Also:

Eisenhower, Dwight D. • Foreign Policy • Hiss, Alger • House Un-American Activities Committee • Politics and Government • Republican Party

NOBEL PRIZES

The six Nobel Prizes awarded annually in chemistry, economics, literature, peace, physics, and physiology or medicine are seen as the highest public accolade for intellectual achievement. During the 1950s more than 30 Americans won prizes for their remarkable efforts.

The Nobel Foundation is a private institution based in Stockholm, Sweden, that awards prizes to individuals who "have conferred the greatest benefit on mankind." It was formed in 1900 with funds from the will of Alfred Bernhard Nobel (1833–1896), the Swedish scientist who invented dynamite. Horrified by the wartime uses of his creation, Nobel bequeathed his vast fortune to a fund that would award five annual prizes: one each for chemistry, literature, peace, physics, and physiology or medicine. In 1969 the Bank of Sweden extended this fund to include an award for economics.

Awarded each year on December 10, the anniversary of Nobel's death, the prizes are seen as the highest public accolade that any individual can achieve. They are available to any person irrespective of nationality, race, or beliefs. Each is accompanied with an award that currently stands at about $1 million. If two or three people are deemed equally deserving of this honor in a single year, the money is split. Sometimes the Nobel Foundation does not award a

prize at all; this happened, for example, during the two world wars.

Among the winners of the Nobel Prize are the most esteemed intellectual figures of the past century. Notable recipients include Theodore Roosevelt (1858–1919; Peace Prize in 1906), Albert Einstein (1879–1955; Physics Prize in 1921), Sir Winston Churchill (1874–1965; Literature Prize in 1953), Martin Luther King, Jr. (1929–1968; Peace Prize in 1964), and Mother Theresa (1910–1997; Peace Prize in 1979). Respected organizations such as the United Nations (UN), Amnesty International, and the International Red Cross have also won the Nobel Peace Prize.

Chemistry

The 1950s were a good decade for American chemistry: Four scientists received Nobel Prizes for their important work.

Nuclear chemists Edwin Mattison McMillan (1907–1991) and Glenn Theodore Seaborg (1912–1999) won the 1951 Chemistry Prize for "their discoveries in the chemistry of the

transuranium elements." All substances are chemical combinations of basic elements such as carbon, oxygen, and iron. Scientists know of about 90 naturally occurring elements, with uranium being the heaviest. By artificially creating new atoms in nuclear reactions, McMillan and Seaborg extended the elements past uranium. Neptunium (1940) was the first of these "transuranics," followed by plutonium (1940), americium (1944), curium (1944), berkelium (1949), and californium (1950). These are all highly radioactive elements. Plutonium, the best known, can form the core for atom bombs and nuclear reactors.

In 1954 the eminent American chemist and biologist Linus Carl Pauling (1901–1994) received a Nobel Prize for his work done between 1925 and 1940 on how elements combine into chemical compounds. All matter is made of atoms bonded together into crystals and molecules. These molecules can have complex shapes depending on their component atoms and bonds. Pauling used scattered X-rays to look at these molecular shapes. He also applied

THE SELECTION AND AWARD PROCESS

Selection of the Nobel Prize-winners is a long and detailed process. More than 6,000 eminent scientists, academics, and scholars submit detailed nominations for candidates in the fall one year before the prize is due to be awarded. The six Nobel Prize committees carefully look through this information. After about six months' consideration and consultation they make their recommendations to the four institutions that award the prizes: the Royal Swedish Academy of Sciences, for physics, chemistry, and economics; the Swedish Academy, for literature; the Karolinska Institute, for physiology or

medicine; and the Norwegian Nobel Committee, for peace. Their final decisions are made by November 15.

The winners, or "laureates," are awarded their prizes on December 10 in a ceremony that includes a lecture from each of them. They are then honored at a huge banquet at which more than 1,000 people are present. These events are broadcast on national television and attended by prominent politicians, leaders, and academics. Each prize confers a gold medal, a handcrafted diploma, and a sum that has grown over the years to reach the current 10 million Swedish kronas (about $1 million).

Linus Pauling (above) is one of only a handful of people to have been awarded two Nobel Prizes. He received one for chemistry in 1954 and one for peace in 1962.

The Nobel Prize awarded to Ernest Hemingway (left) in 1954 specially commended his novel *The Old Man and the Sea*, which encapsulates several themes close to the writer's heart.

the new theory of quantum physics to a mathematical theory of chemical bonding. This theory has underpinned modern chemistry since Pauling's book *The Nature of the Chemical Bond and the Structure of Molecules and Crystals* (1939). Pauling also received the 1962 Nobel Peace Prize for his stance against nuclear weapons.

The 1955 Nobel Prize for chemistry was awarded to another American, Vincent du Vigneaud (1901–1978), for "his work on biochemically important sulfur compounds." Throughout his career he examined many sulfur-containing chemicals that occurred naturally in animals and plants. They include the vitamin biotin, which helps the metabolism, and hormones, which are chemicals that our bodies use to regulate the functions of our tissues and organs. Among them is the hormone insulin, which controls blood-sugar levels. Du Vigneaud received particular praise for his 1954 synthesis of oxytocin, a hormone that stimulates milk production. It was the first artificially synthesized protein.

Literature

In the 1950s individuals from France, Iceland, Italy, Spain, the Soviet Union, Sweden, the United Kingdom, and the United States all won the Nobel Prize for literature. Alfred Nobel stated in his will that the winner should "have produced in the field of literature the most outstanding work of an idealistic tendency." This ambiguous phrase has led to much debate and controversy over who should be the recipient of the prize.

American novelist and short-story writer Ernest Miller Hemingway (1899–1961) won the 1954 Literature Prize for "his mastery of the art of the narrative, most recently demonstrated in *The Old Man and the Sea*." Many of Hemingway's books are regarded as literary classics. His straightforward and objective writing style profoundly influenced other writers in the mid-20th century. The book cited in his Nobel Prize commendation is the tale of an old Cuban fisherman struggling against nature and the elements. Hemingway later described this work as "the hardest of all things to do." Many of his other books focused on very masculine themes; they feature honest people engaged in valiant struggles that gradually overwhelm them. Such perseverance when faced with adversity typified Hemingway's own life values.

Peace

The Nobel Prize for peace differs slightly from the other prizes because it can be awarded to organizations and not just individuals. It can also be given for ongoing work rather than finished achievements. Alfred Nobel stated in his will that its winner should "have done the most or the best work for fraternity between the nations, for the abolition or reduction of standing armies, and for the holding and promotion of peace congresses."

Two Americans won the Nobel Peace Prize in the 1950s. This was a fine achievement for any nation, especially given that the Nobel Foundation did not grant a Peace Prize at all in 1955 and 1956.

1950s AMERICAN NOBEL PRIZE-WINNERS

1950 Peace: Ralph Bunche for mediating the Arab–Israeli conflict

1950 Physiology or medicine: Philip S. Hench and Edward C. Kendall for investigating hormones of the adrenal gland

1951 Chemistry: Edwin M. McMillan and Glenn T. Seaborg for discovering the transuranium elements

1952 Physics: Felix Bloch and Edward M. Purcell for developing nuclear magnetic resonance

1952 Physiology or medicine: Selman Waksman for discovering streptomycin

1953 Peace: George C. Marshall for his postwar economic recovery plan in Western Europe

1953 Physiology or medicine: Fritz Lipmann for discovering coenzyme A and its role in metabolism

1954 Chemistry: Linus Pauling for studying the nature of the chemical bond

1954 Literature: Ernest Hemingway for his mastery of narrative, as demonstrated in his novel *The Old Man and the Sea*

1954 Physiology or medicine: John F. Enders, Frederick C. Robbins, and Thomas H. Weller, for culturing the polio virus

1955 Chemistry: Vincent du Vigneaud for work on biochemically important sulfur compounds

1955 Physics: Polykarp Kusch and Willis E. Lamb for measured errors in the theory of electrons

1956 Physics: John Bardeen, Walter H. Brattain, and William B. Shockley for inventing the transistor

1956 Physiology or medicine: André F. Cournand and Dickinson W. Richards for inserting catheter tubes into human hearts

1957 Physics: Tsung-Dao Lee and Chen Ning Yang for investigating parity breaking for the elementary particles

1958 Physiology or medicine: George Beadle, Joshua Lederberg, and Edward Tatum for pioneering work into how genes function

1959 Physics: Owen Chamberlain and Emilio Segrè for discovering the antiproton

1959 Physiology or medicine: Arthur Kornberg and Severo Ochoa for discovering the biological synthesis of DNA and RNA

Moreover, an international body, the Office of the United Nations High Commissioner for Refugees, received the award in 1954.

American scholar, diplomat, and civil rights campaigner Ralph Johnson Bunche (1904–1971) won the 1950 Peace Prize for helping settle the Arab–Israeli conflict of the late 1940s. The Arab countries of Egypt, Iraq, Lebanon, Syria, and Transjordan had declared war on the state of Israel immediately after it came into existence. After the mediator sent by the United Nations was assassinated, Bunche took over the post. Over almost a year of talks he successfully negotiated an armistice agreement between the warring nations. He returned home to national celebration. The first African American to win the Nobel Peace Prize, Bunche also campaigned vigorously for better race relations.

Another eminent American won the 1953 Peace Prize. Wartime general and later Secretary of State George Catlett Marshall (1880–1959) received the prize for his postwar economic recovery plan in Western Europe. Known informally as the "Marshall Plan," his European Recovery Program pumped more than $13 billion into the war-torn continent from 1948 to 1952. It brought about the fastest economic growth in European history and a dramatic improvement in living standards. The Marshall Plan also encouraged Western European nations to work together for the common good. This spirit of cooperation would later form the basis of the European Common Market and the European Union (EU).

Physics

The United States dominated the field of physics in the 1950s, with 11 American scientists winning five of the Nobel Prizes for physics awarded

In 1956 William Shockley (seated), John Bardeen (center), and Walter Brattain won the Nobel Prize for physics for inventing the transistor. Bardeen also won the prize in 1972.

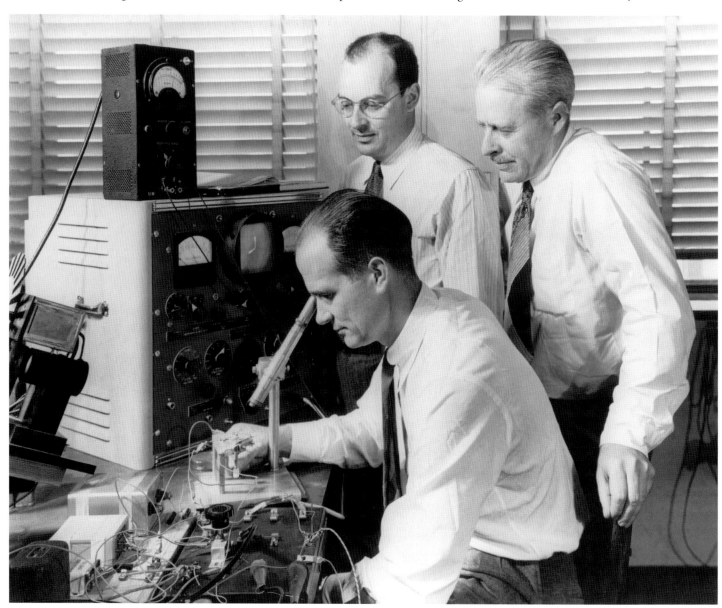

during the decade. Many of these individuals were prominent researchers who had emigrated to America during the thirties and forties. American activities spanned a range of subjects that included the basic properties of matter and the invention of new electronic devices.

Physicists Felix Bloch (1905–1983) and Edward Mills Purcell (1912–1997) shared the 1952 Nobel Prize for physics for their independent discoveries of nuclear magnetic resonance (NMR). This technique detects magnetic fields around the nuclear cores of atoms. Atoms consist of a central nucleus and a system of orbiting electrons. The nucleus behaves like a tiny magnet in a strong magnetic field. Bloch and Purcell's NMR technique used electromagnetic waves to vibrate the magnetic nucleus. At precise frequencies these vibrations built up (resonated), from which scientists calculated the strength of the nuclear magnet, or "magnetic moment." NMR has since become an important tool in chemistry for analyzing the way atoms combine into molecules.

The 1955 Physics Prize was awarded to two American physicists for different but related work. Willis Eugene Lamb (1913–) measured the energy of an electron in a hydrogen atom and found a mistake in its calculated value. Polykarp Kusch (1911–1993) precisely determined the "magnetic moment of the electron." Electrons behave like tiny magnets, with a strength called their magnetic moment. Kusch's work related to Lamb's because both their measurements differed from the predictions of contemporary theories. This showed that the original quantum physics of atoms, nuclei, and electrons was incorrect. Its successor, quantum field theory, has never been proved wrong.

André Cournand won the Nobel Prize for medicine in 1956 with Dickinson Richards and Werner Forssmann. They were recognized for their work on heart catheterization.

In 1956 three Americans shared the Nobel Prize for inventing the transistor. John Bardeen (1908–1991), Walter Houser Brattain (1902–1987), and William Bradford Shockley (1910–1989) created an electronic device that used quantum physics to act like a tiny switch. These transistors quickly became important in radios and other electronic devices. They allowed computers to shrink from room-sized constructions to small boxes; the speed of computers has also greatly increased over the decades. Bardeen is the only person to have won two Nobel Prizes for physics. His second, in 1972, was for his work on superconductivity.

The 1957 Nobel Prize for physics went to Chinese American physicists Tsung-Dao Lee (1926–) and Chen Ning Yang (1922–). They won for their research into the parity laws, which led to "important discoveries regarding the elementary particles." Scientists had believed that the basic laws governing subatomic particles were the same for both matter and its mirror image. They called this symmetry parity. For example, parity reflects objects spinning to the left into objects spinning to the right. In a revolutionary 1956 paper Lee and Yang suggested that this parity symmetry might not hold for the elementary particles. Within a year scientists had measured such parity-breaking effects to find a new feature of matter.

Two American particle physicists also won the 1959 Nobel Prize for physics. Owen Chamberlain (1920–) and Emilio Gino Segrè (1905–1989) jointly discovered the antiproton. The nucleus of an atom contains two types of particles—protons and neutrons—stuck together into a dense clump. Since the 1930s physicists had believed that every particle had an antiparticle twin. It would have the same mass but could annihilate its partner. Physicists knew of an antiparticle for the electron—the positron—but could find no others. Segrè and Chamberlain confirmed a central feature of particle physics by finding such antiprotons in energetic collisions of protons with copper nuclei.

Physiology or medicine

Since discoveries in health often result from teamwork, the Nobel Prize for physiology or medicine is usually awarded to two or more individuals. American scientists made the majority of these important discoveries in the second half of the

20th century. In particular, seven of the ten Nobel Prizes from the 1950s involved American researchers.

Two American scientists, Philip Showalter Hench (1896–1965) and Edward Calvin Kendall (1886–1972), shared the 1950 Nobel Prize with the Swiss biochemist Tadeus Reichstein (1897–1996) for "their discoveries relating to the hormones of the adrenal cortex," a main gland on the kidneys that produces hormones such as adrenaline in animals' fight-or-flight reflex. Hench, Kendall, and Reichstein examined several such adrenal hormones. One of the most important for medicine was the steroid cortisone, which eases the pain of rheumatoid arthritis.

The American biochemist Selman Abraham Waksman (1888–1973) won the 1952 prize for his important discovery of the antibiotic streptomycin. Antibiotics kill some types of bacteria. In particular, Waksman's discovery was the first one to effectively combat the microorganism that caused tuberculosis. In the 1950s tuberculosis was a devastating infection of the lungs that crippled or killed tens of thousands of people every year.

Half of the 1953 Nobel Prize was awarded to the American biochemist Fritz Albert Lipmann (1899–1986) for his work on how our bodies create energy through metabolism. Lipmann discovered a natural chemical, coenzyme A, which our cells use to turn fat into energy. Modern health-food stores sell this substance in diet supplements for losing weight.

In the following year three American microbiologists won the 1954 Nobel Prize after managing to grow the polio virus in a tissue culture. John Franklin Enders (1897–1985), Frederick

George Beadle's research in the field of genetics earned him a Nobel Prize for medicine in 1958. He shared this honor with Edward Tatum and Joshua Lederberg.

Chapman Robbins (1916–2003), and Thomas Huckle Weller (1915–) pioneered this new technique of culturing viruses and applied it to several diseases. Their work led directly to the discovery of a cure for the devastating disease polio, which had previously crippled thousands of children each year.

The two American physicians André Frédéric Cournand (1895–1988) and Dickinson Woodruff Richards (1895–1973) shared the 1956 Nobel Prize for physiology or medicine with the German physician Werner Forssmann

(1904–1979). They continued the German's pioneering work of inserting small tubes, or catheters, down a vein and into the heart. Catheters were used to give drugs directly to the heart and to examine its health. Forssmann initially experimented on himself, but his research was stopped because others (wrongly) thought that it would be too dangerous.

Three American geneticists won the 1958 Nobel Prize for their pioneering research into how genes work. Genes are the basic units for inheriting biological traits from our parents and correspond to sequences of chemicals in our DNA. George Wells Beadle (1903–1989) and Edward Lawrie Tatum (1909–1975) examined genetic mutations in mold and concluded that each gene regulated a particular biochemical process. Meanwhile, Joshua Lederberg (1925–) investigated genetic processes in bacteria. Their collective work was instrumental in creating the modern science of genetic engineering.

The 1959 Nobel Prize for physiology or medicine was also won by two American scientists for an important discovery in genetics. Biochemists Severo Ochoa (1905–1993) and Arthur Kornberg (1918–) won their prize for discovering how DNA and RNA are biologically synthesized. DNA and RNA are the basic chemicals for storing and copying our genetic code.

See Also:

Bunche, Ralph • Computer Science • Hemingway, Ernest • Literature • Medicine • Pauling, Linus • Physics • Polio Vaccine • United Nations

NORTH ATLANTIC TREATY ORGANIZATION (NATO)

The creation of the North Atlantic Treaty Organization in 1949 played an important part in drawing the lines between the opposing sides in the Cold War: the United States and its allies on the one hand, the Soviet Union and its sphere of influence on the other.

The North Atlantic Treaty Organization (NATO), the mutual-defense pact between the United States, Canada, and many of the countries of Western Europe, was of great significance in the decades following World War II (1939–1945). NATO was the principal expression of the American policy of containment toward the Soviet Union, serving as a barrier to the westward spread of communism. Its importance is reflected by the fact that in joining NATO, the United States committed itself to a permanent military alliance for the first time, reversing 150 years of American beliefs about itself and the world.

Historical alliances

American reluctance to join an alliance of other world powers dates back at least to the farewell address of the first president, George Washington, in 1796. As commander of American forces in the Revolutionary War (1775–1783) Washington had relied on his French allies. However, when France went to war with Great Britain after the French Revolution of 1789, Washington refused to ally with either side. America's geographic isolation, the result of the wide ocean that separated the country from the warring states of Europe, provided its best defense. America should remain neutral whenever possible, Washington declared, and should avoid "entangling alliances" that might drag the country into a war halfway around the world. America's relative isolation and its fidelity to Washington's advice prevailed for the next hundred or so years. Although the United States engaged

in normal diplomatic relations with the other nations of the world, it stayed out of any formal alliances with European countries or with anyone else, for that matter.

In 1917 the United States entered World War I (1914–1918), which had already been raging for three years. It sided with France and Britain against Germany, in part out of sympathy with the French and British, although some Americans saw the war as a conflict in which they had no stake. President Woodrow Wilson (1913–1921), however, saw an opportunity to bring an end to war. He pushed for the creation of the League of Nations, an international organization dedicated to

peaceful resolution of diplomatic crises. In the aftermath of the shattering conflict, however, most Americans were more interested in returning to "normalcy" than in committing the United States to a greater role in world affairs. Wilson's refusal to compromise with Senate Republicans led to the peace treaty, and thus membership in the League of Nations, being rejected by his own country.

American neutrality lasted again until the end of the 1930s. In December 1941 the Japanese attack on Pearl Harbor brought the United States into World War II (1939–1945). Once more America belatedly joined a wartime alliance with the democracies

---

NATO AND WARSAW PACT MEMBERS IN THE 1950s

NATO (formed in 1949)	WARSAW PACT (formed in 1955)
United States	Soviet Union
United Kingdom	East Germany (GDR)
Canada	Romania
France	Bulgaria
Italy	Czechoslovakia
Belgium	Hungary
The Netherlands	Poland
Luxembourg	Albania (left in 1968)
Denmark	
Norway	
Portugal	
Iceland	
Greece (joined 1952)	
Turkey (joined 1952)	
West Germany (FRG) (joined 1955)	

of Britain and France, but this alliance also included the Communist Soviet Union. With the defeat of Japan and Germany in 1945 the United States began to repeat the pattern of rapid disengagement of 1918: Almost immediately after the end of the fighting U.S. troops started to arrive home. The United States, Britain, and the Soviet Union had agreed at the Yalta Conference in early 1945 to divide a defeated Germany into zones of

occupation. Relatively modest U.S. forces were to remain in Europe on occupation duty in the sectors assigned to the United States at Yalta.

A new approach

There were, however, two very significant differences between the late 1940s and the late 1910s. First, the United States had agreed to join the new United Nations (UN), the successor to the League of Nations. The

President Harry S. Truman (seated, center) discusses plans with the Joint Chiefs of Staff in 1950; in September Truman announced the creation of a standing army in Europe.

UN included provisions for "collective security"—the idea that UN members as a group would come to the aid of any one member that was attacked. The UN Charter also pledged all member nations to peaceful resolution of potential conflicts.

Of even greater importance to the United States' turning its back on isolationism was the persistence of a major threat to its interests. The new threat came from America's wartime ally, the Soviet Union. By the terms of a series of negotiations and agreements that culminated in the Yalta accords, the Soviets occupied the eastern third of Germany and effectively took control of most of the countries of Eastern Europe. However, many observers in the United States and Western Europe feared that Soviet dictator Joseph Stalin (1879–1953) would not settle for the half of Europe

Watched by leading senators including Arthur Vandenberg (right), Leslie Biffle, secretary of the Senate, signs the resolution ratifying U.S. membership of NATO on July 21, 1949.

Secretary of State Dean Acheson signs the North Atlantic Treaty on behalf of the United States in Washington, D.C., on April 4, 1949. President Truman (center) watches him.

he already controlled. The Soviets actively supported Communist parties in France and Italy, which had the potential to win elections or, failing that, to turn to violence. Meanwhile, the Soviet Red Army kept forces in eastern Germany—despite a postwar reduction in troop numbers—which could conceivably march on their former allies at almost any time.

One of the many Westerners to note the threat from the Soviet Union was U.S. diplomat George Kennan (1904–2005), who in 1946 wrote a long analysis of Soviet intentions. Kennan's analysis helped inspire a new foreign policy known as "containment." The Soviets were eager to expand their control, Kennan argued, supported by communism's ideological commitment to a "world revolution." The United States therefore had a vital interest in halting the spread of communism, which it could only accomplish by actively engaging in world affairs and by forming an enduring group of noncommunist allies.

A year after Kennan's analysis President Harry S. Truman (1945–1953) took a major step toward "containment." In the eastern Mediterranean Greece and Turkey faced Communist uprisings and possible invasion from Communist neighbors. Britain had been funneling military aid to both countries for years; but with British resources stretched to their limits after World War II, Truman agreed that the United States should assume the burden. In March 1947 the president announced what came to be called the Truman Doctrine: "I believe that it must be the policy of the United States to support free peoples who are resisting attempted subjugation by armed minorities or by outside pressures." To back up his words, Truman secured $400 million in aid for the embattled Greeks and Turks.

There were other signs to support Kennan's view of Soviet expansionist ambitions. In February 1948 a Communist coup overthrew Edvard Benes (1884–1948), the noncommunist president of Czechoslovakia, who had resisted the Soviet domination of his country under the Yalta accords. The Soviets also presented the democratic government of Norway with an ultimatum: Sign a treaty of mutual security and cooperation with the Soviet Union, or take the consequences.

In response to such Soviet moves, in March 1948 five of the Western Allies of World War II—Britain, France, Belgium, the Netherlands, and Luxembourg—signed the Brussels Pact, a mutual-defense agreement aimed at deterring a possible Soviet attack. Field Marshal Bernard Montgomery (1887–1976), Britain's senior wartime general, was placed in overall command of all the Brussels Pact forces.

In many ways the creation of the Brussels Pact was aimed as much at the United States as at the Soviet Union. It was an attempt to earn U.S. support by convincing the Americans that the Western Europeans were prepared to help resist a Soviet invasion rather than simply rely on the United States. The pact created a new, polarized vision of Europe that offered the United States a stark choice between a league of noncommunist democracies (and old friends of the United States) on the one hand and the Communist dictatorships on the other.

Truman's reaction to the Brussels Pact was positive. He also had the unlikely support of Senator Arthur Vandenberg (1884–1951), a conservative Republican from Michigan and the chairman of the Senate Foreign Relations Committee. Vandenberg had long been a believer in neutrality, but the nature of the Soviet threat to Western Europe convinced him to agree with Truman's call for a new European–American alliance. The so-called Vandenberg Resolution of June 1948, which contained an outline for the new alliance, passed the U.S. Senate by the huge margin of 64 votes to 4.

Signing the treaty

The Vandenberg Resolution served as the basis for the North Atlantic Treaty, the document that would formally create the alliance. The United States, Canada, and 10 Western European countries—including all the members of the Brussels Pact—signed the treaty in Washington, D.C., on April 4, 1949 (*see box on p. 147*).

One of the main concerns of the treaty was mutual defense. In Article 5

THE FULDA GAP

There is little evidence of any Soviet desire or serious intention to capture Western Europe in the 1950s; for much of the Cold War the Soviets did not have the capability to do so even if they wanted to. That did not prevent U.S. planners from devising a number of scenarios in which such an attack might take place. In their view the most critical sector on NATO's defensive front line was the so-called Fulda Gap on the southern border between East and West Germany. Behind the border towns of Erfurt, Eisenach, Fulda, and Bad Hersfeld lay the great city of Frankfurt, the commercial and communications hub of West Germany. Shortly beyond Frankfurt lay the Rhine River, the last geographical barrier at which NATO forces could hope to halt a Soviet invasion of Western Europe. If NATO lost Frankfurt and the Rhine, it would lose the war.

When U.S. forces moved to Germany, defense of the Fulda Gap fell to the U.S. Army's VII Corps. Facing it in East Germany was the Soviet Eighth Guards Army, eight divisions (100,000 men) strong. Any imagined ground invasion by the Warsaw Pact would likely begin with an all-out assault on the Fulda Gap. The American 2nd and 14th Armored Cavalry Regiments would then engage in a fighting retreat until the three U.S. divisions of the VII Corps and the allied divisions of the West German Bundeswehr could concentrate to defend Frankfurt.

Even when the main force assembled, however, NATO troops would be badly outnumbered. The Soviets might also use chemical weapons, and by the mid-1950s they had battlefield nuclear weapons at their disposal. Despite the NATO buildup of the 1950s, the odds were still with the Soviets.

The battle scenarios called for the fall of Frankfurt or a crossing of the Rhine to trigger NATO use of nuclear weapons. Even a limited use of nuclear weapons, however, might cause the Soviets to retaliate with nuclear strikes against the cities of the United States and Europe. The somewhat hysterical wargames played out by NATO commanders in the 1950s led to one chilling conclusion: A battle that began in the Fulda Gap would likely end with the nuclear annihilation of much of life on Earth.

---

the member countries agreed "that an armed attack against one or more of them in Europe or North America shall be considered an attack against them all." Article 3, meanwhile, pledged that "the Parties separately and jointly, by means of continuous and effective self-help and mutual aid, will maintain and develop their individual and collective capacity to resist armed attack." Although the article required that each member of the treaty be strong enough to aid in its own defense, it also implied that the alliance might develop a unified command in which each country might specialize in particular areas of need.

For some observers the various possible interpretations of Article 3 left questions about what form the U.S. contribution to the alliance would take. It could range from a simple promise to supply air and naval units and weapons to the need to station a large American army in Europe on a permanent basis.

The supply of weapons began almost immediately; the United States sent almost $1 billion in weaponry to its NATO allies in 1950 alone. Even more

U.S. troops stationed in Europe famously included rock-'n'-roll star Elvis Presley, drafted in 1958 for a two-year tour of duty in Germany, where he served as a jeep driver.

economic assistance poured in through the Marshall Plan, America's ambitious attempt to rebuild the economies of Western Europe after World War II. But a substantial ground force would take time to build up and would be very controversial at home.

The question of Germany

Another question left open by the North Atlantic Treaty was the role of western Germany, the part of former Nazi Germany that was occupied by Britain, France, and the United States at the end of the war. The country's economy was being slowly rebuilt and its population politically reeducated in the hopes that when the occupation ended, Germany would emerge as a stable democracy. A democratic Germany might prove an important source of manpower for the NATO alliance. In any case, any ground invasion by the Soviets would likely

FRANCE: NATO'S INCONSTANT CORNERSTONE

France played an important role in the planning and creation of NATO; it was a member of the Brussels Pact and a charter member of the NATO alliance, to which it signed up in 1949, although it entered largely as a tradeoff in order to gain U.S. support for its recovery of its colonies in Southeast Asia. France was expected to provide a large proportion of NATO's manpower in Europe, and the alliance itself would be headquartered in Paris.

Almost from the beginning, however, the French worried about their role in NATO and the role of the Americans. France needed the Americans in NATO to give the alliance the strength to stand up to the Soviet Union. At the same time, France wanted to take the leadership role in Western Europe that the Americans had reluctantly assumed.

While France fought colonial wars in Southeast Asia and North Africa throughout the 1950s, it remained a committed member of the NATO alliance. In the 1960s that changed. France withdrew from Asia and North Africa, and turned to building up its European-based forces. Beginning in 1964, French President Charles de Gaulle (1890–1970) pursued the development of a powerful and independent arsenal of nuclear weapons, missiles, and submarines known as the *force de frappe* (strike force).

In 1966 de Gaulle shocked the Western alliance by withdrawing from NATO military operations entirely. He declared that France would defend itself with the *force de frappe*; it would target its weapons *"tous azimuths"*—in all directions—meaning that they would point at Moscow and Washington alike. At the same time that de Gaulle declared his independent foreign policy, he also sought to build up the old Western European Union established by the Brussels Pact, in which France would play the dominant role, as an alternative to NATO.

The remaining members of NATO, however, did not rush to replace American supremacy with French dominance. The alliance continued as before, albeit one member short and with headquarters moved to Brussels in Belgium instead of Paris. For its part France strongly hinted that should the Soviets invade Western Europe, French forces would assist their old NATO allies in resisting. The troops simply would not be under unified NATO command.

After decades of standing outside of NATO, France decided to rejoin at a time when the alliance seemed least in need of its help. In 1993, two years after the collapse of the Soviet Union, France reclaimed full membership in NATO, although it still maintains the *force de frappe*.

French President Charles de Gaulle (left) rides with German Chancellor Konrad Adenauer during Adenauer's 1962 visit to France to cement Franco-German friendship.

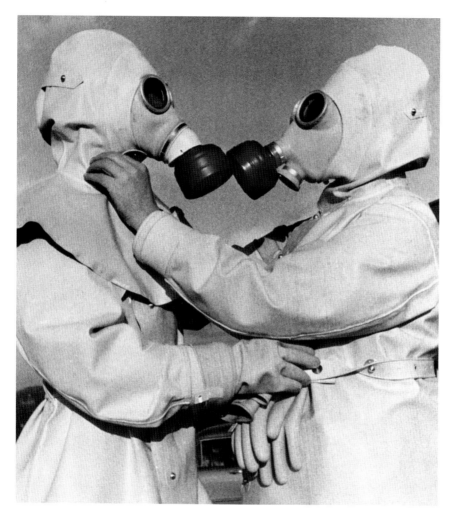

Air-raid wardens demonstrate antiradiation suits in Bonn, West Germany, in 1955. Germany's cities seemed likely to bear the brunt of any Soviet attack on Europe.

strike western Germany first; the United States had considered rearming its defeated enemy in case of a Soviet invasion only a month after the end of the war. Now it seemed clear that bringing Germany into NATO would better allow the alliance to defend its front line.

France, however, had bitter objections to Germany's rearmament and to its membership in NATO. German armies had invaded France in both world wars; France wanted its neighbor to remain weak. French Foreign Minister Robert Schuman (1886–1963), an architect of NATO and the Brussels Pact, promised the French National Assembly: "Germany has no army and should not have one. It has no arms and will not have any.... [It should not] be allowed to adhere to the Atlantic Pact as a nation capable of defending itself or of aiding in the defense of others."

Rather than admit western Germany to NATO, the French proposed instead to form a European Defense Community (EDC), which would create an integrated European army in place of separate national armies. German units could be incorporated into the pan-European army as long as they were safely under other command.

The start of the Korean War (1950–1953) in June 1950 helped break the impasse over the contributions to NATO of both the Americans and the Germans. In the United States the military buildup necessitated by the conflict gave Truman both the political support and the resources to propose a permanent American army for Europe. In September 1950 he committed a large U.S. contingent to the Federal Republic of Germany (as the former Allied-occupied areas had become in May 1949) under a unified NATO command. The fact that such a large

force of U.S. troops would be based in West Germany, under command from NATO headquarters in Paris, in turn helped calm French anxiety over the strength of a rearmed Germany. Planning began in earnest for West Germany's eventual entry into NATO.

Truman's plan was met by conservative antagonism at home, but much opposition was overcome by his nomination of World War II Allied Supreme Commander Dwight D. Eisenhower (1890–1969) as the first NATO Supreme Allied Commander Europe (SACEUR). Although some conservative Republicans still argued for a lesser commitment to NATO, Eisenhower's appointment helped cement America's prominence in the alliance. U.S. leadership of NATO reassured Americans that they would not be dragged into a war by choices made by someone else.

Strengthening the defenses

At a 1952 NATO conference in Lisbon, Portugal, members pronounced an ambitious plan to build up a large permanent army capable of resisting the Soviets. The plan included the French proposal for a European Defense Community (EDC), but the EDC was eventually rejected because of lingering concerns over what role West Germany would take in it. In the same year NATO formally accepted its first new members: Greece and Turkey, longtime rivals that were united by their opposition to Soviet expansion. A new regional command for southeastern Europe, based in Izmir, Turkey, was added to NATO's structure, which already included regional command centers for northern Europe, Central Europe, southern Europe, the Mediterranean, and the North Atlantic.

However, the military buildup proposed by the Lisbon plan was dwarfed by the Soviet forces already in Eastern Europe. Even as the new U.S. forces arrived in Germany, NATO was hopelessly outnumbered on the ground.

In the early 1950s NATO deployed only around 15 divisions (of around 15,000 men each) in West Germany and France, while the Soviets had perhaps as many as 22 divisions in East Germany (the German Democratic Republic) alone, with more divisions and hundreds of warplanes stationed just inside the Russian border. Field Marshal Montgomery warned: "As things stand today and in the foreseeable future, there would be scenes of appalling and indescribable confusion in Western Europe if we were ever attacked by the Russians." One U.S. staff officer was even more succinct: When asked what the Soviets would need in order to march their huge army through NATO territory all the way to Paris and beyond, he simply replied, "Shoes."

The recognition of the poor state of NATO forces had several consequences. One was to accelerate the military buildup already underway: Between 1949 and 1953 virtually every NATO member dramatically increased its defense expenditures. British defense spending doubled, while U.S. defense spending increased by 400 percent, Canada's by 600 percent, France's and Belgium's by 300 percent each, and the Dutch by 200 percent. Another development was closer cooperation among the NATO countries in their military planning. A series of large-scale military exercises, or "wargames," held across Western Europe in 1953 included multiple NATO members practicing fighting side by side. By the end of the year, in the words of defense scholar Roger Hilsman, "NATO had been transformed from a traditional alliance, implying little more than a commitment to stand together, into an integrated coalition army."

West Germany joins NATO

NATO's continuing military inferiority in Europe was also key in facilitating the eventual entry of West Germany into the alliance. In 1955 West Germany gained full sovereignty over its foreign relations when the occupation statute drawn up by the U.S., British, and French governments in 1949 expired, and it joined NATO.

The decision to join the alliance was not without risk. In 1954 a wargame known as Carte Blanche had simulated a Soviet invasion of West Germany that could be stopped only if NATO used nuclear weapons. The scenario estimated that such a battle would leave five million West German civilians dead or irradiated. Even the father of containment, George Kennan, suggested that perhaps Germany might be more secure as neutral territory.

However, West German Chancellor Konrad Adenauer (1876–1967) believed that a democratic West Germany could only survive through close ties to its new allies in Western Europe. Adenauer pledged to build up a new army, the Bundeswehr, and also made West Germany a formal member of both the Brussels Pact and the new European Coal and Steel Community (ECSC; the precursor of the European Common Market and the European Union). Although German soldiers would now play an essential role in protecting Western Europe, membership in such organizations acted as safeguards to prevent the German army from being used again against its Western neighbors.

The Warsaw Pact

West Germany's entry into NATO caused great anxiety in the West. Some observers believed that it would trigger

NATO ABSORBS THE WARSAW PACT

The fall of the Berlin Wall in 1989 signified the collapse of the Soviet puppet governments not just in East Germany but throughout Eastern Europe. One by one the Communist regimes in Hungary, Poland, Czechoslovakia, Romania, Bulgaria, and Albania collapsed. The formerly Communist East Germany was reunited with democratic West Germany. In most of those countries both communism and domination by the Soviets were fiercely resented. As a result, the old Warsaw Pact alliance dissolved almost instantly. With the NATO–Warsaw Pact rivalry gone, a new opportunity arose for NATO to bring some of its old enemies into the alliance.

In January 1994 NATO created the "Partnership for Peace": The program was not a military alliance itself but rather an opportunity for former Warsaw Pact members to cooperate with NATO on specific issues. It was commonly understood, however, that the "PFP" program was a possible steppingstone to full NATO membership. Almost all of the former Soviet republics, including Russia itself, and the Eastern European members of the Warsaw Pact chose to join the partnership. After several years of the "PFP" NATO extended formal invitations to Poland, Hungary, and the Czech Republic to become full members of NATO; they joined the alliance in 1999. In 2002 another round of NATO expansion invited more new members: former Warsaw Pact members Bulgaria and Romania, the former Soviet republics of Estonia, Latvia, and Lithuania, and Slovakia and the former Yugoslav republic of Slovenia. They joined in 2004.

At the same time that NATO's membership expanded dramatically, its mission also changed dramatically. No longer is the principal mandate of the alliance to deter Soviet aggression, nor is it principally aimed at Russia, the largest of the former Soviet republics. NATO remains a treaty of mutual defense but has somewhat less sense than before of what the alliance is defending against.

THE NEUTRALS: SWITZERLAND, SWEDEN, AND SPAIN

Of all the nations of Europe only three remained neutral during both world wars: Switzerland, Sweden, and Spain. In the Cold War contest between NATO and the Warsaw Pact all three nations initially again tried to remain neutral. Being neutral, however, was not the same as being "pacifist" or "unarmed." Although each country hoped to avoid war, each in its own way came to the conclusion that the best way to remain at peace was to be ready for war.

The Swiss had the oldest system of armed neutrality: From the country's birth in 1291 as a confederation of small regions called cantons, every male resident had been expected to be part of an armed militia. From their late teens to their early forties Swiss militiamen had to keep their military rifle at home, ready at all times to mobilize to repel an invasion. The Swiss hoped that the combination of a well-armed populace and the natural defense created by the Alps mountains would deter any likely invader. During World War II the perception of Switzerland as an armed camp may indeed have had the effect of making the country a less attractive target for the Nazis. At the same time, however, the Swiss government bent with the prevailing winds: Early in the conflict it cooperated subtly with the Nazis; when the war turned against the Nazis, the Swiss made themselves subtly useful to the Allies.

In the same way Sweden preserved its neutrality during World War II through a military buildup. Instead of a militia system, however, the Swedes relied on their own fast-growing arms industry, led by the aircraft maker Saab. The Swedes took measures to protect their territory from German attack, but at the same time, they continued to trade extensively with the Nazis during the war until a Nazi defeat seemed certain.

The fascist dictator of Spain, Francisco Franco (1892–1975), came to power in the Spanish Civil War in the late 1930s thanks in part to military assistance from Hitler's Germany. During World War II Hitler repeatedly asked Franco to enter the war on the side of the Nazis and their allies. But Franco drove a hard bargain; ultimately the price of Spanish entry into the war was higher than Hitler would pay, and Spain stayed "neutral."

The path of "neutrality" was similarly varied during the Cold War. Switzerland refused to participate in any international political organizations, rejecting involvement not only in NATO but also in the United Nations (UN). Sweden, meanwhile, was an enthusiastic member of the UN, and advanced Swedish jet fighters took part in a UN intervention in the civil war in the Congo in the late 1950s. The Franco regime in Spain, meanwhile, had no love for the democracies of NATO but was even more fiercely opposed to Soviet communism.

Following Franco's death, Spain reemerged as a democracy and, despite domestic opposition, joined NATO in 1982. The early 1980s also brought Sweden closer to NATO, when Soviet submarines violated Swedish territorial waters and drew intervention from the Swedish air force and navy. After that crisis Sweden was effectively in the Western camp for the remainder of the Cold War, although it never formally abandoned "neutrality" or applied to join NATO.

Spain's General Franco demonstrates the 2,500-mile (4,000-km) distance between Spain and Moscow on a giant globe.

Workers run from a Soviet tank in East Berlin during demonstrations in June 1953. NATO made no effort to interfere to prevent Soviet intimidation of Eastern European nations.

an immediate Soviet invasion, arguing that the Soviets had as much reason to fear German rearmament as the French. Instead, the Soviet reaction was to establish its own version of NATO. In May 1955 the Soviet Union and the countries it dominated in Eastern Europe—including East Germany— signed the Warsaw Pact, a mutual-defense treaty that on the surface closely resembled NATO (*see box on p. 147*). Large Soviet ground and air forces would continue to be stationed in East Germany, often directly facing U.S. forces across the border, and the armed forces of countries such as Poland, Hungary, and Czechoslovakia would collaborate with Soviet forces.

The NATO countries outnumbered the Warsaw Pact countries in terms of total population. Despite this, however, the commitment by the Soviet Union

The opening of the 16th session of the NATO Ministerial Council on May 9, 1955, marked the formal admission of West Germany, represented by Chancellor Konrad Adenauer.

Hungarians place a national flag into the empty boot of a statue of Joseph Stalin pulled down by rioters in October 1956. Soviet troops crushed the uprising against Communist rule.

desire to intervene in the affairs of Warsaw Pact members, which had more reason to be wary of interference from the Soviet Union.

A fragile truce

By the late 1950s the opposing NATO and Warsaw Pact alliances had reached something of a fragile truce. No formal hostilities ever broke out, although both were ready to fight on a moment's notice. NATO's weakness on the ground, however, was never fully resolved. If full-scale war broke out in Europe, any likely scenario would have involved NATO use of nuclear weapons in order to stop a Warsaw Pact advance. Even U.S. Army Chief of Staff Maxwell Taylor accepted that the best NATO ground units could achieve was to act as a short-term delaying force while a strategic nuclear bombing campaign was launched against Soviet targets.

The imbalance remained long after the 1950s. Eventually, however, the balance was tipped in NATO's favor by its economic rather than military strength. The economic conditions of the Warsaw Pact members deteriorated in the 1970s and 1980s. The Soviet Union, beset by political and economic problems, lost the will to preserve the Communist regimes of Eastern Europe, which collapsed in the fall of 1989. The Warsaw Pact died along with the puppet governments (*see box on p. 153*). The Soviet Union itself dissolved in 1991, breaking into Russia and a host of smaller nations. Although the threat of Soviet communism is now a distant memory, NATO itself remains intact, more than 50 years after its creation.

to sustain a massive standing army, and its willingness also to impose that condition on its Eastern European satellites, meant that at any given moment the Warsaw Pact's forces were numerically superior to NATO. However, defense experts believed that NATO forces had somewhat better equipment and technology, while the NATO countries were far wealthier than their pact counterparts. Both those advantages increased over time.

Whatever their similarities, NATO and the Warsaw Pact were very different organizations. NATO was a genuinely cooperative and voluntary effort: No country was coerced into joining, and each member believed that it benefited from the alliance. With the exception of Greece and Turkey, NATO members had stable democratic governments and populations that enjoyed ever increasing prosperity and social rights.

The Warsaw Pact, by contrast, enjoyed little support among the people of Eastern Europe. The governments of all the Warsaw Pact members, save that of the Soviet Union itself, had all been imposed by the Soviets in the wake of World War II. Although the puppet governments joined the pact, the Polish, Hungarian, and Czech populations in particular were opposed to the pact, as they were to the regimes that governed them.

Although ostensibly created to resist a ground invasion by NATO, the Warsaw Pact's real significance lay in the aid it gave to the Soviets in preserving the unpopular regimes they had installed in Eastern Europe. The Soviets cited the terms of the pact as justification to crush anti-Soviet uprisings in Hungary in 1956 and Czechoslovakia in 1968.

Meanwhile, NATO's failure to oppose the Soviet crackdowns reflected both the relative weakness of the alliance on the ground and its defensive nature. NATO had neither a plan nor a

See Also:

Berlin • Cold War • Domino Theory • European Common Market • Foreign Policy • France • Germany • International Aid • Korean War • Soviet Union • United Nations

NUCLEAR POWER PROGRAM

During the 1950s nuclear power—a spinoff from the development of the atomic bomb during World War II—held out the promise of clean and cheap energy. Early optimism about the new technology, however, was balanced by its negative associations with the bomb.

On December 2, 1942, Italian-born American physicist Enrico Fermi (1901–1954) set off the first controlled nuclear chain reaction. Fermi's discovery marked the beginning of the atomic age and culminated in the development of atomic weapons and the subsequent evolution of a nuclear power program.

On August 1, 1946, almost exactly one year after atomic bombs were detonated over Hiroshima and Nagasaki in Japan, President Harry S. Truman (1945–1953) signed into law the Atomic Energy Act. The act established a federal civilian agency, the Atomic Energy Commission (AEC), to supervise the development of nuclear technology in the United States. The commission took over from the Manhattan Engineer District of the U.S. Army Corps of Engineers, which had developed the atomic bomb during World War II (1939–1945). As well as assuming responsibility for nuclear weapons, the AEC took over the development of commercial uses for nuclear energy. David E. Lilienthal (1899–1981), former head of the Tennessee Valley Authority, was appointed the first chairman of the new organization.

During the 1950s most physicists predicted that the cost of nuclear energy would eventually become cheaper than traditional fossil fuels such as coal and oil. Truman summed up the mood of optimism in his State of the Union Address of 1950: "In the peaceful development of atomic energy … we stand on the threshold of new wonders. The first experimental machines for producing useful power from atomic energy are now under construction. We have made only the first beginnings in this field, but in the perspective of history they may loom larger than the first airplane, or even the first tools that started man on the road to civilization."

Practical development

The first moves toward nuclear power generation were taken on December 20, 1951, when the Experimental Breeder Reactor I (EBR I) produced enough power to illuminate four 150-watt lightbulbs. The EBR I was built at the National Reactor Testing Station near Idaho Falls, Idaho, by the University of Chicago's Argonne National Laboratory—the laboratory where Fermi had made his groundbreaking discovery nine years earlier.

In the eyes of the American public, however—and of many others around the world—so soon after the end of World War II the word "nuclear" remained a negative one, inextricably associated with the destructive power of the atomic bomb. As a result, the U.S. government took steps to distance the new technology from the negative associations. On December 8, 1953, President Dwight D. Eisenhower (1953–1961) delivered an address—the so-called "Atoms for Peace" speech—before the General Assembly of the United Nations in which he called for international cooperation in the development of atomic energy for peaceful purposes.

Two years later the Argonne National Laboratory was again instrumental

Chairman of the Atomic Energy Commission Lewis L. Strauss (right) and Congressman Clinton Anderson study a photograph of the atomic energy plant under construction at Shippingport, Pennsylvania, in May 1956.

PROJECT PLOWSHARE

The high hopes for future applications of nuclear power included far more than electricity generation. In 1958 Hungarian-born American physicist and director of the Lawrence Livermore National Laboratory Edward Teller (1908–2003) announced Project Plowshare at the Second International Conference on the Peaceful Uses of Atomic Energy, held in Geneva, Switzerland. Project Plowshare aimed to develop nuclear explosives for use in the mining and heavy construction industries. A series of 35 tests were carried out at sites in Nevada between 1961 and 1973 before the plan was abandoned. The power unleashed by the explosives was huge. The second test, dubbed Project Sedan and carried out on July 6, 1962, produced a crater more than 1,200 feet (365m) in diameter and 320 feet (97m) deep and displaced 12 million tons (11 million tonnes) of earth.

in the design of the first reactor to power an entire town. On July 17, 1955, Arco, Idaho, a community of about 1,350 people, started receiving electricity from the experimental boiling-water reactor BORAX III. Earlier that year the AEC had announced the launch of the Power Demonstration Reactor Program. Based on a 1954 amendment to the Atomic Energy Act, the new program allowed for commercial investment in nuclear energy.

Technicians monitor activity in the reactor in the control room of the experimental boiling-water reactor BORAX III near Arco, Idaho, in 1955.

Private enterprise

Speaking at the first United Nations International Conference on the Peaceful Uses of Atomic Energy in Geneva, Switzerland, in 1955, Lewis L. Strauss (1896–1974), the chairman of the AEC, urged the commercial development of nuclear power. The first large-scale commercial nuclear power reactor in the United States began operations at Shippingport, Pennsylvania, on December 2, 1957. The 60-megawatt reactor plant was designed by the electric power company Westinghouse, built by the Duquesne Light Company, and jointly operated by the AEC. It remained in operation until 1982.

The Shippingport plant was the first American commercial reactor to be licensed by the AEC, but private industries remained reluctant to sign up for the expensive new technology. No more plants were ordered despite the AEC's encouragement and research until finally, in 1959, the first nuclear plant constructed entirely as a private commercial enterprise was built by Commonwealth Edison in Morris, Illinois. Built at a cost of $18 million, the plant, known as Dresden Unit 1, was modeled on the BORAX III experimental reactor. Dresden Unit 1 was a 200-megawatt, dual-cycle boiling-water reactor. It opened in 1960 and operated until 1979.

Unfulfilled promise

More nuclear power plants were built throughout the 1960s and 1970s, increasing steadily in size and power. However, the nuclear power program proved to be much more expensive than the optimistic early predictions had suggested; reactors cost huge amounts to build. A series of accidents—the first major fatal incident was at Idaho Falls on March 14, 1961—also raised fears about the safety of nuclear reactors. As a result of these two factors, no reactor has been commissioned in the United States since 1978.

See Also:

Economy • Environment • Los Alamos • Oppenheimer, J. Robert • Science and Technology • Teller, Edward

FLANNERY O'CONNOR 1925–1964

Despite her short life and relatively small output, Flannery O'Connor enjoys a reputation as one of the most talented writers to give authentic expression to the American South. Her vivid storytelling, strange characters, and distinctive voice continue to win admiration.

Mary Flannery O'Connor was born on March 25, 1925, in Savannah, Georgia, the only child of Regina Cline and Edward Francis O'Connor, a real estate agent. The family moved to Atlanta in 1938 and from there to the Cline family home in Milledgeville, Georgia. O'Connor's father died in 1941. O'Connor herself inherited the same autoimmune blood disease that killed him, lupus erythematosus; it disabled her for over a decade and eventually killed her too.

Unlike comparatively cosmopolitan Savannah, Milledgeville was a staunchly Protestant town. For O'Connor, a devout Catholic of Irish extraction, the tension between the Protestant community and her own faith helped shape both her subject matter—the relationship between people and God—and her highly individual fictional landscape, a "Christ-haunted" place of unsophisticated preachers, mad prophets, and drunk visionaries.

Education of a writer

After studying at Peabody High School in Milledgeville, O'Connor graduated from Georgia State College for Women in 1945. She then enrolled at the prestigious Writers' Workshop of the University of Iowa, where she initially majored in journalism rather than creative writing and earned a fine arts degree in 1947.

However, by 1945 O'Connor was already thinking of a writing career. She asked permission from her mother to drop the name Mary and call herself Flannery O'Connor for publication purposes. She published her first short story in the journal *Accent* in 1946. The following year the collection of short stories she prepared for her degree

Taken in the 1950s, this photograph of Flannery O'Connor shows the author with the crutches she needed as a result of her medical condition.

thesis won the Rinehart-Iowa Fiction Award; in addition to a grant of $750 the award gave Rinehart the option to publish O'Connor's first novel.

For the next five years O'Connor concentrated on her writing away from Georgia, including a period at Yaddo, an invitation-only artist colony in upstate New York. In December 1950, however, she was forced to return to Georgia when lupus struck her. As her health started to deteriorate, she and her mother moved to Andalusia, a farm outside Milledgeville, where her illness forced her into a sedentary life. She wrote for two to three hours a day and then read, lunched with her mother, and tended her flock of peafowl.

When O'Connor submitted the first section of her novel to Rinehart, however, the publisher was dismayed by its unconventional approach. Instead, the book, *Wise Blood*, was published in 1952 by Harcourt, Brace. The novel's protagonist, Hazel Motes, whom Flannery described as a Christian despite himself, baffled the critics. Their response was to miss the novel's humor and depth, instead attacking its absurd and grotesque imagery.

Finding novel writing increasingly difficult, O'Connor concentrated on short stories. Between the fall of 1952 and mid-1955 she enjoyed her most productive period. The resulting stories were published in 1955 as *A Good Man Is Hard to Find*. The collection won O'Connor many admirers and established her reputation as a short-story writer rather than a novelist. Three of her stories won the prestigious O. Henry Awards, and her work regularly appeared in the annual collection of *Best American Short Stories*.

When her declining health allowed, O'Connor continued to travel, making a trip to Europe in 1958. She lectured at colleges across the United States. Her second novel, *The Violent Bear It Away*, was published in 1960.

Since her death on August 3, 1964, O'Connor's stature has grown dramatically, helped by the inclusion of previously unpublished works in *The Complete Stories* (1971). Despite her small output—two novels, 31 short stories, and various essays—she is now considered one of the finest writers the South has produced.

See Also:

Literature

OLYMPIC GAMES

The Olympic Games held during the 1950s witnessed the arrival of the formidable athletes from the Soviet Union, who presented a challenge beyond most nations' abilities. Also during the decade, there were politically inspired boycotts by various countries.

The United States topped the medal table at every Olympic Summer Games from 1912 to 1952, with the exception of the Berlin Games of 1936, when Germany took the top spot.

The big story of the 1952 games, held in Helsinki, Finland, was the presence for the first time of athletes from the Soviet Union. This was followed by their first appearance at the 1956 Winter Games in Cortina d'Ampezzo, Italy.

In 1952 the United States managed to hold on to the top spot. But four years later it was toppled from its perch by the Soviet Union; 1956 was also the year in which Germany returned to the Summer Games after not receiving an invitation for the 1948 London Games and competing as West Germany in 1952. The International Olympic Committee, which at the time was presided over by the U.S. athlete and businessman Avery Brundage, ignored Cold War antagonisms and forced West Germany and East Germany to enter a combined team, a format that was also presented at the 1960 and 1964 games.

Melbourne hosted the 1956 Summer Olympics, the first city from the Southern Hemisphere to do so. For the first time, also, international politics had a direct influence on the sporting events. Egypt, Iraq, and Lebanon boycotted the games in protest against the military action by Israel, France, and Britain following the nationalization of the Suez Canal Company by the Egyptian President Gamal Abdel Nasser.

Spain, the Netherlands, and Switzerland also withdrew from the games in protest against the Soviet crushing of the Hungarian uprising of November 1956. (The Swiss public was so outraged by the decision that its government recanted, but by then it was so late in the day that many Swiss competitors did not make it to Australia in time.)

As a mark of its indignation at the continued recognition by the West of the Nationalist government in exile on Formosa (Taiwan), Communist China also withdrew from the 1956 Olympics; it did not take part in the games again until 1984, in Los Angeles.

Sporting spectacle

By present-day standards in the 1950s the Olympic Summer Games were still on a small scale, with 149 events in 1952 and 145 in 1956—much larger than the 43 events at the first modern games held in Athens in 1896 but dwarfed by the 301 events at the 2004 Athens Games.

In all, 69 nations, represented by 4,955 athletes, competed in Helsinki, a jump of 10 from the 1948 London Games. Four years later the number of nations rose to 72, but the long journey from most of the leading nations to Australia meant that the roll of competitors fell to 3,314.

Another bizarre consequence of the choice of Melbourne as the Olympic city was that owing to Australia's strict quarantine regulations, the 1956 equestrian events were held separately in Stockholm, Sweden, far away from the rest of the games.

Robert Mathias (right), winner of the gold medal in the decathlon at the 1952 Helsinki Games, wins the 110m hurdles, beating the British athlete Geoffrey Elliott.

NATIONAL RANKING TABLES

The Soviet Union—or Union of Soviet Socialist Republics (USSR)—entered the Olympic arena in 1952. It dislodged the United States from its habitual place at the top of the summer rankings in 1956. The USSR did not enter the Winter Olympics until the 1956 games in Cortina d'Ampezzo, Italy, where it immediately topped the tables.

SUMMER

1952	G	S	B
USA	40	19	17
USSR	22	30	19
HUNGARY	16	10	16
SWEDEN	12	13	10
ITALY	8	9	4
CZECHOSLOVAKIA	7	3	3
FRANCE	6	6	6
FINLAND	6	3	13
AUSTRALIA	6	2	3
NORWAY	3	2	0

1956	G	S	B
USSR	37	29	32
USA	32	25	17
AUSTRALIA	13	8	14
HUNGARY	9	10	7
ITALY	8	8	9
SWEDEN	8	5	6
GERMANY	6	13	7
GREAT BRITAIN	6	7	11
ROMANIA	5	3	5
JAPAN	4	10	5

WINTER

	G	S	B
NORWAY	7	3	6
USA	4	6	1
FINLAND	3	4	2
AUSTRIA	2	4	2
GERMANY	3	2	2
CANADA	1	0	1
ITALY	1	0	1
GREAT BRITAIN	1	0	0
NETHERLANDS	0	3	0
SWEDEN	0	0	4

	G	S	B
USSR	7	3	6
AUSTRIA	4	3	4
FINLAND	3	3	1
SWITZERLAND	3	2	1
SWEDEN	2	4	4
USA	2	3	2
NORWAY	2	1	1
ITALY	1	2	0
GERMANY	1	0	1
CANADA	0	1	2

In the 1950s the games were a male-dominated spectacle. There were only 519 female competitors in Helsinki and 376 in Melbourne. The main reason was that there was no women's boxing, wrestling, or weightlifting, nor were there any rowing events for women. Another reason was the belief that women were too fragile to take part in certain events—for example, there were no track races for women at distances greater than 200m.

Helsinki 1952

On the Helsinki track the legendary Czech distance runner Emil Zatopek stole the show, winning the 5,000m, the 10,000m, and then, with only three days' rest, the marathon—all of them in record Olympic times. It was one of the greatest feats in the history of athletics.

In the short-distance events American men ruled the roost. Lindy Remigino won the 100m sprint, maintaining U.S. dominance of the event since 1932; the United States also won all three medals in the 200m sprint (Andrew Stanfield, Thane Baker, James Gathers) and, in a repeat of the 1948 performance, the 110m hurdles (Harrison Dillard, Jack Davis, Arthur Barnard). Americans also won gold in the 800m (Malvin Whitfield) and the 400m hurdles (Charles Moore). Horace Ashenfelter, who trained at night using park benches as hurdles, caused a major upset when he beat the world-record holder from the Soviet Union, Vladimir Kazantsev, in the 3,000m steeplechase. The American press quipped that for the first time an FBI agent had allowed himself to be followed by a Russian. It was only the second—and the last—U.S. victory in the event. America also won the 4x100m relay and came in second to Jamaica in the 4x400m relay.

American men shone in the field events, too. Walter Davis, stricken by polio at the age of eight and unable to walk for three years, won the high jump; Kenneth Wiesner took the silver medal.

High-jump record-breaker Mildred McDaniel was one of only two American female athletes to win a medal for a field event at the 1956 Olympics in Melbourne.

In the pool Patricia McCormick was the star of both Olympics, winning diving golds from both the springboard and the platform (where Paula Jean Myers and Juno Irwin took silver and bronze in 1952 and bronze and silver in 1956). Zoe Ann Olsen won a bronze in the springboard in Helsinki. Diving was also a successful event for the men in 1952. Sammy Lee, who in 1948 had become the first Asian American to win an Olympic gold, repeated his victory in the platform diving, while David Browning led an American sweep of the springboard medals (Miller Anderson and Robert Clotworthy took silver and bronze). Browning was arrested after his victory for shinnying up a flagpole and trying to steal an Olympic flag. U.S. female swimmers garnered only two bronzes, but the men won four golds (the 4x200m relay and individual wins for Clarke Scholes in the 100m freestyle, Ford Konno in the 1,500m freestyle, and Yoshinobu Oyakawa in the 100m backstroke).

Americans won four of the seven golds available in weightlifting and five of the 10 boxing divisions. Charlie Adkins won a split decision over Viktor Mednov in the light welterweight final, the first bout ever between an American and a Soviet prizefighter. Floyd Patterson, the future world heavyweight champion, breezed through the middleweight competition, and Edward Sanders won the superheavyweight gold when his opponent in the final, Sweden's Ingemar Johansson—another future world heavyweight champion—danced round the ring without throwing a single punch and was disqualified for "not giving of his best." Nathan Brooks won the flyweight gold and Norvel Lee the light heavyweight. Four Americans bagged medals in various categories of freestyle wrestling: Bill Smith (gold), Jay Evans and Henry Wittenberg (silver), and Josiah Henson (bronze). The U.S. team also won gold in basketball.

The United States also won gold and silver in the pole vault (Robert Richards, Donald Laz), the long jump (Jerome Biffle, Meredith Gourdine), and the javelin (Cyrus Young, William Miller). Robert Mathias retained the gold medal in the decathlon, where fellow Americans Milton Campbell and Floyd Simmons took silver and bronze. The shot put launched the international career of William Patrick "Parry" O'Brien, who revolutionized the sport by beginning with his back to the front of the throwing circle and gaining momentum by twisting as he moved forward for the put. In 1954 he became the first man to put the shot more than 60 feet (18.29m)—60 feet 5 inches (18.42m). Darrow Hooper and James Fuchs, who had won 88 consecutive meets before being beaten by O'Brien at the 1951 AAU (Amateur Athletic Union) Championships, won silver and bronze. In the discus the American gold-medalist Sim Iness bettered the previous Olympic record with each of his six final throws.

Varied successes

The performance of America's women competitors was less stellar. On the track they won no medals in either 1952 or 1956, although they managed to take gold in the 1952 4x100m relay and bronze in the same event in 1956.

The field events at both games were dominated by Soviet female athletes. Having failed to bring home a single medal from Helsinki, U.S. women competitors did slightly better in Melbourne. Mildred McDaniel won the high jump with a world-record jump of 5 feet 9¼ inches (1.76m), and Willye White, who would read the Bible between leaps, gained an unexpected silver medal in the long jump.

Other American medals won at Helsinki were in the canoe (one gold), rowing (two golds, one bronze), sailing (two golds, one silver), shooting (one gold, one bronze), and equestrian events (two bronzes). A crew from the U.S. Naval Academy won the rowing eights, while the winners of the coxless pairs were Charles Logg and Thomas Price. Neither had sat in a pair-oared shell until two months before the games, and 19-year-old Price had taken up rowing only in the previous January.

Melbourne 1956

The American public saw almost nothing of the 1952 games and little from Melbourne. Highlights from films flown back to the United States were shown on television, but live transmission did not begin until the 1960 Rome Games. The centerpiece of the 1956 games was the men's 1,500m, in which no American made it to the final. In 1954 the English runner Roger Bannister had become the first man to break the four-minute barrier for the mile. Later that year he retired, and in 1956 the favorite for the Olympic 1,500m gold was the Australian John Landy, who had broken Bannister's world record and compiled a series of sub-four-minute miles. The field included no fewer than six competitors who had run the mile under four minutes, but sadly for the expectant home fans, Landy finished a disappointing third. Just before the race Landy said to the young Ronald Delany of Ireland, "I think you can win this one, Ron," and Delany did.

Elsewhere on the track American male athletes were, apart from the long-distance events, simply invincible. They won gold in the two relays and the two hurdles (Lee Calhoun in the 110m and Glenn Davis in the 400m). Baby-faced Bobby Joe Morrow achieved the most coveted Olympic "double," winning both the 100m and the 200m. The United States also won the 100m silver

(Thane Baker) and the 200m silver and bronze (Andrew Stanfield, Thane Baker). Charles Jenkins won the 400m. In the dramatic 800m race the American winner, Thomas Courtney, was so exhausted by his effort that he collapsed after crossing the finishing line, and the medal ceremony had to be delayed for an hour while he recovered.

The United States also reigned supreme in the field, bringing home golds in the high jump (Charles Dumas), pole vault (Robert Richards), long jump (Gregory Bell), shot put (Parry O'Brien), hammer throw (Harold Connolly), discus (Al Oerter), and decathlon (Milton Campbell). O'Brien was

the first repeat winner of the shot put since 1908, and he was to add a silver in 1960. In the discus Fortune Gordien and Desmond Koch completed a medal sweep for the United States. Rafer Johnson, the world-record holder in the decathlon, was hampered by injury and finished second (he was to win gold in 1960), but the most awaited field final was the hammer throw. In the run-up to the games a rivalry had built up between Connolly and the Soviet Mikhail Krivonosov. The latter had set a new world-record throw of 220 feet 10 inches (67.31m), only to see Connolly better it 11 days later by 4 feet (1.22m). Three weeks later

Hammer-throw champion Harold Connolly waves to the crowds as a disappointed Mikhail Krivonosov resigns himself to second place at the Melbourne Olympics.

WINTER OLYMPICS

The 1952 Winter Olympics, held in Oslo, were a triumph for the host country of Norway, the birthplace of modern skiing. The United States made its best showing ever, winning 11 medals in all to trail Norway by five. (In 1992, in Albertville, France, the United States won 11 medals again, but by then there were 57 gold medals on offer, compared to only 22 in 1952.)

The outstanding American performer was Andrea Mead Lawrence, who won both the slalom and giant slalom skiing competitions—the first American skier to win two Olympic gold medals. She fell in the first slalom run, recovered to finish fourth, and with a brilliant second run finished an incredible two seconds ahead of the field. She won the giant slalom by nearly three full seconds.

Press attention at home focused on figure skater Richard "Dick" Button, who repeated his gold-winning performance at St. Moritz in 1948. Button brought a new level of athleticism to the sport. In 1948 he had become the first ice-skater to complete a double-axel jump, and in 1952 he landed a triple loop. The loop is the easiest of ice-skating's jumps, but Button's was the first successful triple of any kind in competition. The fourth American gold was won by Kenneth Henry in the 500m speed skating.

The 1956 games, held in Cortina d'Ampezzo, Italy, saw the USSR in its debut appearance top the table and win the ice-hockey gold—a Canadian preserve of every previous Winter Games except 1936. The United States finished second, pushing Canada down into the bronze-medal position. The outstanding American performance came in the men's figure skating, in which Hayes Alan Jenkins and his brother David took gold and bronze, and Ronald Robertson the silver. That was a repeat of their medal sweep at the 1955 World Championships. Tenley Albright went one better than in 1952, taking the women's figure-skating title ahead of her compatriot Carol Heiss.

The 1956 Winter Olympics in Cortina d'Ampezzo, in the Italian Alps, were dominated by the USSR, which was competing for the first time.

Russians, Finns, and allies watch the Olympic flag being raised at the opening ceremony of the 1952 Helsinki Games. These were the first Olympic Games for the Soviet Union.

the two faced each other in Melbourne, and Connolly won with a throw of 207 feet 3 inches (63.17m) to Krivonosov's 206 feet 9 inches (63.02m). Connolly also added spice to the games through his romance with the Czech discus gold-medalist Olga Fikotova, whom he married after considerable Cold War diplomatic maneuvering in Prague.

Melbourne saw another notable American–Soviet encounter. In 1952, after losing to the United States 86–58 in the basketball Round Robin, the USSR had attempted to "freeze" the final but still lost 36–25. Four years later the Americans, led by future Boston Celtic stars Bill Russell and K.C. Jones, handed out an 89–55 drubbing to the Soviets. The game of

basketball was just starting to catch on outside the United States, and throughout the tournament no team came close to the Americans, whose minimum winning margin was 30 points.

American boxers James Boyd and Pete Rademacher both won gold medals (in the light heavyweight and superheavyweight divisions respectively). In the light middleweight division the American José Torres lost to Laszlo Papp of Hungary, who became the first boxer to win three Olympic golds. American weightlifters won four of the seven golds on offer, as well as two silvers and a bronze. The United States also picked up two freestyle wrestling medals.

Rowing and pool sports

American rowers won both the coxed and coxless pairs and took gold in the blue-ribbon event, the eights. Sailing, too, produced one gold, but in the pool

there was a marked decline from 1952. Robert Clotworthy won the springboard diving gold and Gary Tobian the platform silver, but 200m butterfly specialist William Yorzyk was the lone American swimming gold medalist for the men. Having set a world record of 17:52.9 in the 1,500m freestyle heats, George Breen could only finish third in the final, won by Australia's Murray Rose in a time of 17:58.9. American women fared no better. A clean sweep in the inaugural 100m butterfly provided the only gold, won by Shelley Mann, who had taken up swimming to regain strength in her limbs after being crippled by polio at the age of six.

See Also:

Basketball • Boxing • Cold War •
Soviet Union • Sports • Sports and TV

ON THE WATERFRONT

On the Waterfront *was one of the most acclaimed movies of the 1950s. The controversial story of a dockworker who testifies against his corrupt and violent union boss, the film helped turn its star Marlon Brando into an American icon.*

The movie *On the Waterfront* (1954) is set in the dockyards of New York City, a world ruled by ruthless union boss Johnny Friendly (Lee J. Cobb) through a mixture of violence and intimidation. The Waterfront Crime Commission is certain that Friendly is responsible for a string of murders but cannot find a witness to connect him to his crimes. Reliant on Friendly and his mob for work, the dockworkers adopt a policy of acting "D and D" (deaf and dumb) and refuse to cooperate.

Errand boy Terry Malloy (Marlon Brando), an inarticulate ex-boxer "owned" by Friendly, inadvertently sets up, then witnesses, the murder of fellow dockworker Joey Doyle. Initially intending to keep quiet, Malloy meets and falls for Doyle's sister, Edie (Eva Marie Saint). He also learns that Doyle was killed to prevent him testifying against Friendly. Tormented by his conscience, Malloy resolves to denounce Friendly no matter what the cost.

Real-life background

Inspired by the 1948 murder of a waterfront boss and by journalist Malcolm Johnson's Pulitzer Prize–winning articles about union corruption, *On the Waterfront* exposed the world of extortion and brutality of the New York docks. Screenwriter Budd Schulberg took what he described as an "unorthodox approach to the writing of the screenplay, applying not a month or two, but years of my life to absorbing everything I could about the New York waterfront." Independent

Marlon Brando and Eva Marie Saint play Terry Malloy and Edie Doyle in Elia Kazan's *On the Waterfront*. Both actors won Oscars for their performances.

producer Sam Spiegel was rejected by every major studio on the premise that audiences would be uninterested in the lives of longshoremen, but eventually persuaded Columbia to take on the project. The movie cost $906,000 to make and was shot on location in Hoboken, New Jersey, over 36 days.

Director Elia Kazan (1909–2003) assembled a strong cast, with seasoned Hollywood actors Cobb and Rod Steiger providing compelling support to Brando and Saint, who was making her screen debut. Brando initially

turned down the part of Malloy, and it was offered to Frank Sinatra. Brando, however, changed his mind before Sinatra could sign a contract and delivered a powerful and much imitated performance. The star employed a naturalistic style of acting known as method acting. Brando's most famous scene takes place in the back of a taxi, when Malloy, talking to his brother, laments his wasted life, claiming that he "coulda been a contender." Kazan later commented: "If there is a better performance by a man in the history of American film, I don't know what it is."

On the Waterfront is often viewed as a justification of the role of the informer. In 1952 director Kazan admitted his 1930s membership in the Communist Party and gave the names of fellow Communists to the House Un-American Activities Committee. His betrayal of his former friends caused a great amount of resentment in Hollywood.

Despite such controversy, *On the Waterfront* proved to be both a commercial and critical success, grossing over $9.5 million on its original release and winning eight Oscars, including best picture. More recently the film was voted number eight in the American Film Institute's list of the 100 greatest movies.

See Also:

Blacklist • Brando, Marlon • House Un-American Activities Committee • Movie Industry • Oscars

J. ROBERT OPPENHEIMER 1904–1967

J. Robert Oppenheimer was scientific director of the U.S. nuclear weapons program in the early 1940s and became a national spokesman for atomic physics. However, in 1953 his political career was cut short following an investigation into his alleged communist sympathies.

Born in New York City on April 22, 1904, J. Robert Oppenheimer grew to be a young man of great intellectual ability whose talent for mathematics and science was matched by his love of classics, languages, and literature. After studying at the universities of Harvard and Cambridge, he found his true vocation as a theoretical physicist at Göttingen University, Germany. In 1927 Oppenheimer was awarded a doctorate with distinction and returned to the United States, where in 1929 he took up a post as joint assistant professor of physics at the University of California, Berkeley, and the California Institute of Technology (Caltech).

Absorbed in the abstract world of theoretical physics, Oppenheimer paid little attention to the political instabilities of the 1930s that would eventually lead to global conflict. Being of German-Jewish descent, however, he finally took an interest in the rise of fascism in Europe, and like many intellectuals of his day, he became sympathetic with communist ideals. While he stopped short of actually joining the Communist Party, he became a generous benefactor to many left-wing political groups.

In 1941 Oppenheimer was invited to join the U.S. atomic weapons program, dubbed the "Manhattan Project." Within a year he became the project's scientific director, establishing in 1943 the top-secret Los Alamos Scientific Laboratory in New Mexico, where some of the most talented physicists of the day worked on the atomic bomb. On July 16, 1945, their work culminated in the first nuclear explosion at the "Trinity" test site in Alamogordo, New Mexico. Less than

J. Robert Oppenheimer, pictured here in 1954, shortly after his suspension from the Atomic Energy Commission, was considered one of the greatest theoretical physicists in the world.

one month later atomic bombs were dropped on Hiroshima and Nagasaki in Japan with devastating effect. Oppenheimer is often referred to as the "father of the atomic bomb."

Rise and fall

In the years immediately after World War II Oppenheimer gained enormous political influence as the national spokesman for nuclear physics and science in general. In 1947 he was appointed chairman of the General Advisory Committee (GAC) to the

Atomic Energy Commission (AEC), a position from which he lobbied vigorously for the international control of atomic energy and strongly opposed the development of the hydrogen bomb. When President Harry S. Truman (1945–1953) finally gave the go-ahead for the development of the H-bomb, the political climate turned against Oppenheimer. Indeed, he was already under investigation by the Federal Bureau of Investigation (FBI) for his past links with communism and left-wing politics.

In December 1953 the FBI accused Oppenheimer of being a national security risk, and following a much publicized hearing, his security clearance for the AEC was withdrawn. This move ended Oppenheimer's influence on science policy, and he withdrew to a quiet academic life as director of the Institute for Advanced Study at Princeton University, New Jersey.

Oppenheimer's contribution to nuclear physics could not be overlooked. In 1963 President Lyndon Baines Johnson (1963–1969) presented Oppenheimer with the Enrico Fermi Award of the AEC in recognition of "contributions to theoretical physics as a teacher and originator of ideas, and for leadership of the Los Alamos Laboratory and the atomic energy program during critical years." Oppenheimer resigned from Princeton in 1966 and died of throat cancer the following year.

See Also:

Federal Bureau of Investigation
• **H-bomb Tests** • **Los Alamos** • **Physics**
• **Science and Technology**

ORGANIZATION OF AMERICAN STATES

The Organization of American States (OAS) brought together the United States and most of the nations of Central and South America to promote regional peace and economic development; the dominance of the United States was at times a benefit to the alliance and at others a weakness.

Officially formed in April 1948, the Organization of American States had its roots in the Pan-American Union. It was an international organization made up of independent states in the Western Hemisphere that dated back to 1889, when at the urging of the United States it had brought together the United States and most of the states of Latin America. Nine Pan-American conferences between 1889 and 1948 had formulated agreements mainly on judicial and commercial issues.

In February 1945 delegates at an inter-American conference in Mexico City on the problems of war and peace agreed to the signing of a treaty under which the states of the Pan-American Union would consult with one another if any of their national borders were infringed. If necessary they would take joint action to protect their borders, which might include the use of force. The treaty was followed in 1947 by the Inter-American Treaty of Reciprocal Assistance. Signed at a conference in Rio de Janeiro, Brazil, it contained more detail on the arrangements for the peaceful settlement of disputes and collective defense. The treaty did not, however, reflect the desire of the United States to create a continental anti-communist alliance in the face of the growing strength of communism in Europe and Asia. Part of the reason for this failure was that the states of Latin America did not share U.S. fear of a communist threat. They had long regarded the United States rather than the Soviet Union as the country most likely to intervene in their internal affairs. In addition, they were more concerned about dealing with the immediate economic problems that confronted them in the aftermath of World War II (1939–1945) than in responding to a possible threat from a distant communist state. Finally, at the ninth Pan-American conference in 1948, held at Bogotá, Colombia, but led by the United States, delegates agreed that the Pan-American Union should be reconstituted as the Organization of American States, which would be better equipped than its predecessor to deal with any threat from outside.

Composition of the OAS

On April 30, 1948, the OAS Charter was signed by representatives of 21 countries. The signatories were the United States and Mexico; the majority of countries in South and Central America; and Cuba, the Dominican Republic, and Haiti in the Caribbean. Canada was not to become a member until 1990, while other countries— mainly in the Caribbean—were to join as they gained their independence from

This photograph shows José Figueres Ferrer, president of Costa Rica, as he welcomed members of the OAS committee investigating Nicaraguan-backed attempts to overthrow him.

RAFAEL TRUJILLO AND THE OAS

On coming to power in Cuba in 1959, Fidel Castro frequently criticized the OAS for not expelling countries governed by ruthless dictators such as Rafael Trujillo (1891–1961) of the Dominican Republic. Officially president from 1930 to 1938 and from 1942 to 1952, Trujillo in fact enjoyed absolute power for more than 30 years as commander-in-chief of the armed forces and the man to whom the secret police services reported. He was head of the state's only legal political party, all public officeholders owed their position to him, and through various members of his family he controlled almost all sectors of the Dominican economy. Through his accumulation of land and businesses he amassed an estimated fortune of $500 million by the late 1950s.

Many Americans were appalled by Trujillo's behavior. In the aftermath of World War II (1939–1945), however, many also saw him as an important figure in the fight against the spread of communism, no matter what his personal behavior was like. Cordell Hull, secretary of state from 1933 to 1944, allegedly said, "He may be a son-of-a-bitch, but he is our son-of-a-bitch."

The United States' faith in Trujillo was not shared in the Dominican Republic, where from the late 1940s a

Rafael Trujillo was a U.S. ally against communism, although his tyrannical rule later made him an embarrassment.

number of underground organizations tried to oust the dictator from power, including a group of exiles sponsored by Castro who launched a failed invasion from Cuba in 1959.

By 1960 the U.S. government had concluded that if nothing was done about Trujillo, a left-wing revolution would take place in the Dominican Republic. It was also aware that it was not in a strong position to win support from other OAS nations to condemn Castro's government in Cuba while it continued to ignore the tyrannical behavior of Trujillo.

Meanwhile, Trujillo himself was developing an obsessive hatred of Rómulo Betancourt, the liberal president of Venezuela, to whom some Dominican exiles had turned for help. Trujillo backed various plots by Venezuelan exiles to overthrow Betancourt; on June 24, 1960, Trujillo's agents blew up Betancourt's car, injuring but not killing the Venezuelan president. Horrified by this action, the members of the OAS voted unanimously to sever diplomatic relations with the Dominican Republic. Less than a year later Trujillo himself was assassinated by liberal sympathizers within the Dominican Republic.

their various European colonial governors. The stated purposes of the new organization included strengthening peace and security within the Western Hemisphere, the peaceful settlement of disputes between the member states, joint action against aggression from outside, the eradication of extreme poverty, and the cooperative development of economic, social, and cultural interests.

The administration of the OAS was put in the hands of a General Secretariat, based in Washington, D.C., and headed by a secretary-general elected for a five-year term. The first secretary-

general was Alberto Lleras Camargo (1906–1990), a former president of Colombia and director-general of the Pan-American Union. Agreement on policy was the responsibility of the General Assembly, whose annual meetings were to be attended by the foreign ministers or chiefs of state of all the member countries. No member country could use force without the unanimous consent of the others, but other measures required only approval by a two-thirds majority. Day-to-day decisions were to be made by the Permanent Council in Washington, which was made up of ambassadors of

all the member states. Should an act of aggression occur within or between member states, the Permanent Council would handle the matter until the members of the General Assembly had managed to gather together.

Human rights

In 1959 the basic structure of the OAS was augmented by the foundation of the Inter-American Commission on Human Rights. The creation of the commission, again headquartered in Washington, D.C., was based on the adoption by the OAS in 1948 of the American Declaration of the Rights

and Duties of Man. The commission had seven members who were to be elected by the OAS General Assembly. It held its first session in 1960, and by the following year it had begun to visit member countries to investigate either general or specific abuses of human rights. By the end of the 1990s the commission had investigated more than 12,000 such cases.

Early years

Many Latin American countries had hoped that the creation of the OAS would encourage the United States to give them large amounts of economic aid in the same way that it was giving aid to Europe under the Marshall Plan (officially the European Recovery Program). The United States, however, did not regard the economic development of Latin America as a priority. It remained more concerned with promoting economic recovery among the war-ravaged countries of Europe,

partly in order to resist the spread of communism. The lack of aid led to disillusionment among the Latin American states. Only one—Colombia—would contribute troops to the U.S.-led United Nations forces in Korea when war broke out there in 1950.

Meanwhile, the OAS had become involved in a dispute between Costa Rica and Nicaragua. In 1948 the dictator of Nicaragua, Anastasio Somoza (1896–1956), was accused of giving aid to the forces of ex-President Rafael Calderón Guardia of Costa Rica, who were engaged in fighting José Figueres Ferrer (1906–1990) and supporters loyal to the new president-elect. An OAS investigation upheld the charges and reprimanded Somoza. Figueres himself became president of Costa Rica in 1953. Somoza backed Calderón in an attempted coup in 1955. Another OAS investigation discovered that the rebels' supplies were coming from Nicaragua.

With his pistol tucked into the top of his trousers Carlos Castillo Armas addresses his followers during his U.S.-backed invasion of Guatemala in June 1954.

U.S. interference

The Korean War (1950–1953) heightened the fear of communism in the United States. The increased level of fear inspired a number of U.S. interventions in the internal affairs of countries in Central or South America, both with and without OAS support. In Guatemala, for example, where Jacobo Arbenz (1913–1971) became president in 1951, the United States acted on its own. Arbenz introduced a number of reforms aimed at lessening the extreme poverty in his country, including, in 1953, the confiscation of unused portions of landholdings for redistribution among the peasants. This had a major effect on the U.S.-owned United Fruit Company, which held huge swaths of Guatemala's land. The

United States saw the appropriation of land as being communist in its inspiration and asked the OAS to condemn it at the tenth inter-American conference in Caracas, Venezuela, in March 1954. The other countries, however, rejected the U.S. request; instead, the conference passed a general resolution that condemned communist domination of any American state.

The U.S. response was to ignore the OAS and act alone. In late May 1954 the United States signed an agreement with the government of Honduras, which was concerned about the effects of strikes against foreign-owned fruit companies within its own borders.

Cuban leader Fidel Castro condemns the United States in a three-hour televised speech in 1960; the next year the United States broke off diplomatic and commercial ties with Cuba.

Under the agreement Honduras received large quantities of American arms, many of which it passed on to a covert force of Guatemalan exiles organized by the United States. In June 1954 the exiles launched an invasion of Guatemala. When the Guatemalan army refused to fight for Arbenz, his appeals to the United Nations Security Council to intervene were met by a proposal to refer the matter to the OAS. Arbenz was forced to resign, and the leader of the invasion, Carlos Castillo Armas, became the new president. The United States' success was a reminder of the fundamental weakness of an international organization in which one member was much more powerful than the others.

Although the eleventh inter-American conference, scheduled to be held in 1959 in Quito, Ecuador, was

postponed, the foreign ministers of OAS members met once in 1959 and twice in 1960. Among the issues they discussed were the actions of Rafael Trujillo, the dictator of the Dominican Republic (*see box on p. 169*). In 1959 they denounced his dictatorial rule, while in 1960 they launched an inquiry into an allegation that he had been behind an attempt to assassinate President Rómulo Betancourt (1908–1981) of Venezuela. As a result, the OAS imposed sanctions on the Dominican Republic that remained in place until 1962.

Cuba

Another country with which the OAS became concerned in 1960 was Cuba. After an army revolt in Cuba in 1952 Fulgencio Batista (1901–1973) had established himself as dictator at the

THE INTER-AMERICAN DEVELOPMENT BANK

Long before the creation of the OAS in 1948 the countries of Latin American and the Caribbean had felt the need for an institution that would provide finance for a wide variety of social and economic development projects throughout the region. In 1958 President Juscelino Kubitschek of Brazil put forward a proposal for an Inter-American Development Bank that won widespread support from other OAS countries. As a result the bank—the first in the world set up to encourage regional development—was created under an agreement signed in 1959.

The agreement to establish the bank was immediately ratified by the United States and 17 other OAS countries. Two other countries ratified in 1960, leaving Cuba as the only original OAS country not to ratify. The bank began operations in October 1960 with 87 officials and 101 administrative and secretarial staff based in Washington, D.C. In its first year it granted loans for improved water and sewage systems, housing, transportation, energy, and agriculture in many countries. It has continued to support a wide range of national, state, provincial, and municipal projects run by public or private bodies, which often require the type of long-term loan that commercial banks are reluctant to make. The bank has also served as a model for other regional banks, such as those in Asia and Africa.

Juscelino Kubitschek, president of Brazil from 1956 to 1961, first proposed the creation of the Inter-American Development Bank.

head of a brutal and corrupt regime. The following year a young lawyer, Fidel Castro (1926–), led an unsuccessful attempt to overthrow Batista. After another failed revolt in 1956 Castro had launched a two-year guerrilla campaign that culminated in the collapse of the government. Batista fled the country on January 1, 1959; Castro became premier in February and by July was Cuba's undisputed leader. His planned economic and social reforms, particularly nationalization and land reform, alarmed the United States.

One of Castro's priorities was to end Cuba's dependence on the United States for exports by finding other nations to buy Cuba's main export: sugar. In his search for new customers he turned to the Soviet Union, and in February 1960 he concluded a trade agreement that allowed Cuba to buy Soviet oil. In May Cuba established diplomatic relations with the Soviet

Union, and in June it began to buy arms from the Soviet Union and other communist countries. In the same month Castro seized U.S.- and British-owned oil refineries in Cuba after they refused to refine Russian oil.

OAS policy on Cuba

The United States hoped for the support of other OAS countries to put pressure on Castro to pull back from his increasing involvement with the Soviet Union. However, while a conference of OAS foreign ministers in August 1960 condemned Soviet and Chinese intervention in Latin America, it refused to single out Cuba. A proposal for inter-American mediation between Cuba and the United States got nowhere. As in Guatemala, the U.S. government decided to act on its own.

The United States stopped the purchase of sugar from Cuba, to which Castro responded by nationalizing U.S.

property in the country. The United States then imposed a complete commercial boycott against Cuba and, in January 1961, ended diplomatic relations. It also supported an invasion of Cuba by 1,400 Cuban exiles in April 1961, which ended in failure.

One of Castro's aims was to export revolution to neighboring countries, and he supported subversive activities in countries such as Haiti and the Dominican Republic. In 1961 he announced that he was a Marxist. The OAS responded in 1962 by suspending Cuba on charges of subversion. It has been suspended ever since.

See Also:

Argentina • Brazil • Central America • Cold War • Cuba • Foreign Policy • Guatemala • International Aid • South America • U.S.–Mexican Relations

OSCARS

The Oscars, or Academy Awards, have long been established as the most prestigious and coveted of all movie awards. The annual awards ceremony, which takes place in Los Angeles, was first televised in the 1950s.

Presented annually by the Academy of Motion Picture Arts and Sciences, the Academy Awards of Merit, commonly known as Oscars, had been a feature of American life for some three decades before the 1950s. The first awards, whose nickname apparently came from the statuette's resemblance to a relative of an academy employee, were handed out by the academy president, Douglas Fairbanks, at a banquet at the Hollywood Roosevelt Hotel on May 16, 1929. It took just five minutes to give out the 15 statuettes.

An hour of the second awards banquet was transmitted live on Los Angeles radio in 1930, and the ceremony has been broadcast ever since. A further development came in 1940, when the late edition of the *Los Angeles Times* printed a list of the 1939 winners before they were announced at the evening's ceremony. Consequently, the academy stopped providing advance information about winners to the press, introduced the sealed envelope, and established a code of secrecy. In 1944, when ABC and the Armed Forces radio broadcast the awards ceremony around the world, the Oscars began attracting increased international attention. They have since become more extravagant and high profile with each year.

Eligibility and voting

To be considered for an Oscar, a motion picture must be shown in a 33mm or larger format to a paying audience at a commercial movie theater in Los Angeles for at least one week between January 1 and December 31 in a given year. Foreign language films are put forward by their country of origin, while documentaries and short films are recommended by their producers.

Until the awards of 1957 more than 12,000 individuals, including not only academy members but also industry guilds and unions, made the annual nominations; only the estimated 2,000

MGM art director Cedric Gibbons designed the Oscar statuette of a knight standing on a reel of film, clasping a sword; the gold-plated figure is 13½ inches (34cm) tall and weighs 8½ pounds (3.9kg).

WINNER OF THE OSCAR FOR BEST MOTION PICTURE

1950	*All about Eve* (20th Century-Fox)
1951	*An American in Paris* (Arthur Freed, producer)
1952	*The Greatest Show on Earth* (Cecil B. DeMille, producer)
1953	*From Here to Eternity* (Buddy Adler, producer)
1954	*On the Waterfront* (Sam Spiegel, producer)
1955	*Marty* (Harold Hecht, producer)
1956	*Around the World in 80 Days* (Michael Todd, producer)

1957	*The Bridge on the River Kwai* (Sam Spiegel, producer)
1958	*Gigi* (Arthur Freed, producer)
1959	*Ben-Hur* (Sam Zimbalist, producer)

Charlton Heston (front) was the star of *Ben-Hur*, an epic about Jews and Romans at the time of Christ. The movie won the Oscar for best picture of 1959, and Heston won the best actor award.

academy members were eligible to participate in the final vote. Since 1957, however, both nominations and the final vote have been restricted to members of the academy. The academy is divided into different areas of film production expertise, and each branch takes responsibility for nominations in its field; actors nominate actors, directors nominate directors, and so on. The entire academy decides on the nominations for best picture and votes for the winners in the majority of categories.

Changing format

The Oscars ceremony has undergone numerous changes. During World War II (1939–1945) the traditional banquet was rejected as being too extravagant; since 1944 the ceremony has been held in a theater. Throughout the 1950s the venue was the RKO Pantages Theatre on Hollywood Boulevard. On March 19, 1953, the theater became the venue for the first televised ceremony. Having consistently refused to sell the TV rights to cover the ceremony, the academy finally relented when a number of studios, including Warner Brothers and Columbia, withdrew their funding for the event. NBC bought the television rights for $100,000; the broadcast drew what was then the largest single audience in network television history. The next year approximately 43 million people tuned in to watch the ceremony.

Although many stars were forbidden by their contracts from appearing on television, and others were too nervous about appearing live to attend the ceremony, it was clear that television could be useful to Hollywood. For actresses worried about which outfits would look best on camera, NBC provided fashion adviser Edith Head; the network also offered to tint actors' shirts blue so that they would photograph better. Beginning with the 1957 awards (held in 1958), the movie industry sponsored TV coverage itself, using the broadcast to promote new releases, until costs forced the abandonment of the initiative after three years.

Televising a live ceremony presented problems with running over or under time. In 1954 William Holden, winner of the 1953 award for best actor, was left with only enough time for a "Thank you" before the show ended. The ceremony in 1959, on the other hand, ran short by 20 minutes. Cohost Jerry Lewis dragged out the final number, an all-star rendition of "There's No Business Like Show Business," until NBC found a sports program to fill the gap.

Until 1957 simultaneous Oscar ceremonies were held in Hollywood and New York City to enable the

---

WINNER OF THE OSCAR FOR BEST ACTOR

1950	José Ferrer, *Cyrano de Bergerac* (Cyrano de Bergerac)
1951	Humphrey Bogart, *The African Queen* (Charlie Allnut)
1952	Gary Cooper, *High Noon* (Will Kane)
1953	William Holden, *Stalag 17* (Sefton)
1954	Marlon Brando, *On the Waterfront* (Terry Malloy)
1955	Ernest Borgnine, *Marty* (Marty Pilletti)
1956	Yul Brynner, *The King and I* (The King)
1957	Alec Guinness, *The Bridge on the River Kwai* (Colonel Nicholson)
1958	David Niven, *Separate Tables* (Major Pollock)
1959	Charlton Heston, *Ben-Hur* (Judah Ben-Hur)

---

participation of the stars performing on Broadway. The television show cut between the two occasions and sometimes went even farther afield. For example, the 1953 awards show, staged in 1954, included cut-ins from Philadelphia and Mexico as well as New York, where a police escort rushed Audrey Hepburn from her Broadway theater to the awards to receive her Oscar for best actress. After 1957 the show was broadcast in its entirety from Hollywood.

A range of awards

In the 1950s the Oscars were awarded in up to 30 categories, including best picture, actor, actress, actor in a supporting role, actress in a supporting role, directing, original screenplay, adapted screenplay, film editing, special effects, and sound recording. Musical excellence was rewarded in three categories: song, music score of a musical picture, and music score of a dramatic or comedy picture. Awards were bestowed separately for black-and-white and color films in the categories of art direction, cinematography, and costume design. Feature-length and short documentaries were also honored, as were short animations and, until 1956, one-reel and two-reel shorts; from 1957 the two categories were replaced by a single live action award. Foreign language films were originally awarded honorary Oscars until 1956, when they were granted a category of their own.

The board of governors could choose to make honorary awards to distinguish "exceptional contributions to the state of motion picture arts and sciences, or for outstanding service to the Academy." In the 1950s Louis B. Mayer, Gene Kelly, Bob Hope, and Greta Garbo all received honorary awards. The academy also rewards those who influence or advance the industry through scientific or technical innovation; among the many honored in this way during the decade were Technicolor, for its improvements to color motion picture photography, and Professor Henri Chrétien and Twentieth Century-Fox, for developing and creating CinemaScope. The Irving G. Thalberg Memorial Award, established in 1937 to remember the achievements of the legendary producer

---

WINNER OF THE OSCAR FOR BEST DIRECTING

1950	Joseph L. Mankiewicz, *All about Eve*
1951	George Stevens, *A Place in the Sun*
1952	John Ford, *The Quiet Man*
1953	Fred Zinnemann, *From Here to Eternity*
1954	Elia Kazan, *On the Waterfront*
1955	Delbert Mann, *Marty*
1956	George Stevens, *Giant*
1957	David Lean, *The Bridge on the River Kwai*
1958	Vincente Minnelli, *Gigi*
1959	William Wyler, *Ben-Hur*

and MGM vice president who died age 37, was awarded for "consistently high quality" in motion picture production; 1950s winners included Darryl F. Zanuck (*All about Eve*), Arthur Freed (*An American in Paris*, *Showboat*) and Cecil B. DeMille (*The Greatest Show on Earth*). The Jean Hersholt Humanitarian Award was established in 1956 to commemorate the charity work of the actor and academy president (1945–1949) who died in that year. Among the first to be recognized as individuals whose "humanitarian efforts have brought credit to the industry" were Y. Frank Freeman, Samuel Goldwyn, and Bob Hope.

A decade of records

Several Oscar records set during the 1950s stood unchallenged until the end of the 20th century. The 1950 Oscars got off to a record-breaking start, with *All about Eve* garnering 14 nominations, an achievement unmatched until 1997's *Titanic*. Its stars, Bette Davis and Anne Baxter, went head-to-head for best actress, and Celeste Holm and Thelma Ritter competed against each other for best actress in a supporting role. A satirical sideswipe at the world of Broadway, the movie eventually won six awards, including best picture, best screenplay, and best actor in a supporting role for George Sanders. A second satirical look at the entertainment industry, this time directed at Hollywood, *Sunset Boulevard* was nominated for 11 Oscars and eventually won three, for best art direction, best music score of a dramatic or comedy picture, and best story and screenplay.

The big winner at the 1953 Oscars, *From Here to Eternity*, almost matched *All about Eve* with 13 nominations; it bettered it by winning eight awards, including best picture and best actor in a supporting role for Frank Sinatra. *Gigi* in 1958 set a new record by

Bob Hope was the academy's preferred master of ceremonies for the Oscars during the 1950s; he also received a special award for his charity work.

winning all nine awards for which it was nominated. But it was the 1959 film *Ben-Hur* that became the Oscar success of the decade, winning awards for 11 of its 12 nominations, a feat unequaled until *Titanic* in 1997 and *Lord of the Rings: The Return of the King* in 2003. Other highly nominated films of the 1950s included *Giant* (1956), which was nominated for 10 and won one; *Sayonara* (1957), nominated for 10 and won four; and *On the Waterfront* (1954), nominated for 12 and won eight.

During the fifties the ceremony was most often presented by actor and comedian Bob Hope (1903–2003). Hope was master of ceremonies for the award shows of 1952, 1954, and 1959, and shared the job for the awards of 1957 and 1958 with some of the

decade's biggest stars, including Jack Lemmon, David Niven, James Stewart, and Donald Duck, who hosted an animated history of Hollywood. Other presenters included Fred Astaire (1950), Danny Kaye (1951), Donald O'Connor (1953), and Jerry Lewis (1955 and 1956).

A night of surprises

Oscar night was often full of surprises and notable events. The 1951 awards saw Humphrey Bogart win his first and only Oscar for his role in *The African Queen*, unexpectedly beating favorite Marlon Brando. Also unexpected in 1951 was the best picture victory for *An American in Paris*, which was only the third musical ever to win that award. The 1955 awards were the setting for Grace Kelly's last public appearance before her marriage to Prince Rainier of Monaco brought about her retirement from Hollywood.

The awards for 1956 saw Ingrid Bergman's triumphant return to Hollywood after a six-year exile caused by her affair with Italian director Roberto Rossellini, when she won best actress for *Anastasia*. Bergman could not attend the ceremony because she was appearing on stage in Paris, but the academy had clearly signaled it was ready to accept her back into the movie industry fold.

The 1956 ceremony also marked a less generous action on the part of the academy, with its decision not to reward individuals who had suspected links with communism. This concession to the atmosphere of Cold War paranoia had serious repercussions in the writing categories. Many writers blacklisted by the House Un-American Activities Committee (HUAC) had adopted pseudonyms to enable them to work. The winner of best motion picture story for 1956 was Robert Rich for *The Brave One*; Rich was later discovered to be an alias of blacklisted writer Dalton Trumbo, who was not

WINNER OF THE OSCAR FOR BEST ACTRESS

1950   Judy Holliday, *Born Yesterday*
          (Billie Dawn)
1951   Vivien Leigh, *A Streetcar Named Desire*
          (Blanche DuBois)
1952   Shirley Booth, *Come Back, Little Sheba*
          (Lola Delaney)
1953   Audrey Hepburn, *Roman Holiday* (*right*)
          (Princess Anne)
1954   Grace Kelly, *The Country Girl*
          (Georgie Elgin)
1955   Anna Magnani, *The Rose Tattoo*
          (Serafina Della Rose)
1956   Ingrid Bergman, *Anastasia*
          (The Woman)
1957   Joanne Woodward, *The Three Faces of Eve*
          (Eve White/Eve Black/Jane)
1958   Susan Hayward, *I Want to Live!*
          (Barbara Graham)
1959   Simone Signoret, *Room at the Top*
          (Alice Aisgill)

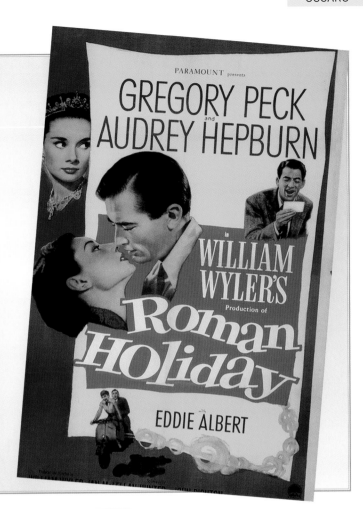

PARAMOUNT presents
GREGORY PECK and AUDREY HEPBURN in WILLIAM WYLER'S Production of Roman Holiday
EDDIE ALBERT

Screenwriter Dalton Trumbo was one of the Hollywood Ten, blacklisted in 1947 for their refusal to testify before the House Un-American Activities Committee; he won an Oscar in 1956, writing under the name of Robert Rich.

presented with his award until shortly before his death in 1976. Less fortunate were writers Michael Wilson and Carl Foreman, whose Oscar for best adapted screenplay for *The Bridge on the River Kwai* in 1957 was actually given to the original author, Pierre Boulle. It was not until after their deaths that the academy in 1984 voted posthumous Oscars to both writers and amended its records accordingly.

See Also:

Blacklist • Brando, Marlon • *High Noon* • House Un-American Activities Committee • Movie Industry • *On the Waterfront* • Sinatra, Frank • Television • Western Movies

THE ADVENTURES OF
OZZIE AND HARRIET

A staple of American television comedy in the 1950s was the family sitcom based on a lightly fictionalized real-life couple, often using their own names. I Love Lucy *is today the most famous, but the longest running was another show based on a bandleader and his wife.*

The show *The Adventures of Ozzie and Harriet* was, along with the similar *I Love Lucy*, among the most successful television sitcoms of the 1950s. It focused on the real-life Nelson family—Ozzie, Harriet, and their sons David and Ricky—and mixed fiction and reality to create a portrait of 1950s America that only ever existed as an ideal.

The half-hour weekly program aired for the first time in 1952 and ran for 14 seasons until 1966. Ozzie Nelson (1907–1975) and his wife Harriet Hilliard (1914–1994) were a real-life show-business couple, he a bandleader and she a singer. During the 1940s Ozzie's band appeared regularly on Red Skelton's radio show, taking it over in 1944 when Skelton was drafted. The show continued with the big-band routine but also introduced sketches about married life. Ozzie, however, wanted to do a domestic comedy based on his own family, so from 1946 the show became a straight radio sitcom, though still centered on Ozzie's role as bandleader. Until 1949 the roles of the two sons were played by child actors.

Transition to television

In that year Ozzie decided to let his own sons, 13-year-old David and 9-year-old Ricky, appear as themselves, which they did with great success. Ozzie negotiated a 10-year contract with ABC that guaranteed the family a basic salary whether they worked or not. ABC was interested in transferring

Ozzie Nelson was already well known as a bandleader, and his wife Harriet Hilliard as an actress and singer, by the time they turned real life into a long-running comedy.

the show to television and so made a pilot movie, *Here Come the Nelsons* (1952), in which Ozzie's persona shifted from bandleader to advertising executive. The film's success led ABC to commission a television series that year. For the next two years the radio show continued to run concurrently with the one on television, but with completely different scripts. Ozzie maintained his bandleader role in the radio version, which finished its run in 1954.

The television show represented an ideal of an American family. The emphasis was on the family's ordinariness, and the real Nelson family did nothing to dispel that image. The television family's house was almost

identical to the Nelsons' own. Ozzie's white-collar job was part of an effort to make him more like an ordinary father and husband. Harriet, like other 1950s moms, stayed home and took care of the family.

During the decade America watched David and Ricky grow up and get married. David was the typical older brother, responsible and steady. Ricky was the typical younger brother who challenged authority but always in minor ways that could be resolved in each episode. He became the family's biggest star when he covered a Fats Domino song, "I'm Walkin'," during an episode in 1957. Released as a single, the song was a hit. Ricky Nelson was the bestselling rock-'n'-roll star in the country the following year; a performance on the show effectively provided a free ad for each new release.

In reality Ozzie Nelson was far removed from his bumbling on-screen character. A workaholic, he was script writer or consultant on every episode. In 1959, due to the success of Ricky's singing career, the show was recommissioned for five more years. It spawned many imitations, including *Make Room for Daddy* (1953–1965), *Leave It to Beaver* (1957–1963), and *Father Knows Best* (1954–1963).

See Also:

Ball, Lucille • Leisure Industry • Popular Music • Radio • Teenage Culture • Television Comedy

CHARLIE PARKER 1920–1955

In his brief career saxophonist Charlie Parker revolutionized the world of jazz. He was largely responsible for creating a new genre—bebop—and was hailed as a musical genius. However, his life was cut short by the effects of alcohol and drug addiction.

Charles "Bird" Parker, Jr., was born on August 29, 1920, in Kansas City, Kansas, and raised in Kansas City, Missouri. He took up the alto saxophone when he was 13 years old and dropped out of school one year later to concentrate on developing his instrumental skills. At 16 Parker was married for the first of four times. Over the next two years he gained experience playing with jazz and blues bands both in and outside Missouri, and between 1940 and 1942 he toured with the big band of pianist Jay McShann, with whom Parker recorded his first solos.

The advent of bebop

In 1942 Parker moved to New York City, where he played in a number of informal, small combos with trumpeter Dizzy Gillespie (1917–1993), a former bandmate. Together, Parker and Gillespie were responsible for developing a revolutionary new form of jazz known as bebop. Bebop was distinguished by complex improvisation, with soloists using innovative harmonies and unusual rhythms. Solos were often played at breakneck speed. Bebop was greeted with bewilderment by both the general public and many established jazz musicians. However, the genre also had many devoted followers who saw Parker as a genius.

In 1945 Parker traveled with the Gillespie sextet to California, but there 10 years of heroin addiction and heavy

The saxophonist Charlie Parker was one of the most talented and influential jazz musicians of his generation.

drinking caught up with him. After setting fire to his hotel bed one night, Parker was confined to a state mental hospital for six months.

On returning to New York in 1947, Parker performed as leader of a quintet that included Miles Davis (1926–1991) on trumpet. The group recorded many numbers that have become classics. In late 1949 a Broadway club opened that was named for Parker—Birdland. It was to become the most famous jazz club of the 1950s, and Parker himself played there many times.

In 1949 and 1950 Parker made a number of recordings with a string backing, which appealed to a wider audience than his earlier, more innovative, work, and he made several appearances with a string orchestra. He then embarked on a period of travel around the United States, playing with local groups or, as a guest soloist, accompanying bands such as that of Woody Herman.

The final years

Parker continued to produce great performances in the early 1950s, but they became more sporadic. He had begun to suffer from the long-term effects of his drug and alcohol addiction—habits that younger, hero-worshipping jazz musicians had imitated. Parker frequently failed to turn up for engagements, and eventually he was fired from Birdland. In 1954, in the midst of a period when his two-year-old daughter died and his fourth marriage collapsed, he made two attempts to commit suicide.

Parker died on March 12, 1955, at the home of jazz benefactor Baroness Pannonica de Koenigswarter. At the time of his death Parker was only 34 years of age, but in his brief career he had exerted an enormous influence on the world of jazz.

> **See Also:**
>
> **Davis, Miles • Jazz**

LINUS PAULING 1901–1994

Linus Pauling was both an exceptional scientist and a devoted peace activist whose contribution to both fields culminated in the award of two Nobel Prizes in 1954 and 1962. He was also a tireless campaigner against the dangers of nuclear warfare and testing.

Born in Portland, Oregon, on February 28, 1901, Linus Carl Pauling was the son of a druggist of German descent. After completing a degree in chemical engineering at Oregon Agricultural College in 1922, he received a doctorate from the California Institute of Technology (Caltech) in 1925 and joined the faculty in 1927. He used his talent for chemistry, physics, and mathematics to investigate the nature of chemical bonds. Pauling became one of the first scientists to apply the new field of quantum mechanics to the study of chemistry, taking inspiration from the work of some of the leading physicists of his day. He supplemented his theoretical work using an experimental technique called X-ray crystallography. Pauling published his results in a scientific paper in 1931, but the true body of his work on chemical bonding appeared in 1939 in a definitive book entitled *The Nature of the Chemical Bond and the Structure of Molecules and Crystals*. In recognition of his work on chemical bonding Pauling was awarded the 1954 Nobel Prize for chemistry.

In 1931 Pauling became a full professor at Caltech, assuming responsibility for the undergraduate chemistry program. His modern approach to the study of chemistry proved popular among his students, and he eventually collated his lectures into a textbook entitled *General Chemistry* (1947).

During the 1930s and early 1940s Pauling shifted the focus of his research to the biological sciences. He worked on the structure of proteins and other complex molecules in living organisms.

Nobel Prize-winner Linus Pauling, seen here at the Anti-A-Bomb Convention in 1959, was one of the leading voices in the campaign against the advancement of nuclear technology.

Pauling successfully determined the structure of hemoglobin—the oxygen-transport molecule in red blood cells—and went on to examine the roles of antigens and antibodies in immunity. He later developed the theory of molecular disease through his research into sickle cell anemia.

Pauling and peace

Shortly after the United States dropped atomic bombs on Hiroshima and Nagasaki to end World War II (1939–1945), Pauling joined many other distinguished scientists to speak out against the dangers of nuclear

warfare. His involvement in the peace movement would consume the rest of his life. In November 1950 he was subpoenaed to appear before the Senate Investigating Committee on Education of the State of California and testified about his objections to loyalty oaths that involved inquiries into political beliefs. In 1952 he was denied a passport because the State Department believed it "would not be in the best interest of the United States."

In 1958 Pauling presented a petition to the United Nations. Signed by 11,000 scientists from all around the world, including 38 Nobel Prize-winners, it called for a ban on nuclear testing. That year Pauling published *No More War!*, which discussed the effects of radioactive fallout and the hazards of nuclear testing and warfare. On August 5, 1963, the United States, Britain, and the Soviet Union signed a partial nuclear test-ban treaty. Pauling's campaign was finally vindicated, and the Nobel Committee announced that he had won the 1962 Nobel Prize for peace.

From the late 1960s until his death in 1994 Pauling strove to educate the public about the dangers of smoking and the benefits of vitamins, writing a number of popular scientific books. He received many honors in recognition of his outstanding contributions to science, technology, and society.

See Also:

H-bomb Tests • Nobel Prizes • Physics • Science and Technology

BOOKS

Altschuler, Glenn C. *All Shook Up: How Rock 'n' Roll Changed America*. New York: Oxford University Press, 2003

Ambrose, Stephen E. *Eisenhower: Soldier and President*. New York: Simon and Schuster, 1990

Bell, Daniel *The End of Ideology: On the Exhaustion of Political Ideas in the Fifties*. Cambridge, MA: Harvard University Press, 2000 (originally published 1960)

Boddy, William *Fifties Television: The Industry and Its Critics*. Urbana, IL: University of Illinois Press, 1990

Cross, Gary S. (ed.) *Encyclopedia of Recreation and Leisure in America*. Farmington Hills, MI: Charles Scribner's Sons, 2004

Doherty, Thomas *Teenagers and Teenpics: The Juvenilization of American Movies in the 1950s*. Philadelphia, PA: Temple University Press, 2002 (rev. edn)

Fried, Albert (ed.) *McCarthyism, the Great American Red Scare: A Documentary History*. New York: Oxford University Press, 1997

Galbraith, John Kenneth *The Affluent Society*. Boston, MA: Houghton Mifflin, 1998 (originally published 1958)

Hendershot, Cyndy *Anti-communism and Popular Culture in Mid-century America*. Jefferson, NC: McFarland, 2003

Johns, Michael *Moment of Grace: The American City in the 1950s*. Berkeley, CA: University of California Press, 2003

Judge, Edward H. and John W. Langdon (eds.) *The Cold War: A History Through Documents*. Upper Saddle River, NJ: Prentice Hall, 1999

Kaledin, Eugenia *Daily Life in the United States, 1940–1959: Shifting Worlds*. Westport, CT: Greenwood Press, 2000

Klingaman, William K. *Encyclopedia of the McCarthy Era*. New York: Facts on File, 1996

LaFeber, Walter *America, Russia, and the Cold War, 1945–2002*. Boston, MA: McGraw-Hill, 2004

Layman, Richard (ed.) *American Decades: 1950–1959*. Detroit, MI: Gale Research, 1994

Levy, Peter B. *The Civil Rights Movement*. Westport, CT: Greenwood Press, 1998

McCullough, David *Truman*. New York: Simon and Schuster, 1992

Oakley, J. Ronald *Baseball's Last Golden Age, 1946–1960: The National Pastime in a Time of Glory and Change*. Jefferson, NC: McFarland, 1994

Olson, James S. *Historical Dictionary of the 1950s*. Westport, CT: Greenwood Press, 2000

Palladino, Grace *Teenagers: An American History*. New York: Basic Books, 1996

Pierpaoli, Paul G., Jr. *Truman and Korea: The Political Culture of the Early Cold War*. Columbia, MO: University of Missouri Press, 1999

Salamone, Frank A. *Popular Culture in the Fifties*. Lanham, MD: University Press of America, 2001

Thumin, Janet (ed.) *Small Screens, Big Ideas: Television in the 1950s*. New York: I.B. Tauris, 2002

Young, William H. with Nancy K. Young *The 1950s* (American Popular Culture through History series). Westport, CT: Greenwood Press, 2004

USEFUL WEBSITES

Cold War
http://edition.cnn.com/SPECIALS/cold.war

Cold War International History Project
http://wwics.si.edu/index.cfm?fuseaction=topics.home&topic_id=1409

The Dwight D. Eisenhower Library
www.eisenhower.archives.gov

The Fifties Index
www.fiftiesweb.com

Greatest Space Events of the 20th Century: The 50s
http://www.space.com/news/spacehistory/greatest_space_events_1950s-1.html

The History of Rock 'n' Roll
www.history-of-rock.com

Kingwood College Library: American Cultural History 1950–1959
http://kclibrary.nhmccd.edu/decade50.html

The Korean War
www.korean-war.com

Literature and Culture of the American 1950s
http://www.writing.upenn.edu/~afilreis/50s/home.html

National Baseball Hall of Fame 1950–1959
http://www.baseballhalloffame.org/hof_weekend/hof_game/history/1950s.htm

Pro Football Hall of Fame: The Fifties
http://www.profootballhof.com/history/decades/index.jsp#50s

Voices of Civil Rights
www.voicesofcivilrights.org

PICTURE CREDITS

Front cover images supplied by Library of Congress, National Archives of America, and the Robert Hunt Library

Corbis: 11, 123, 126, Bettmann 6, 13, 25, 43, 46, 48, 64, 66, 84, 85, 87, 116, 118, 119, 120, 136b, 148t, 152, 155b, 157, 158, Hulton-Deutsch Collection 41, Lake County Museum 18; **Getty Images:** 7, 9, 10b, 14, 17, 20, 22, 23b, 24, 29, 30, 31, 35, 44, 45, 47, 51, 53, 54, 56, 59, 67, 76, 77, 78, 82, 83, 91, 92, 96, 121, 122t, 127, 129t, 131, 132, 134t, 134b, 139, 142t, 168, 170, 173, 178; **Lebrecht Collection:** 103b, 106; **Library of Congress:** 8, 10t, 12, 21, 26, 27, 28, 32, 33, 40, 42, 49, 50, 55, 57, 58, 60, 61, 62, 80, 81, 88, 94, 100, 101, 103t, 105, 112t, 112b, 113, 114, 117, 122b, 124, 128, 129b, 133, 137, 148b, 159, 177t, 177b, 179; **NASA:** 109, 110; **Rex Features:** Everett Collection 174; **Robert Hunt Library:** 4, 5, 19, 23t, 34, 36, 37, 38, 39, 52, 68, 69, 71, 73, 74, 79, 89, 93, 97, 98, 140, 151, 154, 164, 165, 167, 171, 172, 176, 180; **The Nobel Foundation:** 142b, 145, 146; **Topham Picturepoint:** 15, 70, 86, 95, 104, 108, 136t, 144, 149, 150, 155t, 156, 160, 162, 163, 166, 169, 20th Century Fox 99, MGM 90, Warner Bros 102.

PRE-1950

1945
April 12 President Franklin D. Roosevelt dies. His vice president, Harry S. Truman, replaces him.

May 12 British Prime Minister Winston Churchill first uses the phrase "Iron Curtain" to describe the invisible barrier that divides Eastern and Western Europe.

August 6 United States drops an atomic bomb on Hiroshima, Japan. A second bomb is dropped on Nagasaki on August 9.

September 2 Ho Chi Minh declares the founding of the Democratic Republic of Vietnam.

October 24 The United Nations Charter is ratified.

1947
March 12 President Truman commits the United States to defending Greece and Turkey against communism.

April 15 Jackie Robinson makes debut his for the Brooklyn Dodgers, becoming the first African American to play baseball for a major-league team.

June 5 Secretary of State George C. Marshall outlines a program of financial aid to help accelerate European economic recovery. The program becomes known as the Marshall Plan.

September 18 The Central Intelligence Agency (CIA) is established to coordinate U.S. intelligence efforts.

October 20 The House Un-American Activities Committee (HUAC) holds its first round of hearings into communist activity in the movie industry.

December 3 Tennessee Williams's play *A Streetcar Named Desire* opens on Broadway to widespread acclaim.

1948
April 30 The Organization of American States is formed.

June 24 The Soviet Union blocks road and rail access to West Berlin.

1949
April 4 The North Atlantic Treaty Organization is formed at a meeting in Washington, D.C.

October 1 The People's Republic of China is formed after the victory of Mao Zedong's Communists over Nationalist forces.

1950

January 21 Alger Hiss, a U.S. government official accused of spying for the Soviet Union, is convicted of perjury. He is later sentenced to five years' imprisonment.

February 9 In a speech delivered to a Republican women's group Senator Joseph McCarthy claims that the U.S. State Department is home to 205 communists.

March 1 Klaus Fuchs is convicted of spying for the Soviet Union and supplying it with top-secret information about British and American nuclear bomb research.

April 14 National Security Report NSC-68 is published. The document warns that the Soviet Union is aiming to bring Europe and Asia under its control.

May 11 The Kefauver Committee hearings into organized crime begin.

June 25 North Korean troops cross the border dividing North and South Korea; the Korean War begins.

July 17 Julius Rosenberg is arrested and charged with spying for the Soviet Union. His wife Ethel is arrested on August 11.

July 20 In a report to the Senate the Tydings Committee finds no substance to the allegations about communist activity made by McCarthy in February.

September 15 UN troops launch an amphibious assault on the port of Inchon to turn the tide of the Korean War.

October 2 "Peanuts," the comic strip by Charles M. Schulz, is published for the first time.

November 1 Puerto Rican nationalists Griselio Torresola and Oscar Collazo attempt to assassinate President Harry S. Truman. The attempt fails.

November 11 The first gay liberation organization, the Mattachine Society, is founded in Los Angeles.

November 26 Chinese troops take part in their first major battle of the Korean War when they surround UN forces at the Chosin Reservoir.

November 30 U.S. troops begin to retreat from the Chosin Reservoir.

December 10 Ralph Bunche wins the Nobel Peace Prize for his efforts to bring peace to the Middle East.

1951

February 1 The United Nations General Assembly denounces China's entry into the Korean War as an act of aggression.

February 27 The Twenty-Second Amendment to the United States Constitution is ratified. The amendment limits presidents to two terms in office.

March 30 The first UNIVAC I computer is delivered to the United States Census Bureau by Remington Rand.

April 11 President Truman relieves General Douglas MacArthur of his command in Korea after the latter openly criticizes the president's foreign policy.

April 18 Six Western European nations sign the Treaty of Paris, establishing the European Coal and Steel Community.

June 25 Arthur Godfrey, Ed Sullivan, and Faye Emerson appear in CBS's first commercial color telecast.

July 16 J.D. Salinger's novel *The Catcher in the Rye* is published.

August 14 U.S. newspaper publisher William Randolph Hearst dies.

September 1 The ANZUS Treaty, a mutual defense pact, is signed by the United States, Australia, and New Zealand.

September 4 The first live coast-to-coast TV broadcast in the United States features President Truman at the opening of the Japanese Peace Conference in San Francisco.

September 8 The end of the Pacific War is officially recognized when 48 countries sign the San Francisco Peace Treaty with Japan.

October 15 The first episode of *I Love Lucy* is broadcast.

November 1 In the Nevada Desert U.S. troops hold the first military exercises aimed at preparing for nuclear war.

November 24 The play *Gigi*, starring Audrey Hepburn, opens on Broadway.

December 20 The nuclear reactor Experimental Breeder Reactor I produces enough power to illuminate four 150-watt light bulbs.

December 25 The black civil rights activist Harry T. Moore is murdered. No one is arrested for the crime.

1952

March 21 The Moondog Coronation Ball takes place at the Cleveland Arena. The show, which was to feature a number of rock-'n'-roll artists, is stopped after just one song because of overcrowding.

March 29 President Truman announces that he will not be running for reelection.

July 2 Scientist Jonas Salk tests an early version of the polio vaccine on children.

July 24 *High Noon* opens. The movie would go on to win four Oscars; star Gary Cooper would win the best actor award.

July 25 Former colony Puerto Rico becomes a self-governing commonwealth of the United States.

August 1 The first Holiday Inn hotel opens in Memphis, Tennessee.

August 29 *4' 33"* by John Cage is performed for the first time.

September 1 *Life* magazine publishes Ernest Hemingway's *The Old Man and the Sea*.

September 19 U.S. Attorney General Thomas McGranery issues an order that actor Charlie Chaplin should be held by immigration services if he tries to return to the United States. Chaplin is suspected of holding left-wing political views.

September 23 Rocky Marciano defeats Jersey Joe Walcott to claim the boxing world heavyweight title.

Vice-presidential candidate Richard M. Nixon appears on television to counter corruption charges.

November 1 The United States successfully detonates its first hydrogen bomb, "Mike," on Enewetak Atoll in the Pacific Ocean.

November 4 Republican candidate Dwight D. Eisenhower defeats Democrat Adlai Stevenson in the presidential election. The Republicans regain control of both houses of Congress.

November 29 Eisenhower fulfills an election campaign promise and travels to Korea in an attempt to bring the Korean War to a close.

December 14 Conjoined twins are successfully separated by surgery at Mount Sinai Hospital in Ohio, the first time that such an operation has been performed.

1953

January 1 Country singer Hank Williams dies of a heart attack at age 29.

January 7 President Truman announces that the United States has developed a hydrogen bomb.

January 20 Eisenhower takes over the presidency from Truman.

January 22 Arthur Miller's play *The Crucible*, an attack on the anticommunist fervor of the decade, opens on Broadway.

February 18 Lucille Ball and Desi Arnaz sign an $8 million contract to continue the *I Love Lucy* TV series until the end of 1955.

February 28 James D. Watson and Francis Crick announce that they have determined the chemical structure of DNA.

March 5 Soviet leader Joseph Stalin dies after ruling the country for 29 years.

April 7 Dag Hammarskjöld is elected secretary-general of the United Nations.

June 19 Julius and Ethel Rosenberg are executed following their conviction for conspiracy to commit espionage in 1951.

July 26 A small band of revolutionaries led by Fidel Castro attacks Moncada Army Barracks in Cuba.

July 27 The Korean War ends. The United Nations Command, People's Republic of China, and North Korea sign an armistice agreement at Panmunjom.

August 12 The Soviet Union explodes its first hydrogen bomb.

September 7 Nikita Khrushchev becomes first secretary of the Soviet Union's Central Committee.

Tennis player Maureen Connolly wins the U.S. National Singles Championship to become the first woman to win all four grand slam titles in a single year.

October 5 Earl Warren is sworn in as chief justice of the U.S. Supreme Court.

December 8 President Eisenhower delivers what becomes known as the "Atoms for Peace" speech to the United Nations; he proposes the formation of an international atomic energy agency.

December 30 The first commercially available color TV set goes on sale.

1954

January 14 Actress Marilyn Monroe marries baseball star Joe DiMaggio.

January 25 The foreign ministers of the "big four"—the United States, Britain, France, and the Soviet Union—meet at the Berlin Conference.

February 23 The first mass vaccination of children against polio begins in Pittsburgh, Pennsylvania.

March 1 The United States conducts a hydrogen bomb test on Bikini Atoll in the Pacific Ocean.

April 7 In a speech at a news conference President Eisenhower outlines the "domino theory," which states that if one nation falls to communism, its neighbors will soon follow.

April 22 Television coverage of the Army–McCarthy hearings in the U.S. Senate begins.

May 7 The siege of Dien Bien Phu ends in victory for the Vietminh over French colonial forces.

May 17 The Supreme Court rules that racial segregation in public schools is unconstitutional in the case of *Brown v. Board of Education*.

June 18 Rebel troops trained by the CIA cross the border from Honduras to topple President Jacobo Arbenz of Guatemala.

July 17 The first Newport Jazz Festival opens. Billie Holiday, Dizzy Gillespie, Stan Getz, and Louis Armstrong are among the musicians to appear.

July 21 An agreement at the Geneva Conference results in the division of Vietnam at the 17th parallel.

September 8 The Southeast Asia Collective Defense Treaty is signed in Manila in the Philippines. It provides the basis for the formation of the Southeast Asia Treaty Organization the following year.

December 2 The U.S. Senate censures McCarthy for conduct that tends "to bring the Senate into dishonor and disrepute."

December 10 Ernest Hemingway wins the Nobel Prize for literature.

December 15 The first episode of *Davy Crockett* appears on television as part of the *Disneyland* show.

1955

January 28 Congress approves a presidential request to allow U.S. forces to defend Formosa (Taiwan) against Communist aggression.

March 12 Jazz saxophonist and bebop pioneer Charlie Parker dies.

March 30 *On the Waterfront* wins the Oscar for best picture. Its star, Marlon Brando, receives the award for best actor, while Elia Kazan is named best director.

May 5 West Germany becomes a sovereign state, with Bonn as its capital. Allied troops remain in occupation to protect the country from Soviet threat.

May 9 West Germany joins the North Atlantic Treaty Organization.

May 14 After a three-day conference in Poland the Soviet Union, Poland, East Germany, Czechoslovakia, Hungary, Romania, Bulgaria, and Albania sign the Warsaw Pact.

May 31 The Supreme Court orders that public schools be desegregated with "all deliberate speed."

June 12 The radio show *Monitor* is broadcast for the first time.

July 9 "Rock around the Clock" by Bill Haley and His Comets reaches number one on the pop charts.

July 17 The Disneyland theme park opens in Anaheim, California.

August 19 Hurricane Diane causes severe flooding in the northeastern United States and claims 200 lives.

September 30 Film star James Dean dies in a car crash.

October 13 Beat writer Allen Ginsberg gives a reading of his poem "Howl" at San Francisco's Six Gallery.

December 1 On a bus in Montgomery, Alabama, Rosa Parks refuses to give her seat to a white man and is arrested for violating the city's racial segregation laws.

December 5 The Montgomery Bus Boycott begins under the leadership of Baptist minister Martin Luther King, Jr.

The American Federation of Labor and the Congress of Industrial Organizations merge to form the AFL–CIO.

1956

February 22 Elvis Presley makes his chart debut with "Heartbreak Hotel." The single reaches number one.

February 25 Khrushchev denounces Stalin at the 20th Soviet Party Congress.

March 12 More than 100 southern representatives and senators sign a manifesto pledging to use "all lawful means" to reverse the Supreme Court ruling on segregation.

March 15 The musical *My Fair Lady* opens on Broadway.

May 21 Bikini Atoll in the Pacific Ocean is almost obliterated during a nuclear test following the first airborne explosion of a hydrogen bomb.

June 29 Actress Marilyn Monroe marries playwright Arthur Miller.

President Eisenhower signs the Federal-Aid Highway Act, authorizing the construction of a 41,000-mile (65,970-km) highway network linking the major urban centers.

July 30 The phrase "In God We Trust" is adopted as the national motto of the United States.

August 11 Abstract expressionist painter Jackson Pollock dies.

August 25 Dr. Alfred Kinsey, author of two groundbreaking reports on sexual behavior, dies.

September 9 Elvis Presley makes his first TV appearance on *The Ed Sullivan Show*.

October 23 Thousands of people take to the streets of Budapest, Hungary, in antigovernment protests.

October 29 The Suez Crisis begins; Israeli troops invade the Sinai Peninsula and push Egyptian forces back toward the Suez Canal.

November 4 Soviet tanks roll into Budapest and crush the Hungarian Uprising.

November 6 In a rerun of the 1952 presidential election Republican incumbent Dwight D. Eisenhower again defeats his Democrat opponent Adlai Stevenson.

November 13 The Montgomery Bus Boycott ends in a victory for civil rights activists when the Supreme Court declares that segregation on public buses is unconstitutional.

1957

January 2 The San Francisco and Los Angeles stock exchanges merge.

January 5 In a speech to a joint session of Congress Eisenhower pledges U.S. military support to any Middle Eastern country threatened by communism. The policy becomes known as the Eisenhower Doctrine.

January 13 The Wham-O Company produces its first frisbee, called the Pluto Platter.

March 13 The FBI arrests Jimmy Hoffa, general president of the Teamsters labor union, and charges him with bribery.

March 25 The European Economic Community is created by the signing of the Treaties of Rome.

April 10 The Suez Canal reopens.

May 2 Joseph McCarthy dies.

July 6 Althea Gibson wins the Wimbledon women's singles title, becoming the first African American to do so.

July 16 United States Marine Major John Glenn flies an F8U supersonic jet from California to New York in 3 hours, 23 minutes, and 8 seconds, setting a new transcontinental speed record.

August 5 The first program of *American Bandstand* is broadcast across the nation.

September 4 The Little Rock crisis begins; Orval Faubus, governor of Arkansas, calls out the National Guard to prevent black students from enrolling at Central High School in Little Rock.

September 9 President Eisenhower signs the 1957 Civil Rights Act, which seeks to protect voting rights.

October 4 The Soviet Union launches the first artificial satellite, *Sputnik 1*, into orbit around Earth. The ball-shaped satellite weighs 184 pounds (83kg).

November 3 The Soviet satellite *Sputnik 2* is sent into orbit around Earth with a dog, Laika, on board.

November 25 President Eisenhower suffers a stroke and is partially incapacitated.

December 6 The first attempt by the United States to launch a satellite, *Vanguard TV3*, fails when the rocket explodes on the launchpad.

1958

January 20 Elvis Presley is drafted into the U.S. Army. He serves until March 1960, largely in West Germany.

January 31 A team led by Wernher Von Braun successfully launches the first U.S. artificial satellite, *Explorer I*. The 31-pound (14-kg) cylindrical spacecraft detects the Van Allen radiation belt that surrounds Earth.

March 17 The U.S. satellite *Vanguard 1* finally makes it into orbit. The 3-pound (1.4-kg) satellite proves that Earth is not a perfect sphere but is slightly flattened at the poles.

March 27 Khrushchev becomes premier of the Soviet Union.

May 13 A group of anti-American demonstrators attack Vice President Richard M. Nixon's car during an official visit to Caracas, Venezuela.

July 14 A military coup in Iraq brings Brigadier Abdul Karim Kassem to power. Under Kassem's leadership Iraq withdraws from the pro-Western Baghdad Pact and forges closer ties with the Soviet Union.

July 24 At the opening of the American National Exhibition in Moscow Khrushchev and Nixon discuss the respective merits of the capitalist and communist economic systems.

July 29 President Eisenhower signs the National Aeronautics and Space Act; the the National Aeronautics and Space Administration (NASA) comes into being on October 1.

August 7 A federal court quashes Arthur Miller's conviction for contempt of Congress. Miller had refused to "name names" of possible communists when called before HUAC.

September 22 Sherman Adams, the White House chief of staff, is forced to resign over allegations that he accepted a gift from a friend who had business dealings with the government.

October 26 Pan American World Airways makes its first scheduled jet fight from New York to Paris.

December 28 The Baltimore Colts beat the New York Giants in sudden-death overtime in the NFL Championship Game, which *Sports Illustrated* calls "the best football game ever played."

1959

January 1 President Fulgencio Batista of Cuba flees the country as rebel troops march on the capital Havana.

January 2 The Soviet space probe *Luna 1* becomes the first artificial object to fly past the moon and escape Earth's gravitational field.

January 3 Alaska is admitted as the 49th state of the Union.

February 3 Rock-'n'-roll stars Buddy Holly, Ritchie Valens, and The Big Bopper are killed in a plane crash.

February 16 Fidel Castro becomes the prime minister of Cuba.

March 9 The first Barbie doll goes on sale.

May 24 Former Secretary of State John Foster Dulles dies.

June 26 The St. Lawrence Seaway, which links the North American Great Lakes to the Atlantic Ocean, officially opens to shipping.

July 15 Steelworkers go on strike in pursuit of higher wages, shorter hours, and better working conditions.

July 17 Jazz and blues singer Billie Holiday dies.

August 17 *Kind of Blue* by trumpeter Miles Davis is released. It is eventually recognized as one of the greatest jazz albums ever recorded.

August 21 Hawaii is admitted as the 50th state of the Union.

September 15 Khrushchev begins a visit to the United States.

October 4 The first photographs of the far side of the moon are taken from the Soviet space satellite *Luna 3*.

October 21 The Solomon R. Guggenheim Museum opens to the public in New York City. It was designed by Frank Lloyd Wright, who died in April.

December 1 The Antarctic Treaty is signed by 12 countries, including the United States and the Soviet Union. It bans military activity on the continent and is the first arms control agreement established during the Cold War.

December 14 Berry Gordy, Jr., founds Motown Records.

POST-1959

1960

May 1 An American U-2 spy plane is shot down while flying over the Soviet Union. The incident places a considerable strain on U.S.–Soviet relations.

November 8 John F. Kennedy is elected president of the United States in the closest election in the country's history.

1961

January 3 President Eisenhower cuts diplomatic ties to Cuba.

April 12 Yuri Gagarin makes the first manned space flight for the Soviet Union.

April 17 Cuban rebels, trained and funded by the CIA, land at the Bay of Pigs in an attempt to topple the Castro regime. In a humiliating setback for the United States they are quickly defeated.

August 13 The Berlin Wall is erected, separating East from West Berlin.

1962

August 5 Actress Marilyn Monroe is found dead after a drug overdose.

October 14 U.S. reconnaissance planes spot a Soviet ballistic missile on a military base in Cuba. The discovery prompts the Cuban Missile Crisis, a period of tension that ends only when the Soviet Union agrees to withdraw the missiles.

1963

August 28 250,000 people take part in a civil rights march in Washington, D.C.

November 22 President Kennedy is assassinated by Lee Harvey Oswald in Dallas, Texas. Vice President Lyndon Baines Johnson takes over as president.

1964

February 9 British pop group the Beatles appears on *The Ed Sullivan Show*. An estimated 73 million viewers watch the performance.

February 25 Cassius Clay defeats Sonny Liston to win the world heavyweight boxing title. Shortly afterward Clay adopts the Muslim name Muhammad Ali.

1965

February 21 African American political activist Malcolm X is shot dead in New York City.

1968

April 4 Martin Luther King, Jr., is assassinated in Memphis, Tennessee.

185

SET INDEX

Volume numbers are in **bold**.
Page numbers in **bold** refer to
main articles; those in *italics* refer
to picture captions.